SINGLE-FAMILY HOUSES

CONTEMPORARY HOMES IN GERMANY

SINGLE-FAMILY HOUSES
CONTEMPORARY HOMES IN GERMANY

Chris van Uffelen

BRAUN

CONTENTS

CONTENTS

SINGLE-FAMILY HOUSES CONTEMPORARY HOMES IN GERMANY

—AN INTRODUCTION

The construction of owner-occupied housing is neither one of the most lucrative nor one of the most prestigious construction tasks. But it is one of the most widespread. In the last decade, between 73 and 95,000 building permits have been issued annually – although not all have been completed. In the 1990s there were always more than 100,000, with a peak value of 188,000 in 1999. Nevertheless, 95,000 are an enormous volume that the construction of museums – where architects can let off steam creatively – or office buildings – much more profitable – can't compete with.

By 2017 there where around 15.7 million single-family homes in Germany, including old buildings, despite the fact that the ownership rate of just over 40 percent in Germany is not too high compared to neighboring countries. At the same time, the average living space of newly built single-family homes is increasing: from 130 square meters in the early 1990s to 151.8 square meters today. The approximately 90,000 single-family homes for which a building permit was issued in 2018 will cost around € 23,677,000,000. So only about 1,000,000,000 less than for the 17,500 houses with three and more apartments. The price increase – by 16 percent in 2015 alone – naturally affected both to a similar extent. The houses with three and more flats account for 531,000 living spaces, the single-family houses only about 10,000 less. The living space per apartment is 76.7 square meters for multi-family houses and 151.8 square meters for single-family houses, as mentioned above.

However, these figures include luxury villas and private palaces that are not part of this book. This book is about the house that the "average earner with above-average taste" can afford. What do the better buildings look like, which make up a large part of housing construction activity?

The energy aspect is becoming increasingly important for the construction of detached houses. In particular, the current Energy Conservation Ordinance (EnEV) and the standards of the public development bank KfW, that are based on primary energy demand and transmission heat loss and which demands higher energy efficiency than the EnEV, are of particular interest for financing. The Effizienzhaus 40 has the lowest energy requirement, only 40 percent of the reference house (from the EnEV 2009). Other ecological aspects, however, hardly play a role, because basically the single-family house construction type is rarely environmentally compatible compared to the multi-family house: a specially equipped construction site, high ground sealing per residential unit by the building, but also by the associated streets and sidewalks or even the private garage and the garden paths and garbage houses ultimately used by only one family. Nevertheless, the dream of one's own home, the illusion of an "idyll in the countryside", remains one of the main wishes of the Germans.

Stylistically, the desires vary widely. On the one hand, the desire for an "idyll in the countryside" is reflected by a rural appearance with (supposedly) rural natural materials (wood), or on the other hand the new building adapts to the classic rural environment with a saddle roof and gable stand. On the other hand, knitted modern cubatures or asymmetrical compositions – possibly also made of exposed concrete – are also popular, and between these poles of shapes and materials almost nothing is unthinkable, even the flat sloping roof of post-war modernism is popular again. The interior layout also reveals an enormous variety: from access areas and corridors to living areas that openly merge into one another. Nevertheless, the room arrangements usually remain classic – rarely do you think you can feel the succession of a Loosian spatial plan. Air-spaces connecting floors, on the other hand, are welcome. They make the main room as spacious as the large glazed areas of the living room, usually the most modern, usually the largest, but also the most imaginative one.

HORREUM

1

2, 3

10

Architects: denzer&poensgen
Year of completion: 2018
Location: Nettersheim, North Rhine-Westphalia
Gross floor area: 140 m^2
Number of bedrooms: 4
Main materials / structure: wood / timber frame construction
Ecological features: heat pump

The property is located on the outskirts of a town, about one kilometer east of the town center of Nettersheim in the Eifel. Originally, this landscape was characterized by field barns, sheds, or other agricultural buildings. By the exploitation of a new development area, Auf Bennfeld, from the old castle up to the Engelgauer street, a heterogeneous development evolved here over the years.

The task for this new building was to implement the future house into the landscape and at the same time create sufficient living space for a family of five. With the concept of transforming a horreum (Latin for warehouse, barn), an attempt was made to add a new historical image to the former landscape. By responding to the conditions of the place where the architecture was created, the genius loci, the poetry of the place is retranslated.

4

5

6

1 Exterior view street side
2 Exterior view garden side
3 View from the studio

4 Inner courtyard towards entrance
5 Inner courtyard towards living space
6 View to the inner courtyard

1

2

3

4

1 Crossover from the living area to the corridor
2 Staircase
3 Entrance
4 Dining area and kitchen

5 Cross section
6 Ground floor plan
7 First floor plan

5

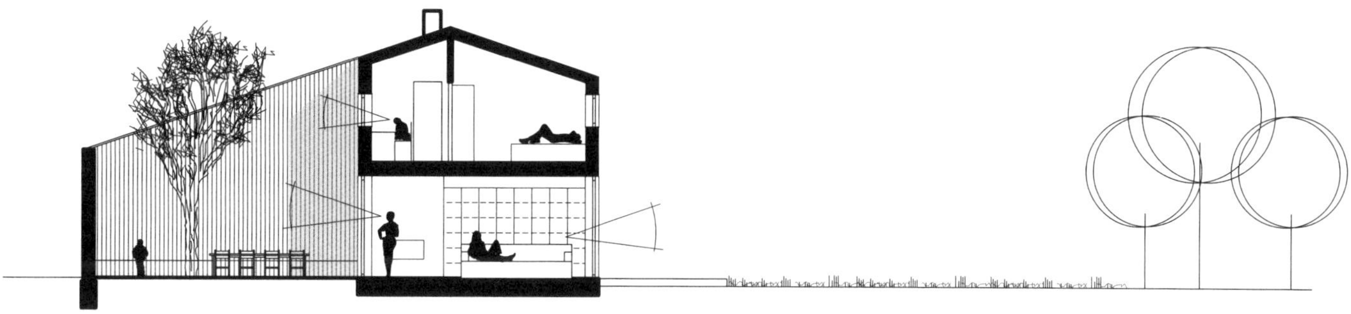

6

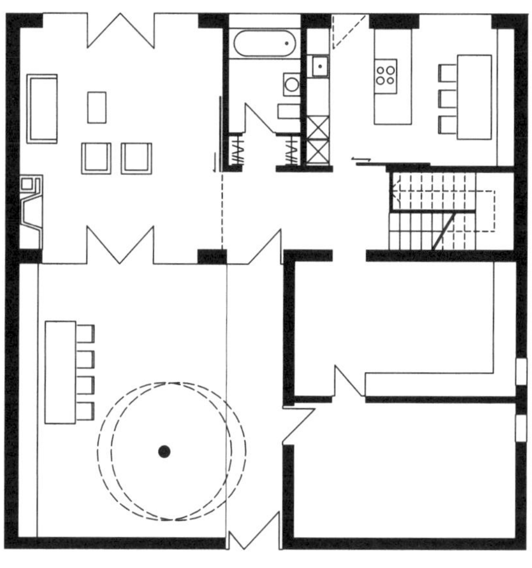

7

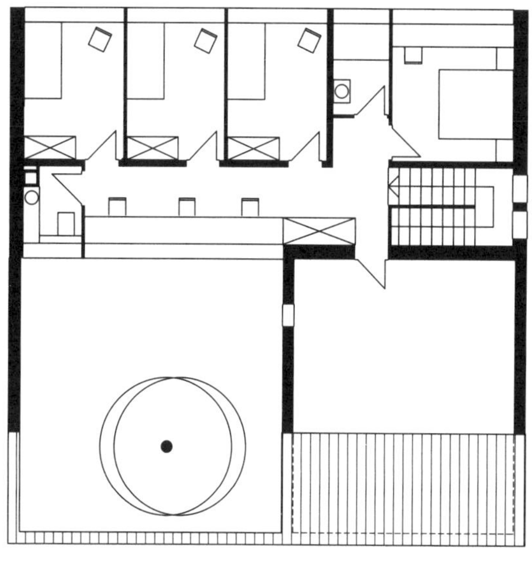

HIDEAWAY. BETZENSTEIN

1

2

3

14

The hideaway is located on the outskirts of Betzenstein, in the middle of the Franconian Switzerland Nature Park. The architecture of the elongated building with its striking double saddle roof is based on the topographical conditions, traditional forms, and materials of the local environment. These have been architecturally reinterpreted using modern means. Embedded in a northern slope, the structure blends unobtrusively into the surrounding hilly landscape with rocks and beech forests. The roof and façade appear as a monolithic structure, completely smooth and as if cast in one piece. Dark shingles take up the regional Upper Franconian building tradition with slate. The clear formal language with its reduction to the essentials and a restrained choice of materials and colors is seamlessly integrated into the interior design.

The reference to the lush green of the outdoor area was an important component of the concept.
The design with natural ponds, native shrubs, fruit orchards and Jurassic limestone from the own property and from a native quarry reflects the typical surrounding landscape in the Franconian Switzerland Nature Park. The species-rich planting and the meadow areas with herbs, flowers and grasses help bumble bees, butterflies, and other insects and ensure biodiversity.

The Hideaway.Betzenstein is based on a holistic, energy-efficient and sustainable concept. The brief demanded the consistent use of regenerative, health and environmentally compatible building materials. Wood, as renewable raw material, dominates. Following aspects of sustainability and energy efficiency, renewable energies were used for the building services.

An active and passive use of solar energy, an almost energy-autonomous operation with the use of 100 percent green electricity, sustainable drainage technology with a rainwater cistern, extensive roof greening and a natural exterior design with paths and areas that can be seeped round off the overall ecological concept.

Architects: Bucher | Hüttinger – Architektur Innen Architektur
Year of completion: 2016
Location: Betzenstein, Bavaria
Gross floor area: 307 m^2
Number of bedrooms: 3
Main materials / structure: solid wood construction
Ecological features: healthy passive house, consistent use of ecological and sustainable building materials

1 Exterior view from southeast
2 Exterior view from south
3 Exterior view from southwest

4 First floor office/work space
5 Cantilever stairs

4, 5

1

2

3

1 Sections
2 Ground floor apartment
3 First floor dining room
4 First floor plan
5 Ground floor plan

4

5

SANDWICH

1

Architects: Atelier ST
Year of completion: 2015
Location: Potsdam, Brandenburg
Gross floor area: 111 m^2
Number of bedrooms: 3
Main materials / structure: solid construction made of exposed concrete with fully glazed aluminium construction
Ecological features: geothermal heat pump, component activation, translucent thermal insulation

2

18

The property with its protected old pine trees provides a view over the shore of the Groß Glienicker See lake. The architecture derives its primary functional and design features from this special situation in accordance with the topographical slope. The single-story building with partial basement completely does without load-bearing exterior walls and columns. In connection with a prestressed, cantilevered ceiling construction, the forces are only transferred by an inner load-bearing longitudinal wall, a transverse wall and three supports.

With the exception of the surrounding glass façade, all surfaces of load-bearing components, including the floor, are made of exposed concrete. The limits of the construction site specified in the development plan are exhausted to the maximum. The glazed outer skin is divided into a façade transparent towards the lake, a fully glazed aluminium construction and three opaque translucent façades made of green shimmering profiled glass (industrial glass) with translucent thermal insulation. The relatively small footprint is optimally utilized by a compact room arrangement and always appears generous due to the all-round glazing. In addition to bathrooms and kitchen, room-high furniture elements made of sea pine ultimately serve as storage space and the space required by the client's library. In contrast to the compact interior, there is a spacious roof terrace, which can only be reached via a secret door inside the furniture wall. This invisible exterior surface occupies the entire floor space and offers views of the lake and landscape. Together with the low height development of the trapezoidal object of the cantilevered roof slab, the architecture is set back from the landscape and nature. Thus, the building is restrained on the outside and blends into the landscape situation in its proportion, color and scale.

3

4

1 Exterior view from northeast
2 Glazed façade from the east

3 Living area with lake view
4 Living area with landscape view
5 Entrance with wardrobe
6 Kitchen with skylight
7 Bathroom with large mirror

5, 6

7

1

2

1 Bedroom
2 Exterior view from north

3 Ground floor plan
4 Ground floor plan
5 Isometry of the concrete structure in its individual parts
6 Isometry of the concrete construction

3

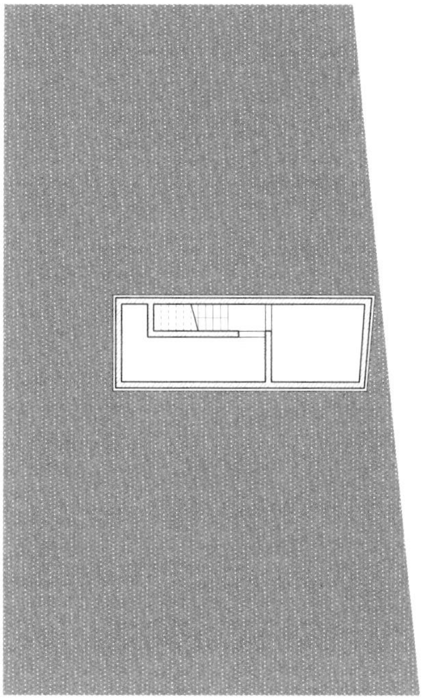

4

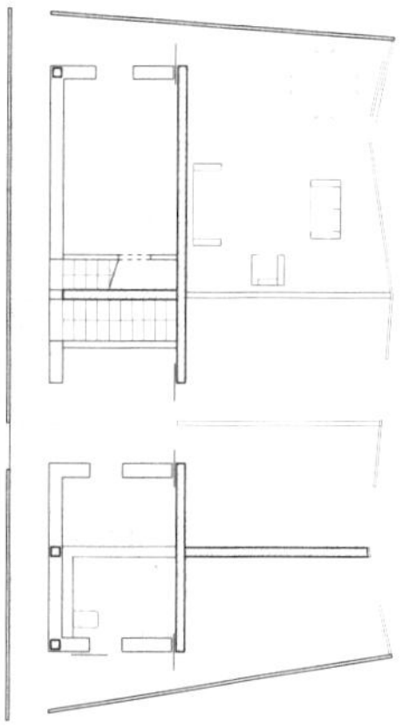

5

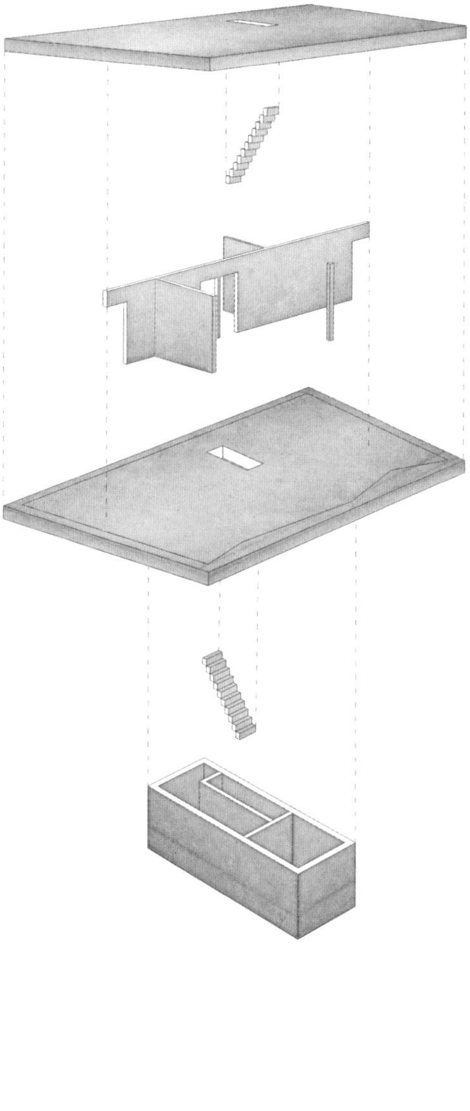

6

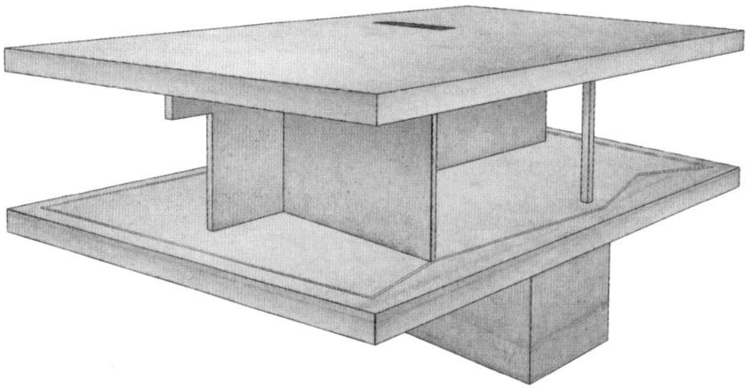

THE SMALL HOUSE

1

2

3

Architects: Architekturbüro Schildhammer
Year of completion: 2014
Location: Passau, Bavaria
Gross floor area: 126 m^2 (without basement level)
Number of bedrooms: 2
Main materials / structure: brick, concrete / solid construction
Ecological features: KfW 55, solar for domestic hot water, heat pump, controlled ventilation, building cooling

"... not be too big, but bright, warm and cozy! And handy in everyday life! I want the rooms to be open and modern. I also need space for my pictures and many books. And when friends come over I need a comfortable dining table, preferably with a view of the countryside ..." This wish list of the building owner is fulfilled by a living concept, which corresponds more to a free-standing dwelling than a house in the classical sense.

On a hillside plot of only 320 square meters on the outskirts of the town, a narrow building with three stories was designed. Cubic, angular and rich in contrast, the house is only 5.60 meters wide. An underground car park provides sufficient space on the small plot for the modern open spaces. The living concept is efficient – in terms of living space, energy and construction costs. Thin-walled room dividers made of light, warm wood, curtains instead of interior doors, a small gallery and generous window openings create an airy and open space continuum. The interiors appear cozy, comfortable and larger than one would expect from such a compact building. The geometry of the floor plan is clear, and there are no protrusions or recesses.

4

5

1 Street view from northeast
2 Entrance
3 Garden view from southwest

4 Gallery
5 Exposed concrete staircase in the interior
6 View from the kitchen to the dining area

6

1

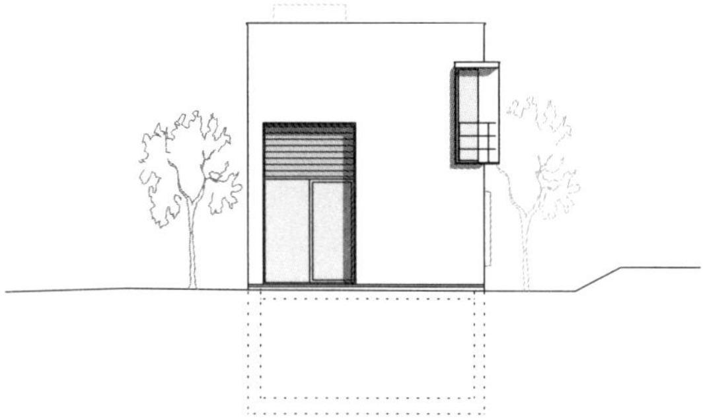

2

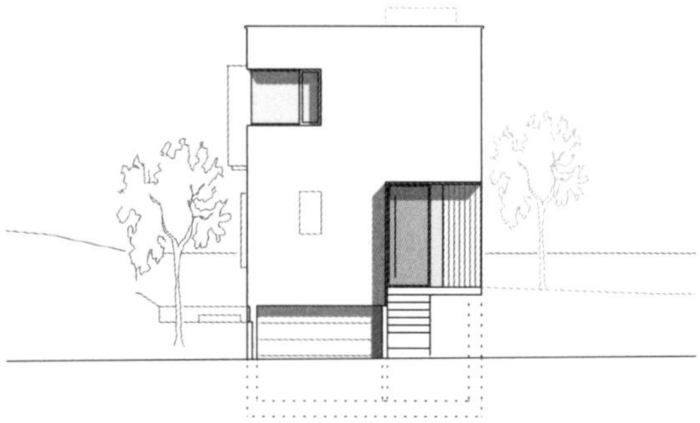

3

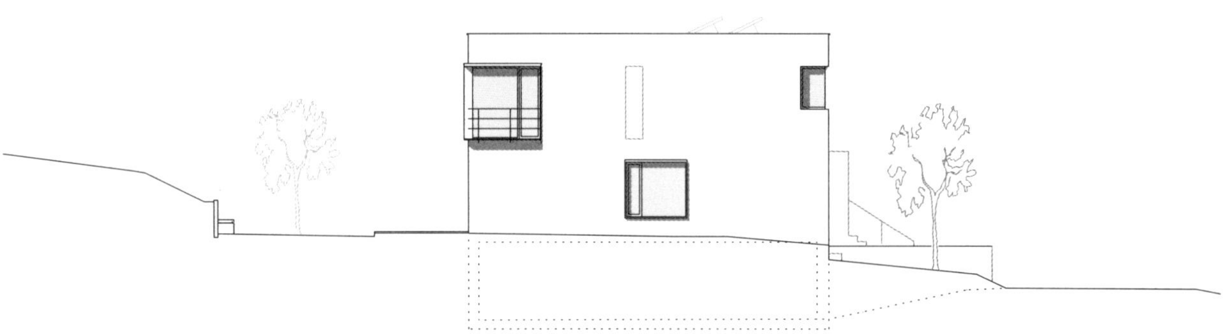

4

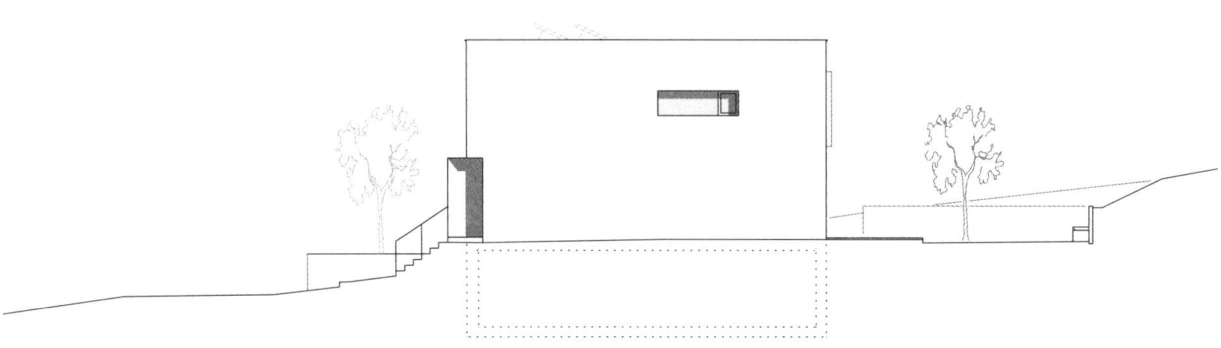

5

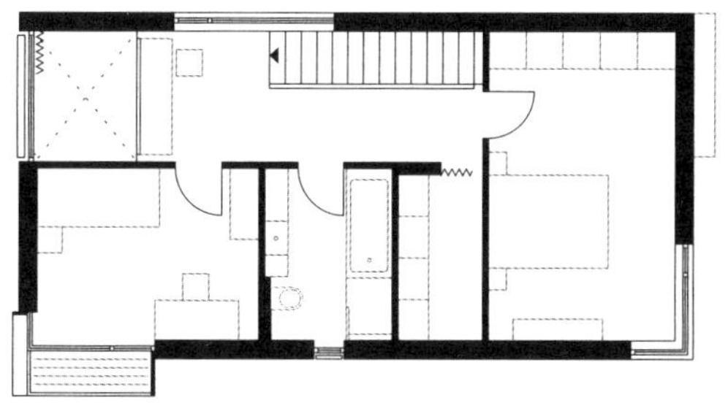

6

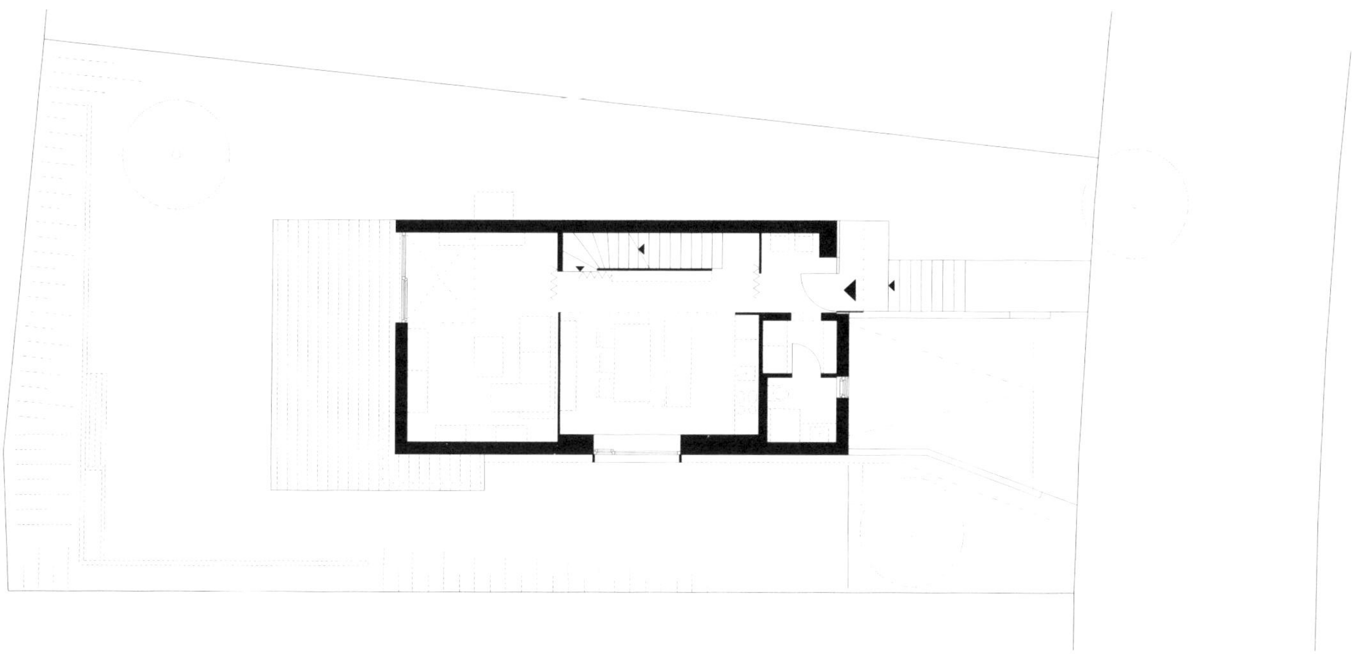

1 Southwest elevation
2 Northeast elevation
3 Southeast elevation
4 Northwest elevation

5 First floor plan
6 Ground floor plan

WOODEN HOUSE BY THE MILL

1

2, 3

Architects: Flacke + Otto Architekten
Year of completion: 2012
Location: Brodowin, Brandenburg
Gross floor area: 112 m²
Number of bedrooms: 3
Main materials / structure: wood, clay building slabs / timber frame construction with cellulose insulation
Ecological features: renewable building materials, clay slabs as a storage mass

On the outskirts of Brodowin, a Berlin family has purchased a plot of land to build a house with a timber frame construction. Its heart is a high, spacious, airy living and dining room with a stove, from which all other rooms are accessible. In contrast to this room, bedrooms, bathrooms, and kitchen are compact and functional, but vary in their proportions and the size of the windows. A guest room with gallery, private bathroom and terrace functions as a separate room so guests can retreat to their own area. The entire south façade has a terrace with a pergola on which wooden gratings can be installed in summer. This sun protection and the storage mass of the clay building slabs creates a pleasant indoor climate in the entire building even in midsummer. The seating area on the sliding, covered terrace next to the kitchen is protected from sun and rain. In addition, the wind is kept away from the extended east façade. Thus the house balances climatic and weather conditions with natural means.

4

5

1 Exterior view from south
2 Exterior view from north
3 Exterior view from east

4 Pergola
5 Terrace

1

2

1 Living area
2 View into the rooms

3 Ground floor plan
4 Longitudinal section
5 Cross section
6 West elevation

3

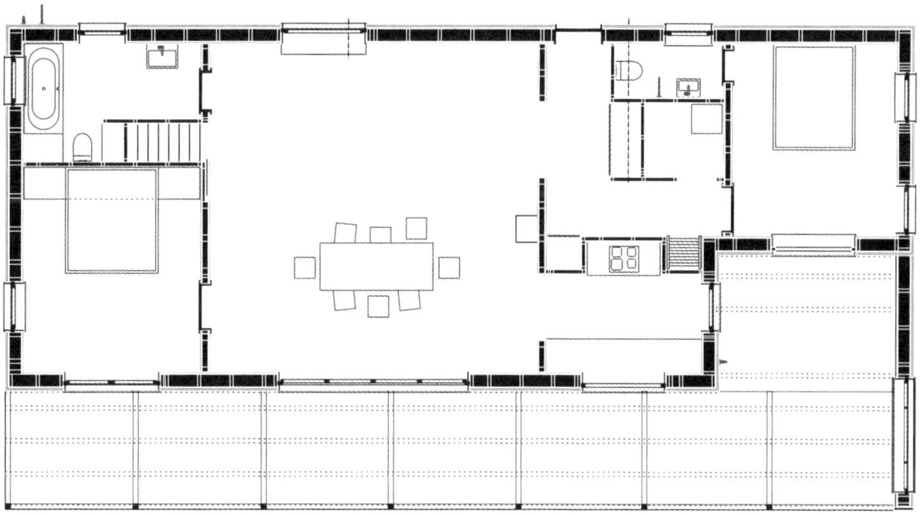

4

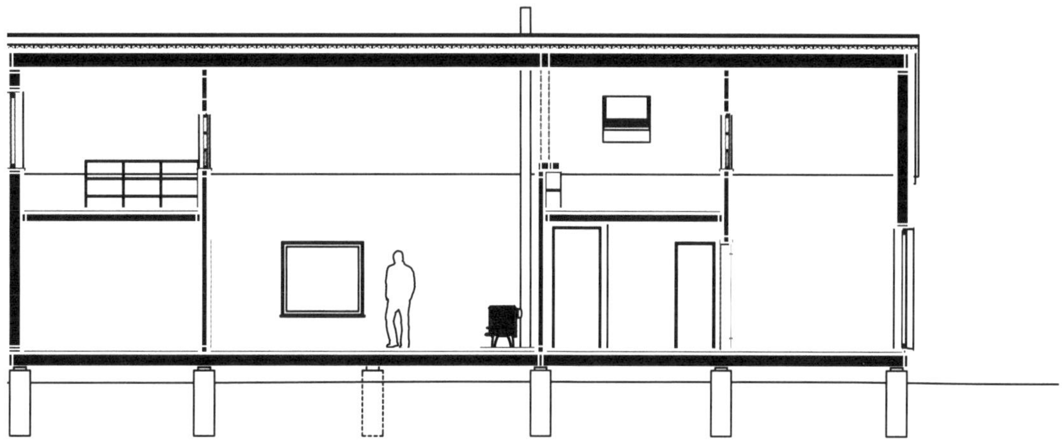

5

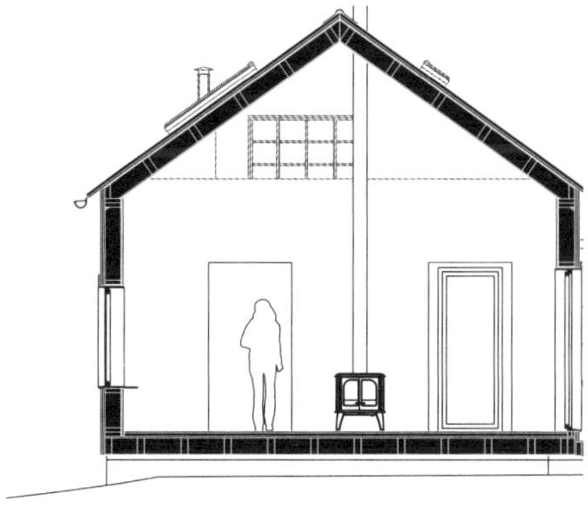

6

HOUSE SPK

1, 2

3

Architects: nbundm* Architekten und Stadtplaner
Year of completion: 2015
Location: Ingolstadt, Bavaria
Gross floor area: 247 m^2
Number of bedrooms: 3
Main materials / structure: insulating bricks, coloured mineral plaster and solid wood Oak / monolithic solid construction
Ecological features: no need for ETICS, sustainable materials

Extremely narrow and at the same time very long the plots of land forced a specific type of house in this part of the city: eaves-style workering classs houses with sloping roofs and attached nave directly on the street. The existing typology served as a model and was further developed. On a surface area of six by 22 meters, the children's house, community house and parents' house are lined up and transformed into a volume. The entire ground floor is used jointly, all private rooms are accommodated on the two upper floors and some have small galleries on the roof floor. The pivot point of the family life remains in the elongated living and dining room with 60 square meters on two floor levels and with different room heights, which has been put through to the garden. Built in solid construction with insulating bricks and oak windows, this building is constructed according to the KfW 70 standard.

4

5

1 View from the staircase into the dining room
2 parent's bathroom
3 View from living room into dining room

4 Garden view from the east
5 Exterior view from southwest
6 Living room and terrace from southeast

6

1

1 Stairs as accessible furniture

2 First floor plan
3 Ground floor plan
4 Longitudinal section through both stairs

2

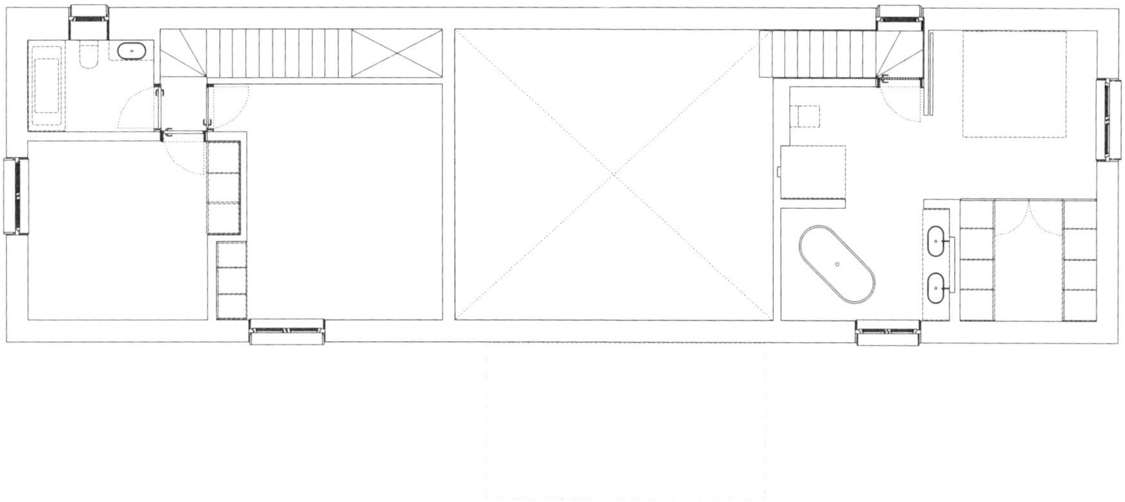

3

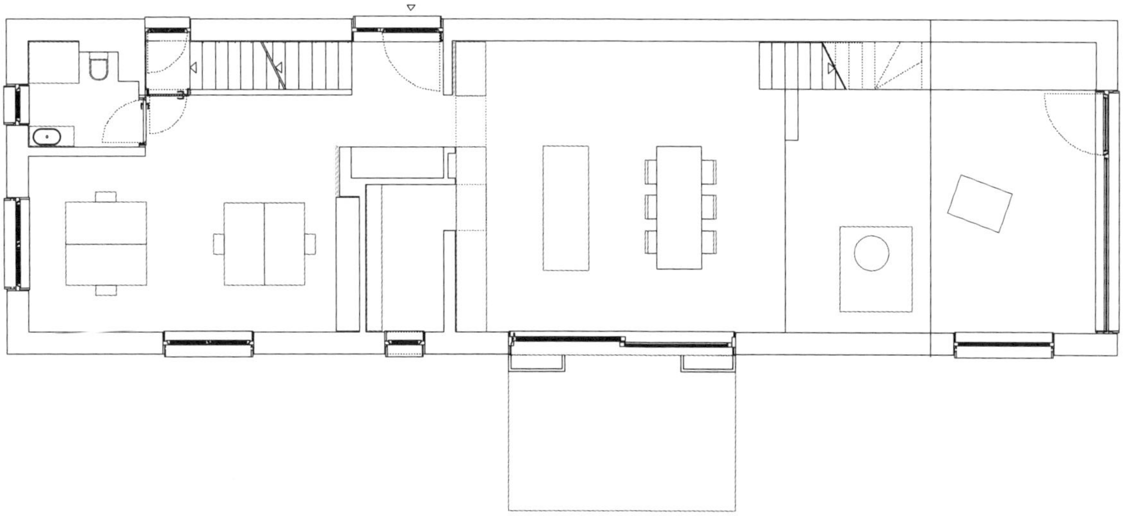

4

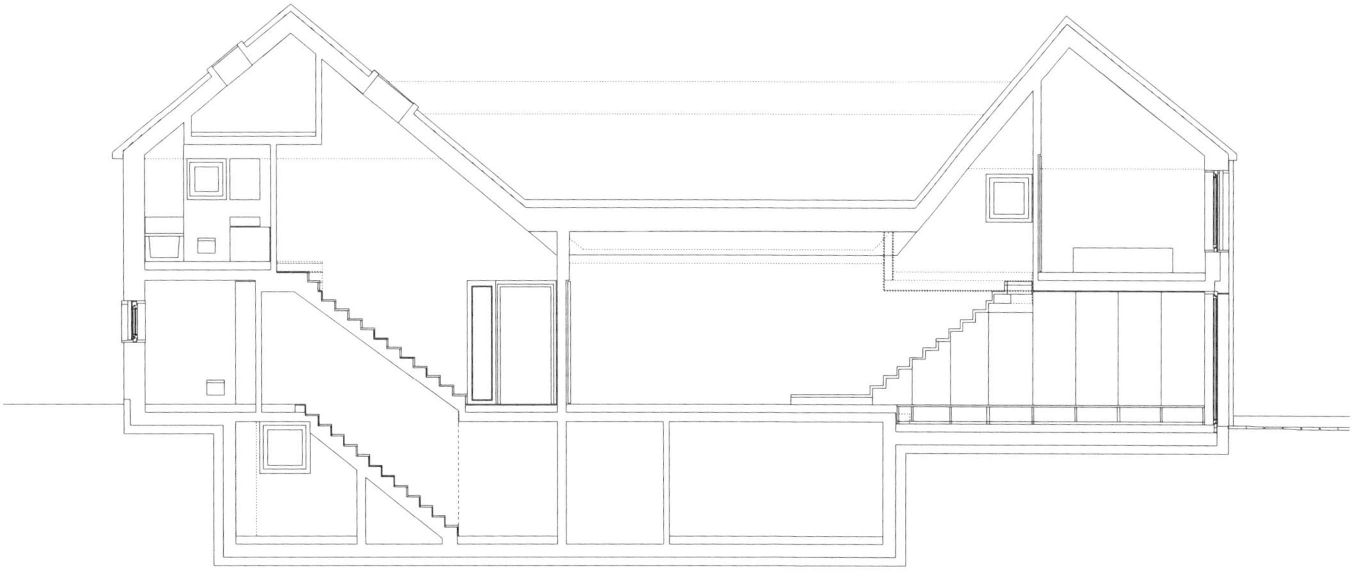

GRANNY WANTS A HOUSE!

1

2, 3

1 Garden view
2 Street view
3 Entrance

4 Ground floor plan
5 Site plan
6 Indoors alignment
7 Living area

34

"It shall be small, fine and barrier-free. But also comfortable, handy and practical in everyday life..." This is how the sprightly elderly woman described her intention to build to the architect.

In the end, two largely identical houses suitable for rent were built on a small plot of land, which are anything but old-fashioned and even appeal to younger prospective buyers. The clear structures and lines in the building concept clearly contribute to the attractiveness of the properties, while the interior lines create a special spatiality. Large openings to the green area at the rear of the houses supply the interiors with plenty of daylight.

The structured construction also allows controlled ventilation of the living space. Thanks to the energy-efficient construction with heat pump, the energy balance of these houses in Fürstenzell is also better than that of many large, expensive villas. So they still exist, the simple, affordable houses.

4

5

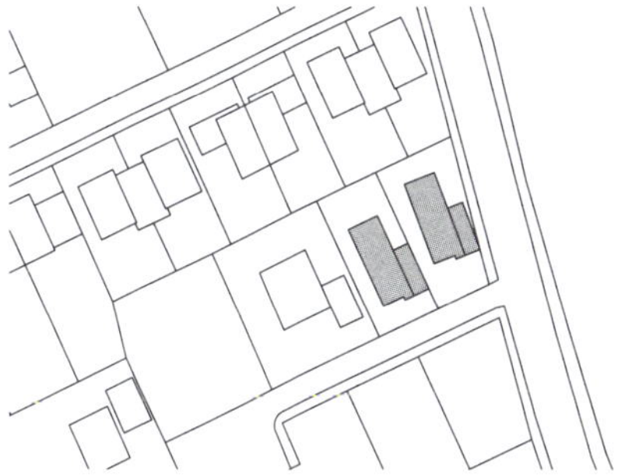

6

Architects: Architekturbüro Schildhammer
Year of completion: 2015
Location: Fürstenzell, Bavaria
Gross floor area: 110 m²
Number of bedrooms: 2
Main materials / structure: brick, concrete, wood / solid construction
Ecological features: KfW 55, heat pump with cooling system

7

CONTEMPORARY RURAL HOME

1

2

Architects: Meyer Terhorst Architekten
Year of completion: 2018
Location: Klein Waabs, Schleswig-Holstein
Gross floor area: 77 m^2
Number of bedrooms: 2
Main materials / structure: pre-grayed larch wood façade, wooden windows, dark clay roof tiles / timber frame construction
Ecological features: wood construction with cellulose insulation, air heat pump

36

In a Baltic coastal village in Schleswig-Holstein, the builders wanted a clear architecture for their 800-square-meter property with old stock. In addition to the deliberate preservation and renovation of the existing settlement house, a simple single-family house was built.

The new development calms and relaxes the surroundings. With the unagitated saddle roof shape, Meyer Terhorst architects react respectfully, restrainedly and at the same time contemporary to the interplay of single-family houses with outbuildings from various eras. Differently sized square windows in a façade of pre-grayed wooden formwork consistently continue the reduced formal language and transform the rural village character into a contemporary context. The construction method is a sustainable timber frame construction with cellulose insulation and air heat pump supply.

Reduction and clarity also characterize the bright interiors. Oak planks, large-format tiles and an open kitchen, transmit an almost urban feeling of living in the surrounding landscape with meadows.

3

1 Exterior view with outbuildings
2 Exterior view in street alignment

3 Staircase to the upper floor
4 Living room with terrace door
5 Bathroom

4

5

1

2

3

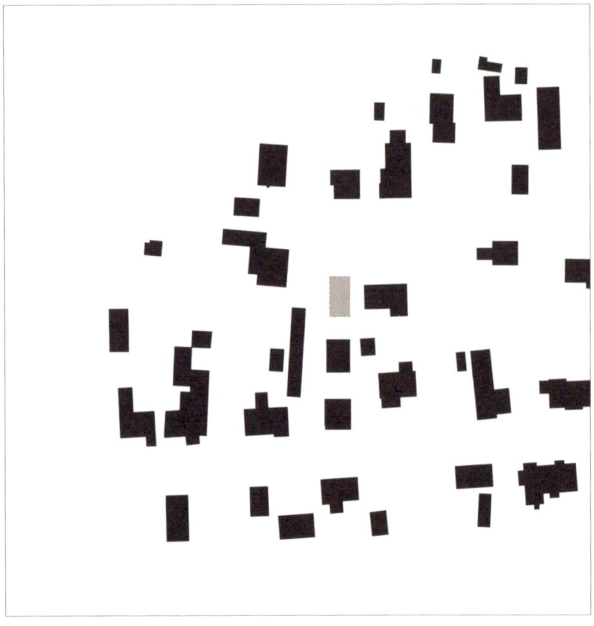

4

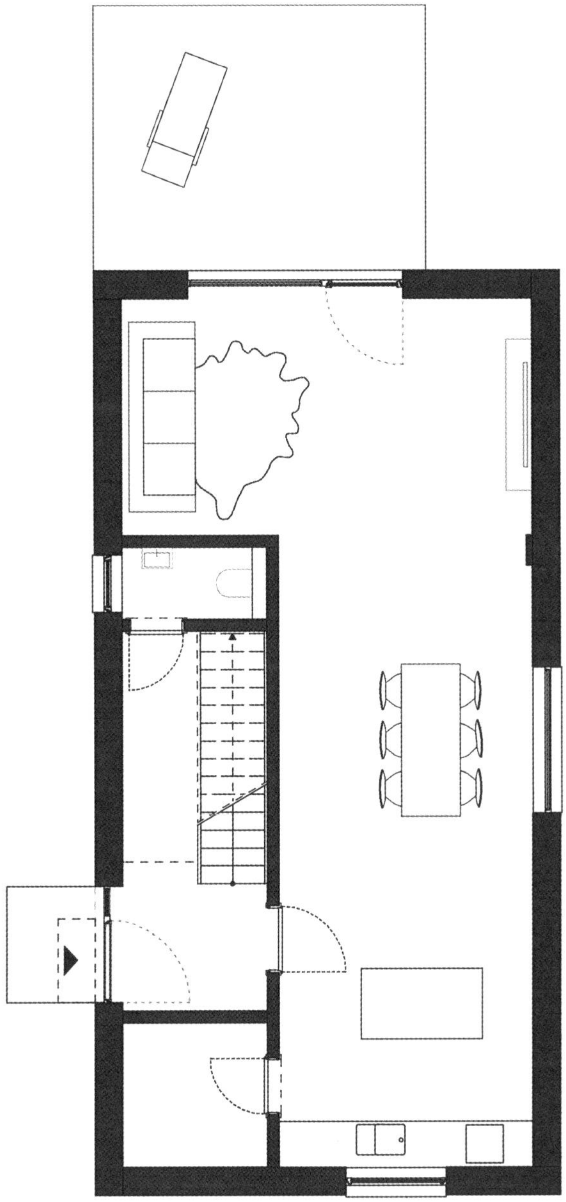

5

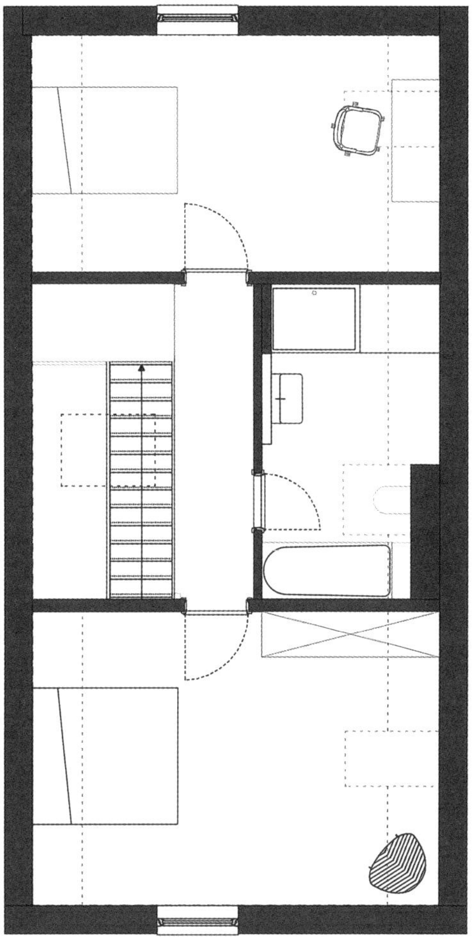

1 Attic floor
2 Entrance area
3 Site plan

4 Ground floor plan
5 First floor plan

HOUSE W

1

1 Exterior view from west
2 Dining area, passageway to the living area
3 Passageway between living area and kitchen

4 Kitchen and dining area
5 Staircase from first to second floor
6 Detailed view of the gallery on the 2nd floor

2

3

Architects: Büro Stoll für Architektur und Design
Year of completion: 2017
Location: Stuttgart, Baden-Württemberg
Gross floor area: 183 m^2
Number of bedrooms: 3
Main materials / structure: autoclaved aerated concrete, lime plaster / monolithic solid construction
Ecological features: reduction of composite materials, use of renewable energies (solar thermal energy and stove with water pocket)

The new building with its simple exterior design holds spatial surprises in store. On the ground floor, an internal core separates the cooking and dining area from the living area. The areas are connected via the entrance to the house and a passageway on the opposite side of the core. Two voids, which reach all the way to the rooftop, enable visual and verbal communication across all floors. On the upper floor, a gallery provides access to three bedrooms. The gallery room reaching up to the roof leads to the top floor, where two open, multi-functional areas have been created. Here, two further rooms could be created by simple conversion measures.

4

The desire for an ecological construction method and a self-regulating room climate determined the choice of materials. The exterior walls, made of cellular concrete, were provided on both sides with a mineral, open-pored plaster system. The façade was given a dark-colored scratch coat. A two-layer base plaster was applied to the interior. Larch aluminum windows, rudimentary polished screed and parquet are essential materials as well.

5

6

1

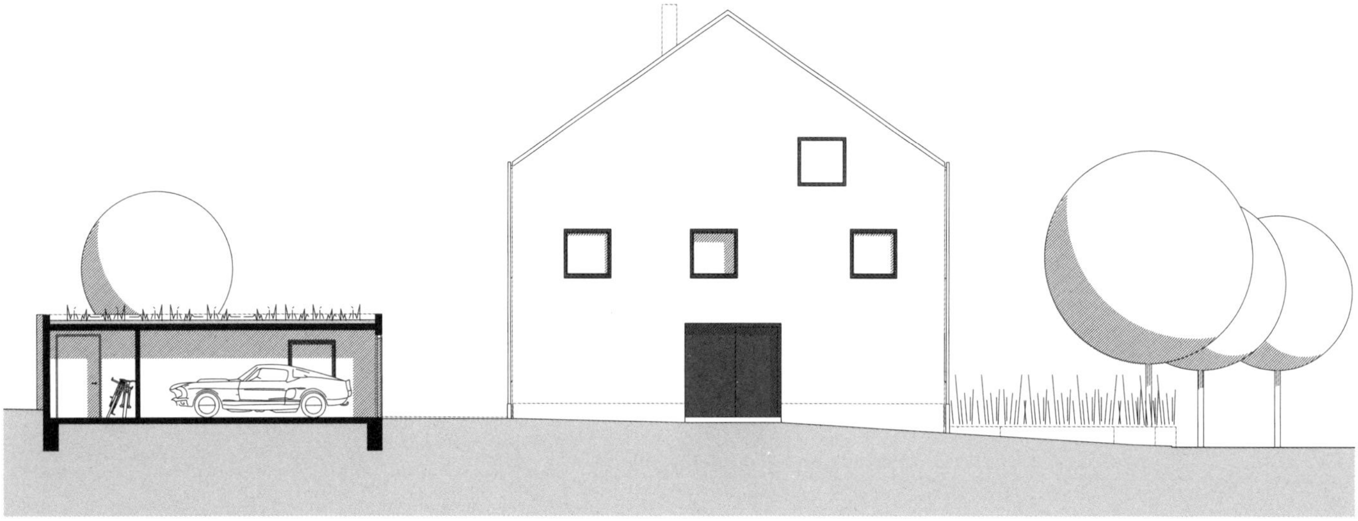

2

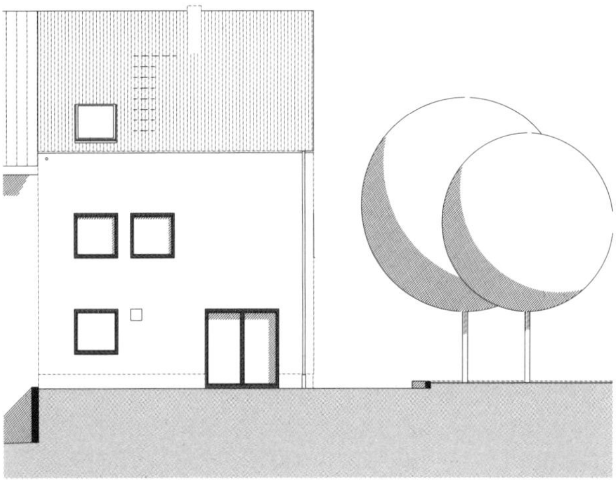

3

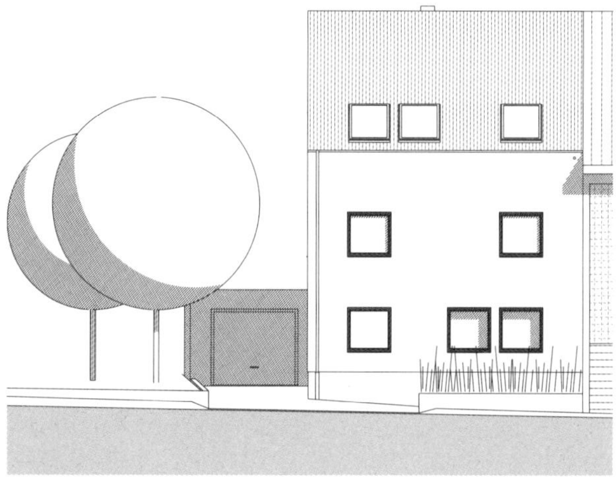

4

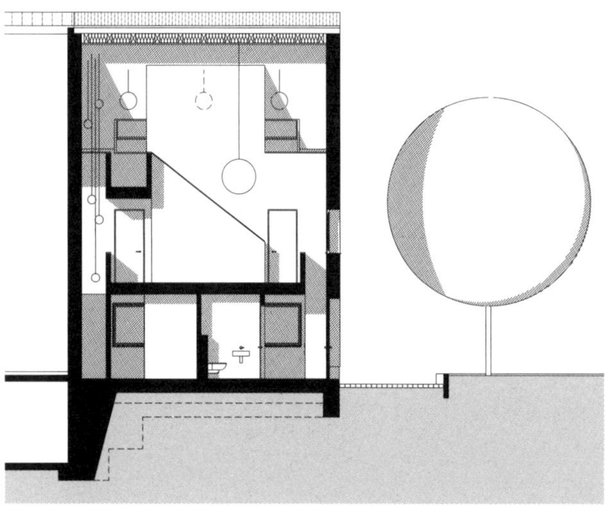

1 North elevation
2 East side elevation
3 West elevation
4 Cross section in ridge direction
5 Attic floor plan
6 First floor plan
7 Ground floor paln

5

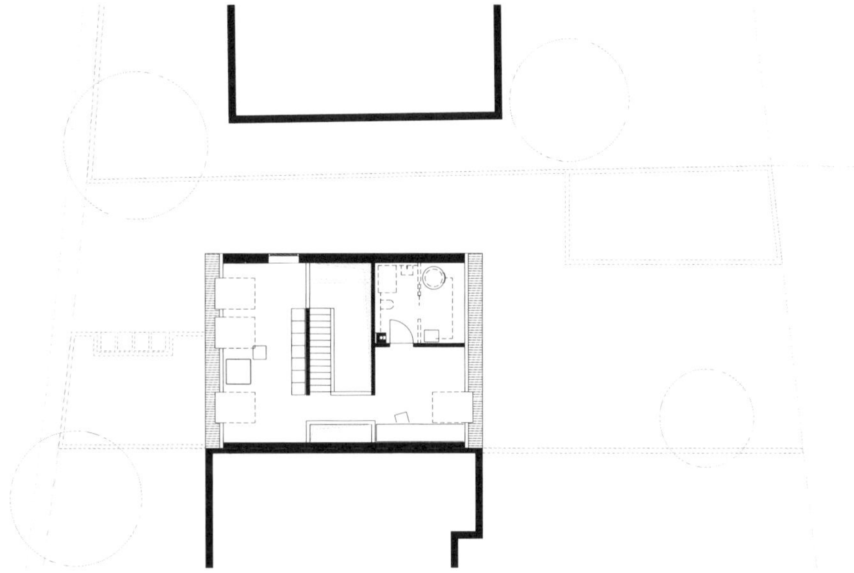

6

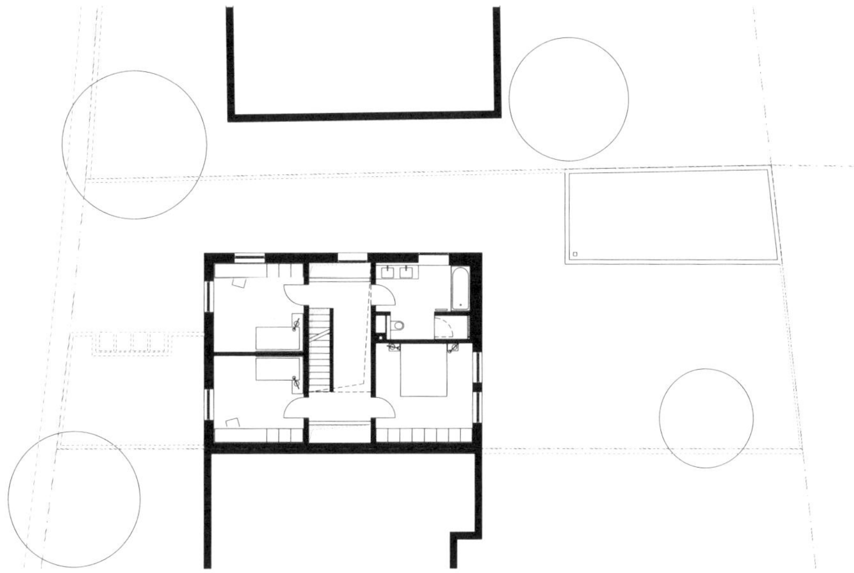

7

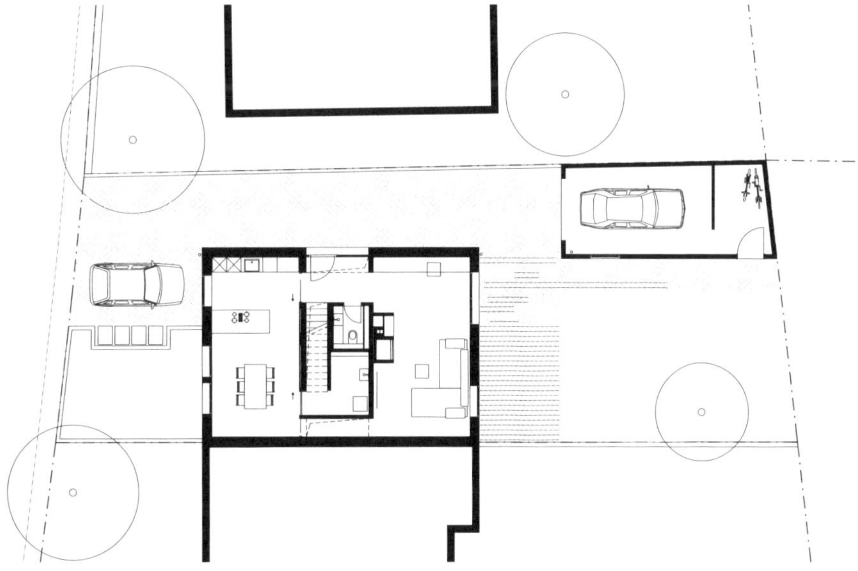

LAKESIDE SUMMER HOUSE

1

Architects: Zappe Architekten
Year of completion: 2008
Location: Kagar, Brandenburg
Gross floor area: 68 m²
Number of bedrooms: 1
Main materials / structure: natural stone (slate, masonry), wood / timber frame construction

2

An old dacha on the site offered the opportunity to use this special location for a new summer house. Since the lake and shore zone belong to a protected landscape, a new construction towards the water would not have been permitted according to the applicable building law.

Zappe Architekten constructed a new replacement building. The building is approached from behind. House and surroundings belong together as a matter of course. The windows offer a view through the living space to the waterline at the end of the property. The picture is complemented by the simple flower meadow, which was deliberately designed as such.

The building is structured by a free ground plan. The kitchen serves as the backbone of the living area, which can be opened together with the sleeping area via wide sliding window fronts. Both rooms, which are only separated by a sliding element, face the terrace and the lake. The exterior façade, which is covered with larch rhombuses, rises above a wide lawn area. In addition, there is an exposed gable made of slate.

3

4

1 Exterior view from southeast
2 Exterior view from noth

3 Living area with a fireplace
4 Living area with kitchen
5 View into the bedroom
6 Bathtub overlooking the lake

5

6

1

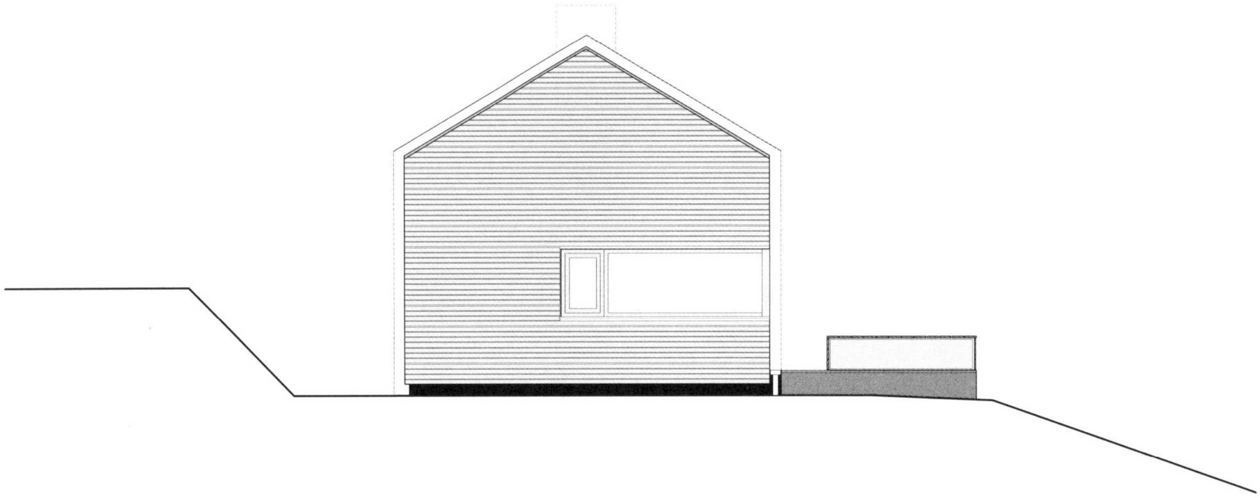

2

3

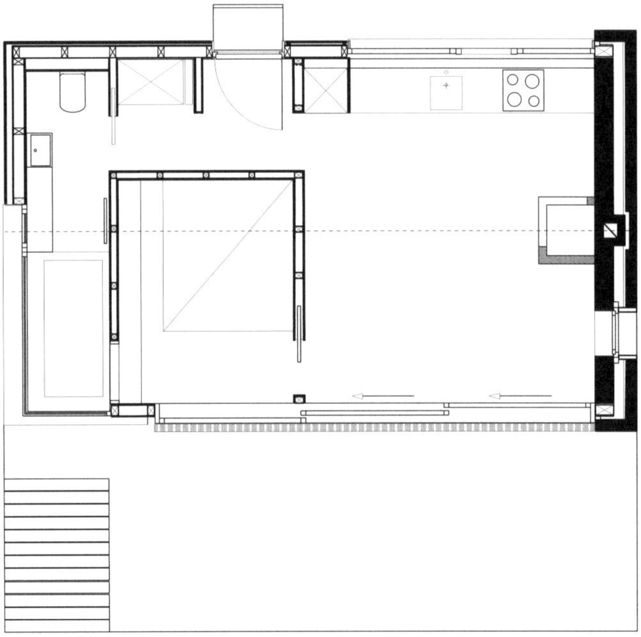

4

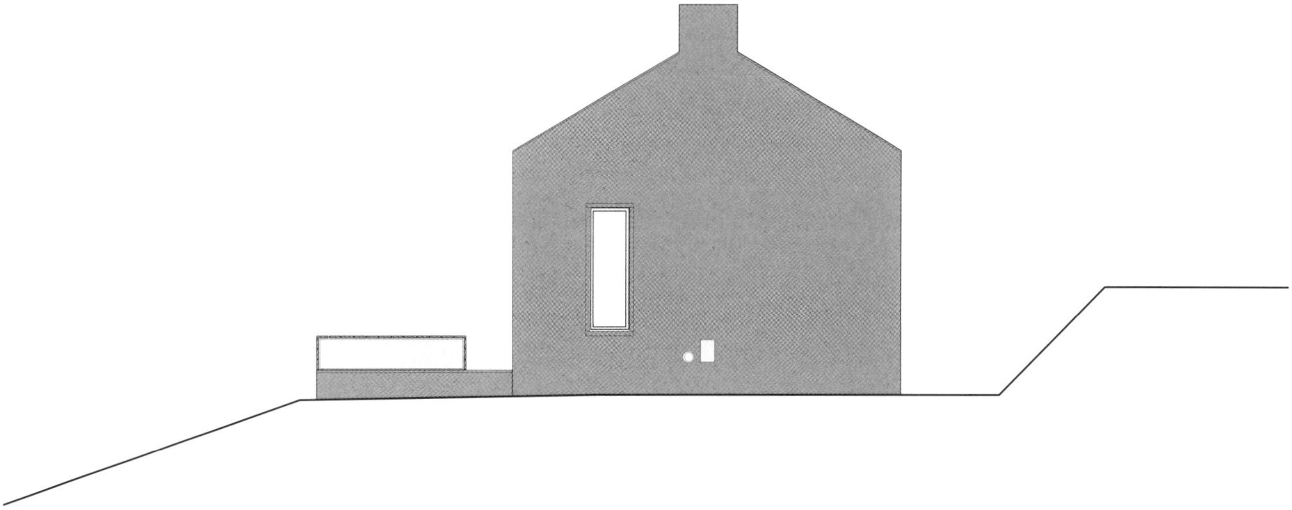

5

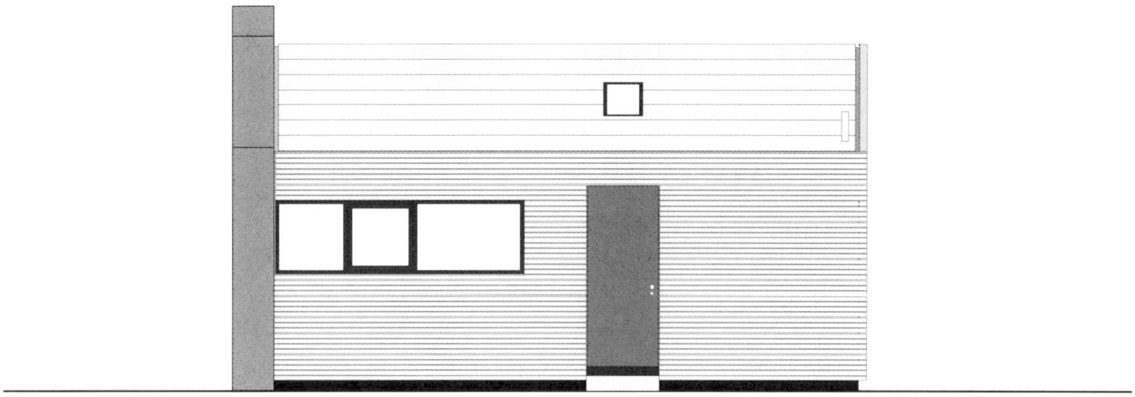

1 West elevation
2 Southeast elevation
3 Ground floor plan

4 East elevation
5 North elevation

HOUSE S

1

Architects: Hullak Rannow Architekten
Year of completion: 2018
Location: Senden, Bavaria
Gross floor area: 219 m²
Number of bedrooms: 4
Main materials / structure: masonry, plaster, solid concrete ceilings / conventional
Ecological features: ventilation system, water-water heat pump, floor heating system

2

48

The extremely narrow property in an existing building area was part of the neighboring property and was considered un-developable. Bernd Hullak, a specialist for difficult site cuts, found the right concept together with the client relatively quickly, resulting in a very narrow, long house with a saddle roof and a towering upper floor on both gable sides. The result was a roofed seating area in the south and an entrance area between the house and garage. In order to avoid problems with the high groundwater level of the nearby Iller, a basement was omitted. The necessary storage areas were accommodated in an additional room behind the garage.

The house is kept very simple. White walls and built-in furniture meet wooden floors and covers. The concrete ceilings are left visible and are color-balanced by the beige tiles in the wet areas. Energetically the house is state of the arts. With a ventilation system, water-water heat pump and underfloor heating, an application could be made for the 10,000 house programme and was built according to the KfW 55 standard.

3

4

1 Exterior façade from northeast
2 Exterior façade from southwest

3 Kitchen on the ground floor
4 Bathroom on the first floor
5 Living- and dining area

5

1

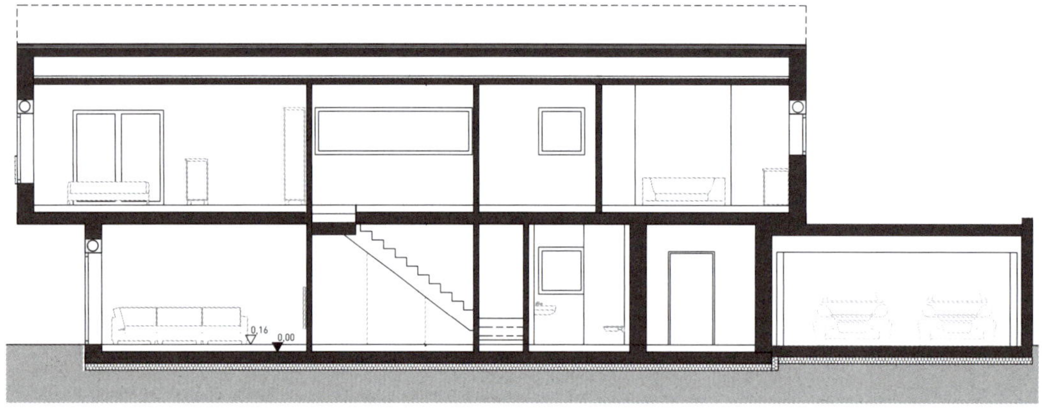

2

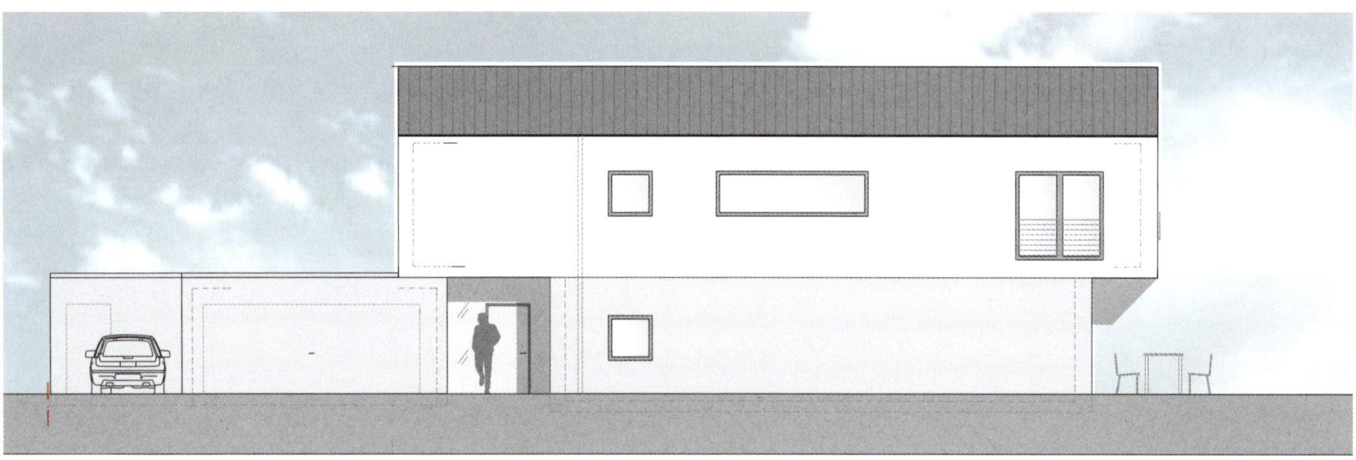

3

4

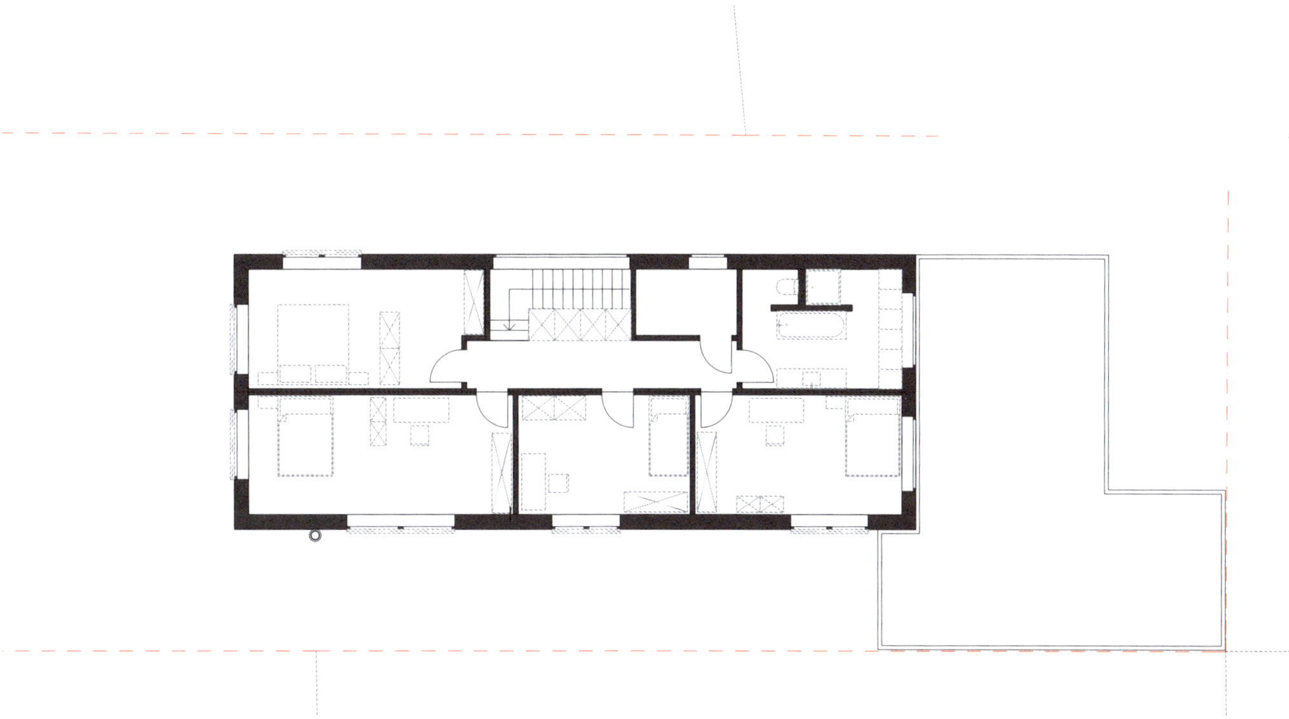

5

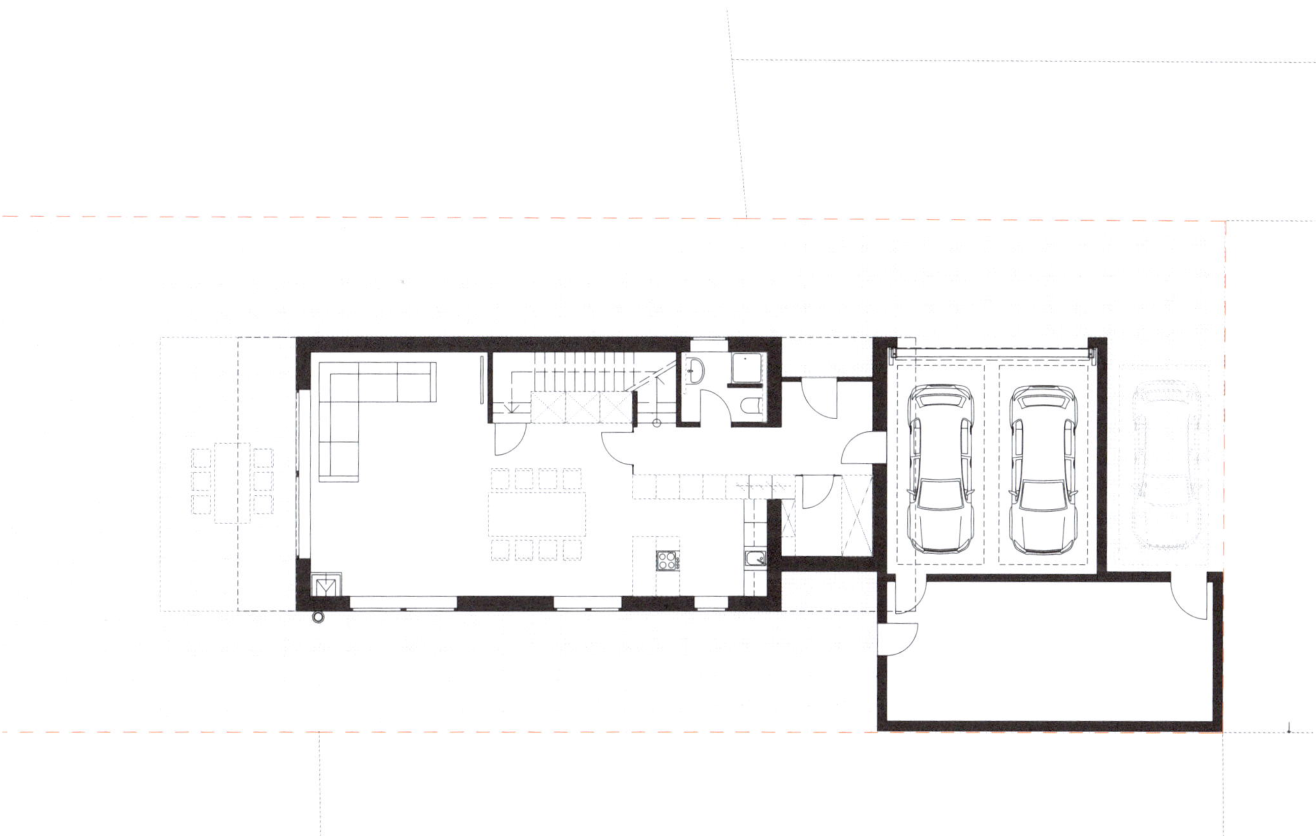

1 Longitudinal section
2 North elevation
3 South elevation

4 First floor plan
5 Ground floor plan

TRUDEL AND SIEGFRIED

1

Architects: Tobias Ruge Architekt
Interior designers: ruge+göllner gmbH
Year of completion: 2015
Location: Dierhagen, Mecklenburg-Western Pomerania
Gross floor area: 120 m^2
Number of bedrooms: 2
Main materials / structure: timber frame construction with reinforced concrete floor slab
Ecological features: timber construction, low-energy house

2

52

The holiday homes Trudel and Siegfried in Dierhagen on the Baltic Sea coast were planned and realized by Tobias Ruge (architect) and Marcus Ruge (interior designer). The brothers developed a modern architecture in timber frame construction with natural materials and delicate details. The holiday homes offer sufficient space for four people on 90 square meters each. They impress with their quiet location, simple beauty and functionality, and blend in carefully with the organic structure of the surroundings.

The white interiors contrast with the naturally graying larch wood façade. Individual color accents let every day begin refreshingly. The solid oak parquet gives the interiors warmth and security.

The ground floor levels are the heart of the holiday home: the dining area is equipped with a high-quality kitchen and merges smoothly into the spacious living area. Between the dining and living areas, the wood-burning stove spreads cosy warmth during the winter months. In the upper floors there are two spacious bedrooms with a double bed and a bathroom. On unclouded nights you can enjoy the starry sky from the skylights above the beds.

The modern, open architecture creates a light-flooded and nature-loving ambience. Large windows offer an impressive view as far as the Saaler Bodden. On the east and west terraces as well as in the garden under old pines beautiful sunny or shady places to eat, rest and play at any time of day can be found.

3

4

1 Front view
2 Back view

3 Staircase
4 View through the living area
5 Dining area
6 Living area
7 Kitchen and dining area

5, 6

7

1

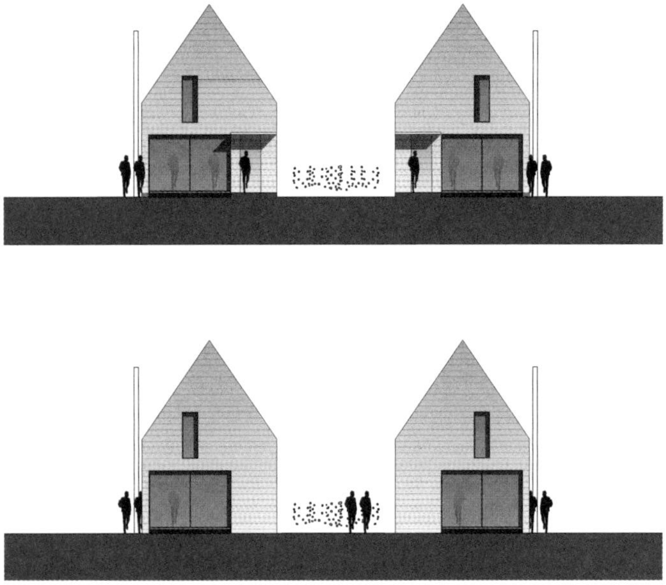

2

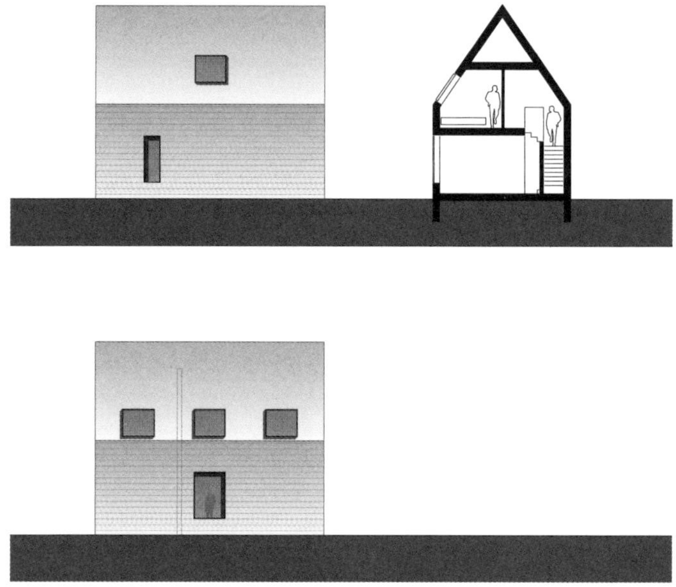

3

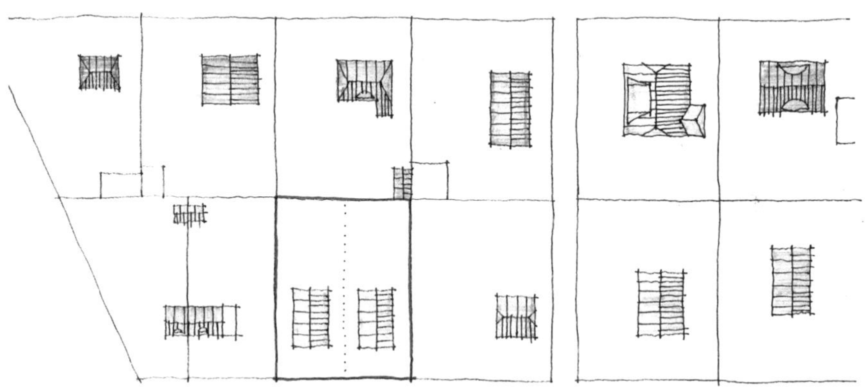

4

1 Front / back elevation
2 Longitudinal elevation / section
3 Sketch location
4 Drawings
5 First floor plan
6 Ground floor plan

5

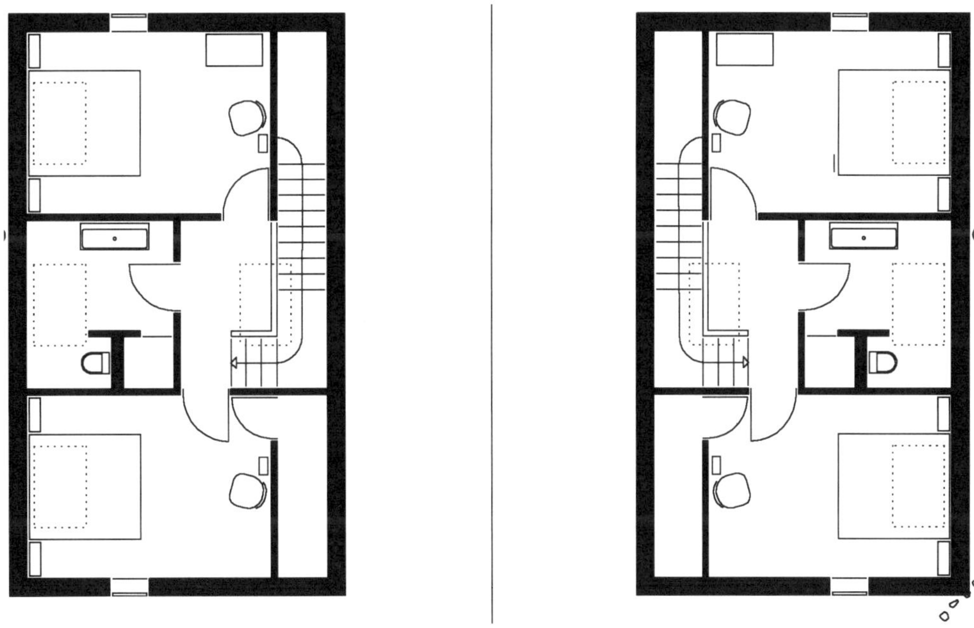

6

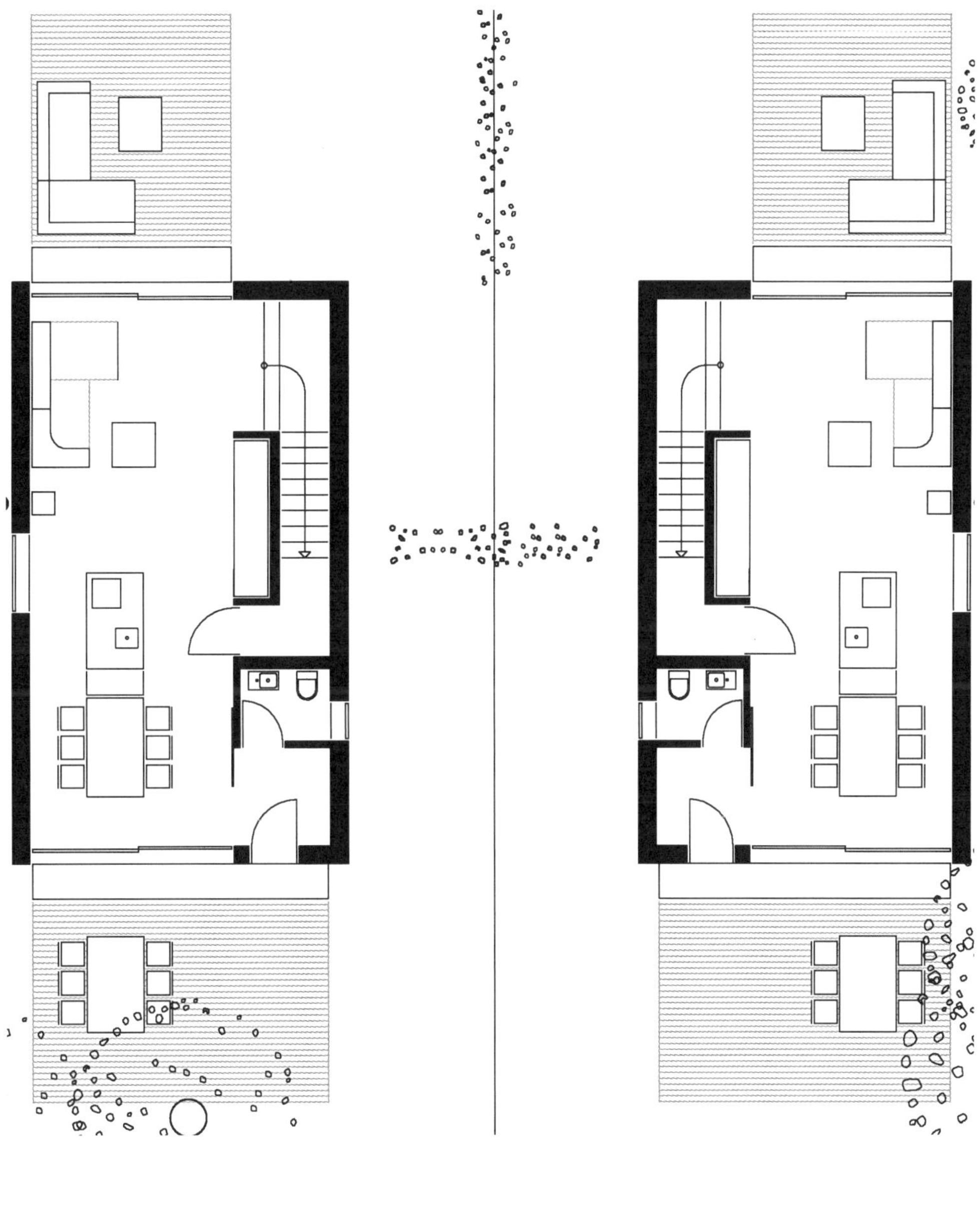

SAARBRÜCKER WEG

1

2

3

Architects: Smyk Fischer Architekten
Year of completion: 2016
Location: Mülheim an der Ruhr, North Rhine-Westphalia
Gross floor area: 344 m^2
Number of bedrooms: 4
Main materials / structure: sand-lime brick with mineral insulation and plaster / solid construction
Ecological features: simple technical equipment without ventilation and roller shutters, economical use of materials

The project was developed out of context. The existing building was demolished in favor of a two-volume new building, which was placed on one side of the left neighboring building. This first part adapts to the surroundings in form and color. The second, front-gabled black volume stands at a 90 degree angle towards the street. This way, the building creates a compromise between restrained integration and a concise appearance without appearing dominant.

The ground floor is dedicated to the commune areas, the entrance, kitchen, dining area and living area. They are designed as open spaces. The contrasting staircase core differentiates the areas and creates exciting room sequences. In terms of design, it picks up on the dark exterior façade. This opens with window elements to the garden and allows the connection to the outside space. The upper floor, with its three rooms, bathroom, and spacious corridor, is primarily dedicated to the children. In the light-flooded attic, the function of the staircase becomes clearly present again. It divides the open floor plan into bedroom, dressing room, and hobby area.

The centrally positioned massive core contributes to cost optimization through material savings. The structure of the building is adapted to the cardinal points for daylight supply. The black house with its saddle roof and traditional plaster façade has been implemented sustainable and efficient using simple means.

4

5

1 Exterior view
2 Garden view
3 Street view

4 Open kitchen with view in the garden
5 Living and dining area
6 First floor hallway
7 Living area with view to the kitchen

6

7

1, 2

3

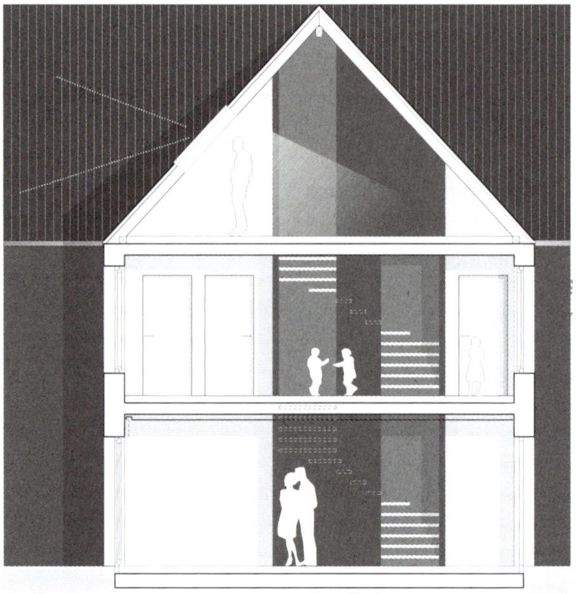

4

1 Attic floor bath- and bedroom
2 First floor nursery
3 First floor bathroom
4 Section

5 Attic floor plan
6 First floor plan
7 Ground floor plan

5

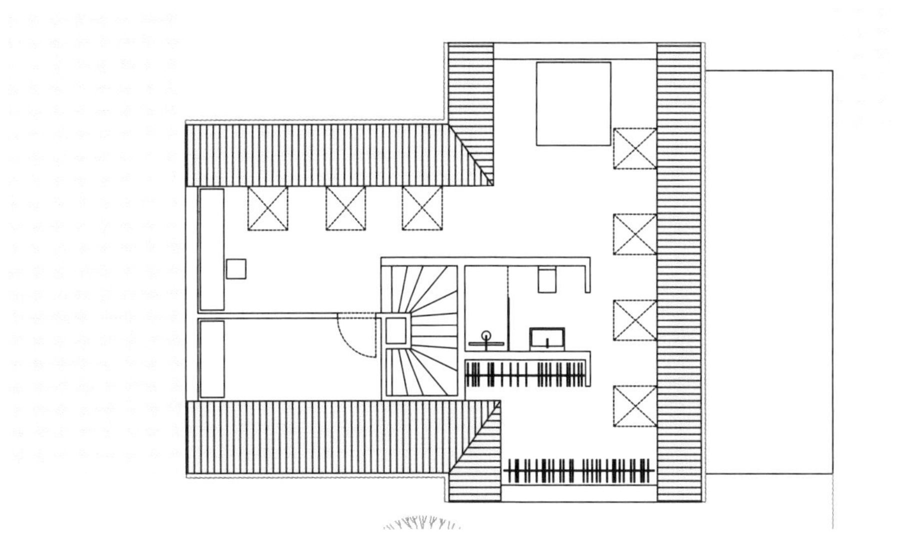

6

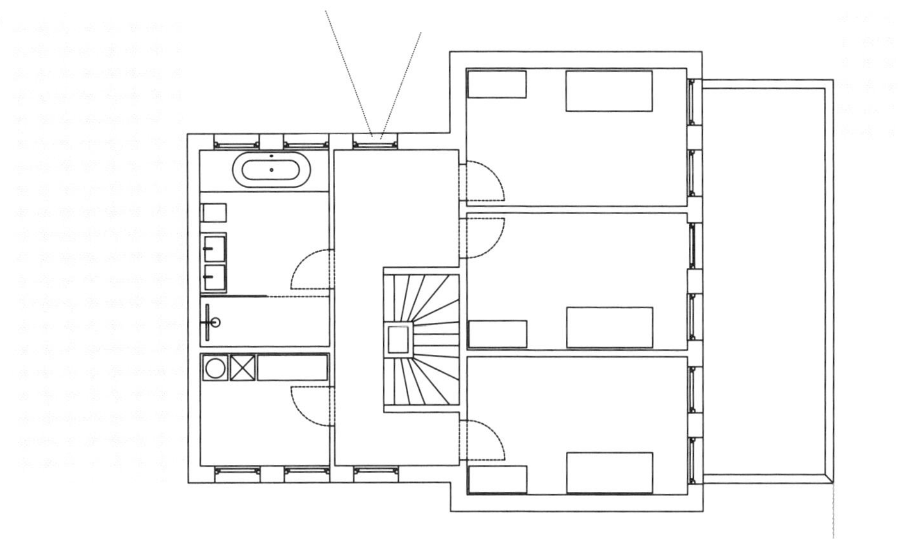

7

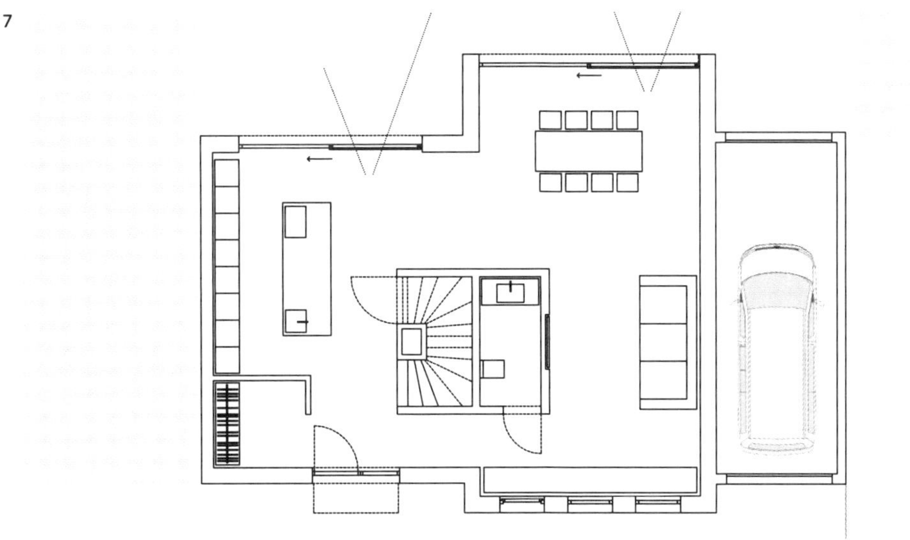

HOUSE ON A SLOPE

1

2

Architects: DWA David Wolfertstetter Architektur
Year of completion: 2018
Location: Dorfen, Bavaria
Gross floor area: 266 m²
Number of bedrooms: 4
Main materials / structure: silver fir, oak, plasterboard / cross laminated timber
Ecological features: KfW 40 Plus standard, 7.4 kWh/m² a, maximization of sustainable building materials

60

The choice of the peripheral site with a total gradient of six meters and only narrow access to the road was decisive for the special development of the design. The house is characterized by ecological building materials, surfaces made of pure high-quality white fir wood, durable materials, large windows, and a high energy standard. Clever solutions for storage spaces made it possible to dispense with basement and storage floors.

A staircase leads to the wooden terrace between two garages. A front door made of glass and a porch deflect the outside. The rooms of daily life are located on the upper floor and on the way upstairs there is a view down into the valley. The course of the sun is used throughout the day, both atmospherically and energetically. All ancillary rooms are located at the core in the center of the upper floor, while the individual rooms on the ground floor face west. The house is currently designed for five people, but has a flexible floor plan. For example, an additional drywall of only two meters in length can be used to separate a two-room apartment, which occupies two thirds of the ground floor area. The heating and electrical systems have already been installed separately for this division, and a second front door has already been installed. There was made use of flexible and adaptable rooms on the ground floor and an open floor plan on the upper floor.

A KfW 40 Plus standard was achieved through the high insulating effect of the wooden construction in combination with triple glazing, decentralized ventilation systems with heat recovery and a photovoltaic system on the roof with battery storage. The material concept is based on a simple basic idea: All materials should be left raw and the coloring in the house is not achieved by painting, but by the material color and texture itself. The façade is made of larch for weather reasons and the boards are left rough. The concrete remains unplastered inside and outside and is overgrown with wine in the long term.

3

1 Exterior view from the west
2 South terrace with view

3 Slope
4 View from east – mountain side

4

1

2

3

1 Kitchen with dining place at the window
2 Kitchen with a house inside the house
3 Living room with a house inside the house

4 Cross section
5 Ground floor plan
6 First floor plan

4

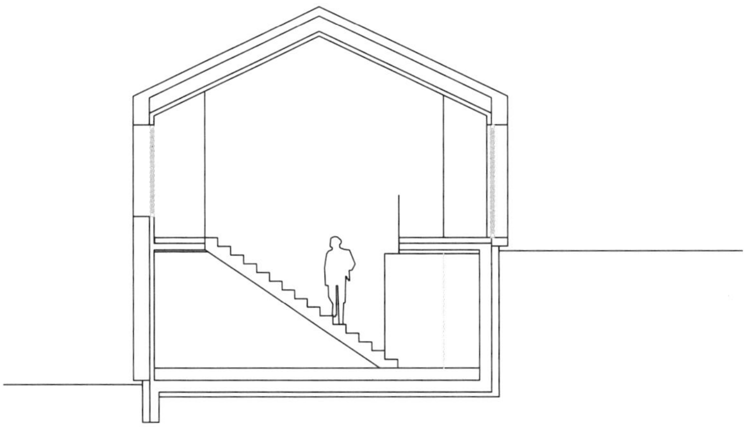

5

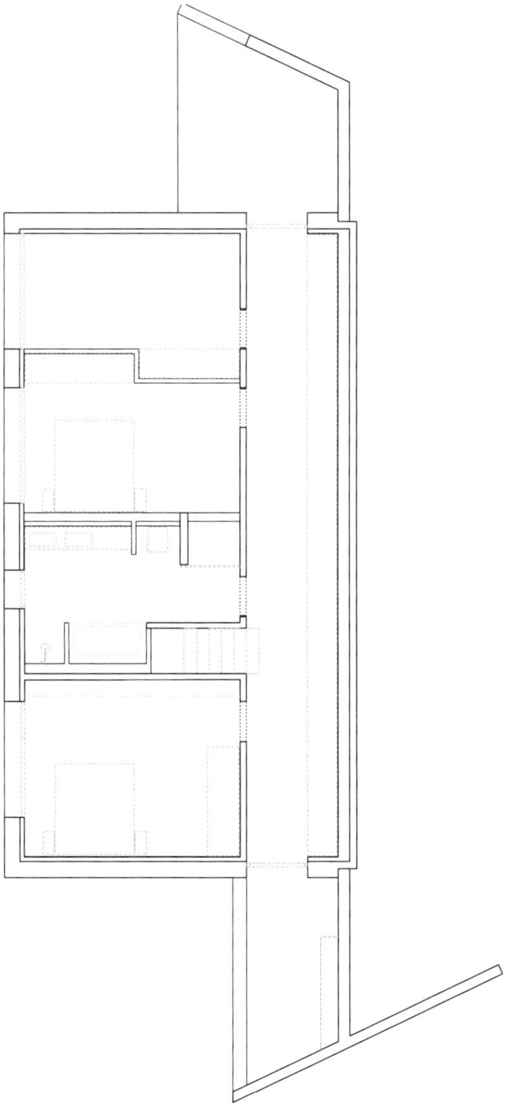

6

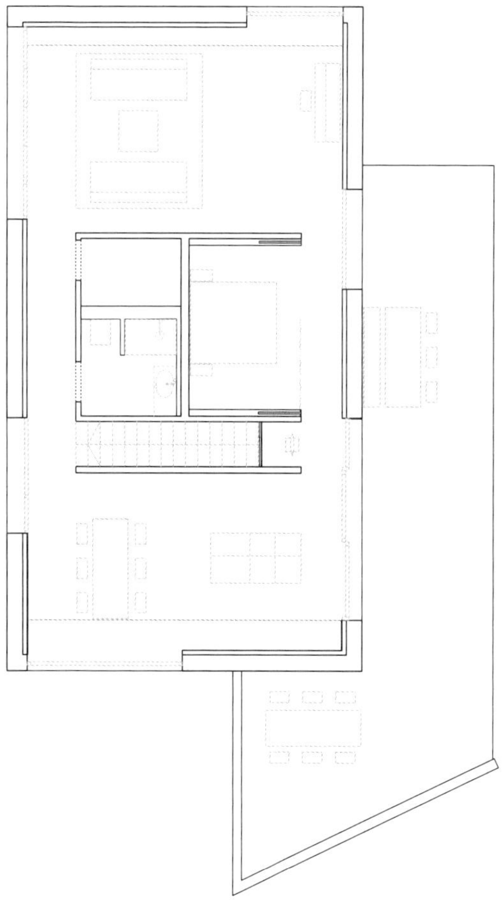

HOUSE NEAR LEIPZIG

1

2

3

64

Architects: Woltereck Fitzner Architekten PartGmbB
Year of completion: 2014
Location: Leipzig, Saxony
Gross floor area: 300 m^2 existing building and 65 m^2 extension
Main materials / structure: concrete and wood / solid construction
Ecological features: inside thermal insulation

4

The one-story pavilion is an extension to a country farm near Leipzig. It is used by a family of seven as dining and living space. Large openings provide a view into the garden. On warm days the windows can be completely pushed to the side. This removes the spatial boundaries; inside and outside merge seamlessly. The façade of the cube is made of light, smooth exposed concrete. The transition to the existing building is formulated as a "glass joint" in order to detach the new building from the existing building with a light yet clear gesture.

The interior of the cube, which is insulated on the inside, is lined with oak wood. The centrally arranged large dining table is illuminated from above with daylight. A fireplace separates a small seating area from the dining area. There is also a wall niche designed as a reading sofa with its own skylight, which serves as a retreat from everyday family life. Room-high curtains protect against unwanted glimpses.

5

1 Walls lined with oak
2 Dining area with skylight
3 Dining area and connection to existing building

4 Terrace view from south at night
5 Terrace view from south
6 Reading sofa in wall niche
7 Detailed connection to existing building
8 Detail exposed concrete

6, 7

8

1

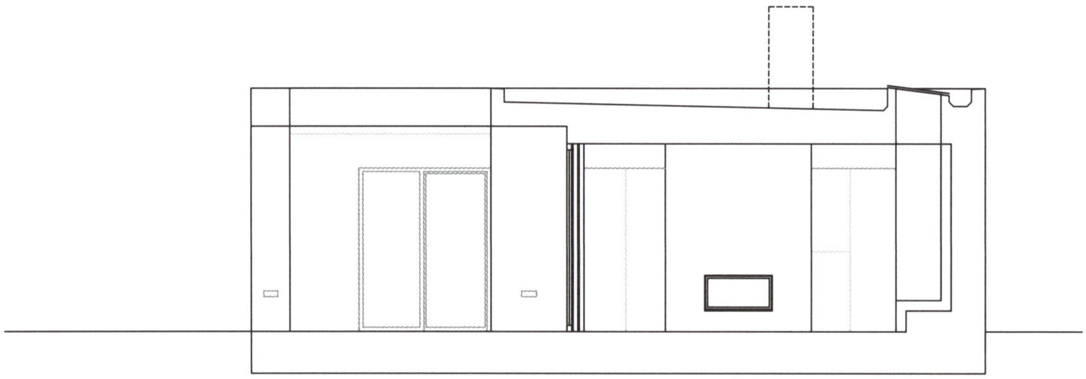

2

1 Cross section
2 Side view from the east with existing building

3 Longitudinal section
4 Ground floor plan

3

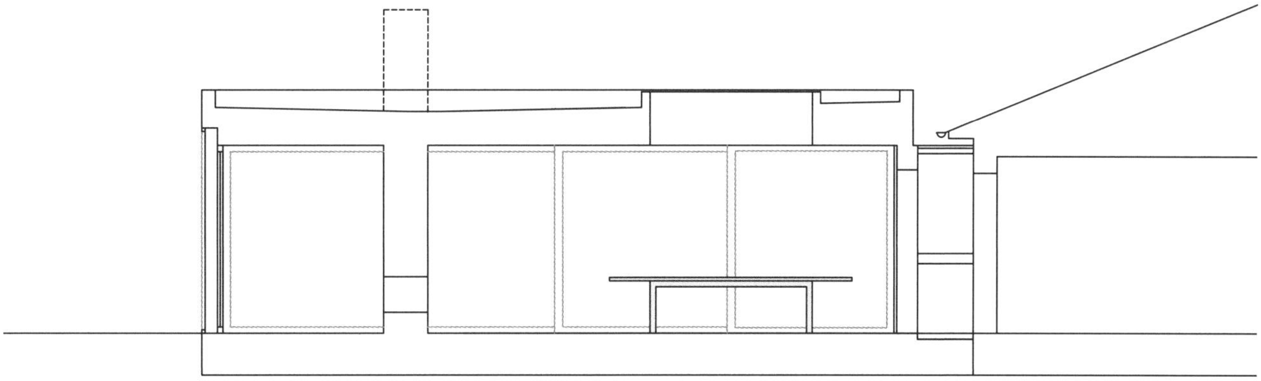

4

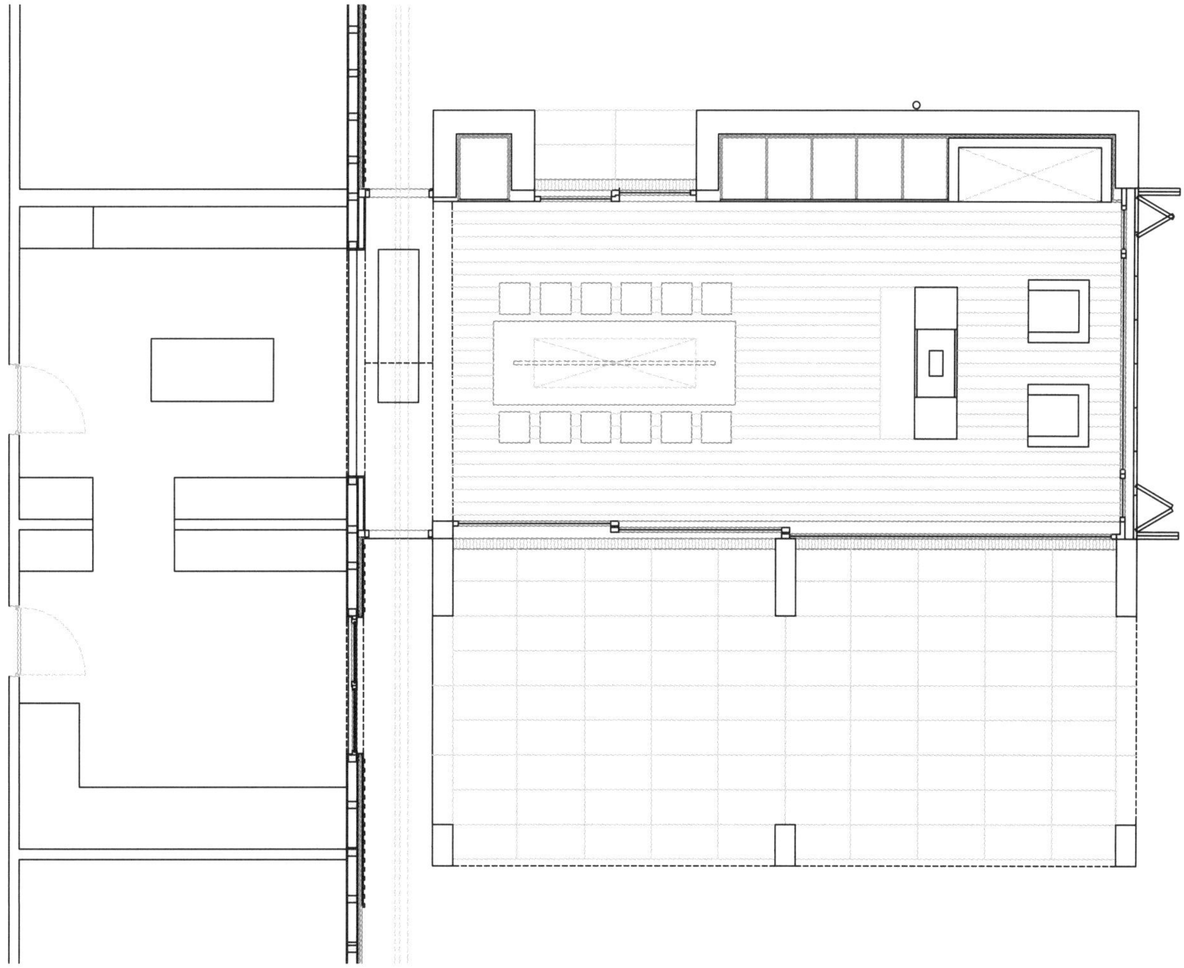

LOW-ENERGY HOUSE S

1

2

Architects: schmidt heinz pflüger architekten
Year of completion: 2017
Location: Neubiberg, Bavaria
Gross floor area: 268 m²
Number of bedrooms: 3
Main materials / structure: bricks, wood / solid construction
Ecological features: built according to KfW energy efficiency standard

The property is situated adjacent to a forest in the municipality of Neubiberg near Munich within a residential area characterized by a loose single-family house development. According to plan, the building was to be constituted from several wooden boxes which are visible in the exterior as well as in the interior. Specific functional areas were allocated to each of these units and as a result, the interior on the ground floor is divided into zones. In height, size and cubature, the single-family house with basement and double garage follows the existing development plan.

On the ground floor there is an entrance area, a guest toilet as well as a spacious living and dining area with an open kitchen and a separate office. The open box containing the terrace extends the living and dining area to the outside. Generous illumination is provided by the wide window front. The individual rooms are located on the upper floor: bedroom with dressing room and bathroom as well as the children's and guests' rooms with their own bathrooms.

The wooden boxes as a constitutional element of the design plan are also visible in the façade: While the main building is plastered in white, the boxes are covered with horizontal wooden slats. Thus their respective functions are also visible from the outside. The building was built according to KfW energy efficiency standard and is equipped with a geothermal heat pump.

1 Exterior view from west
2 Exterior view from south

3 Entrance area with structuring wooden box
4 Bathroom
5 Kitchen with window façade

3

4

5

1

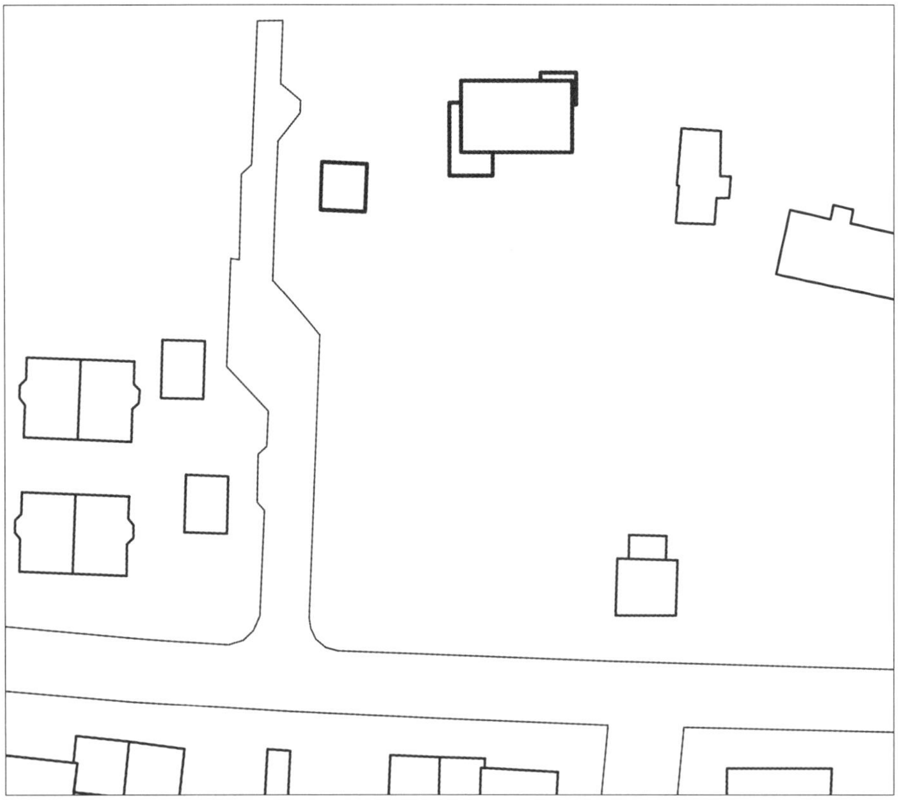

2

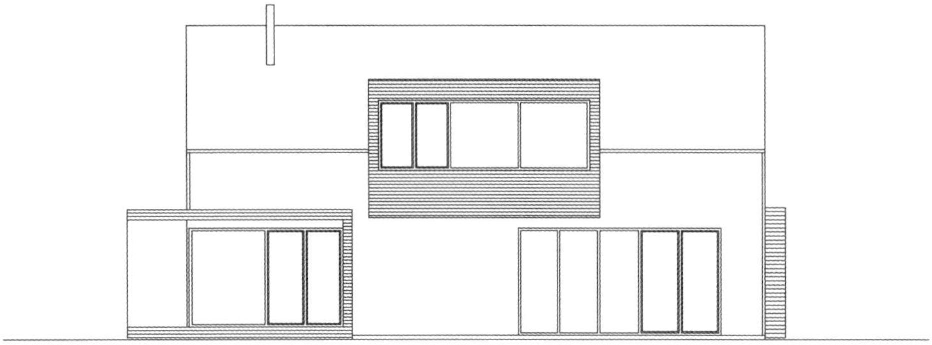

3

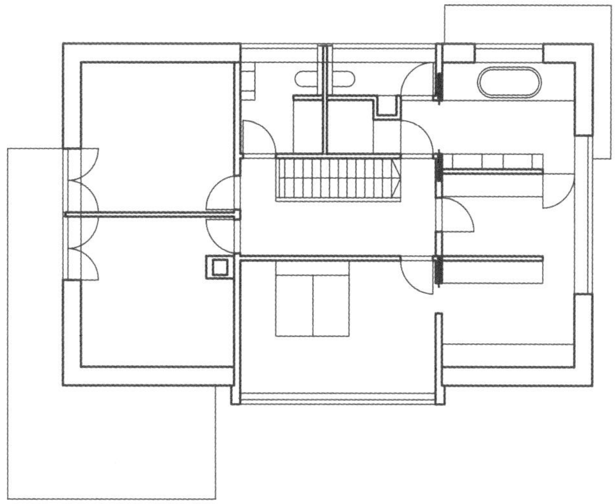

4

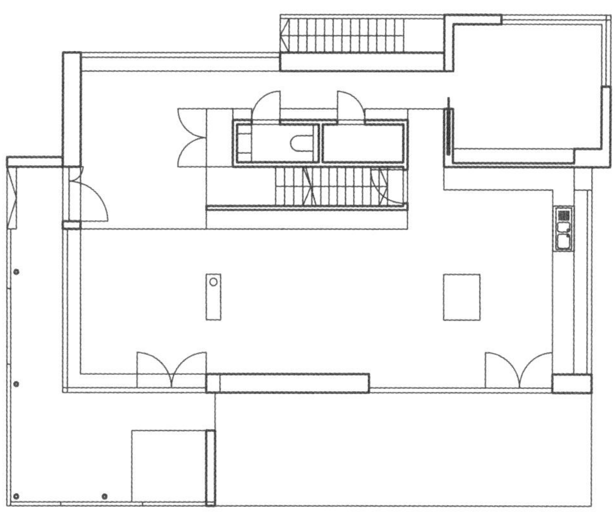

1 Site plan
2 South elevation

3 First floor plan
4 Ground floor plan

HOUSE W

1

2, 3

Architects: Thomas Beyer Architekten
Year of completion: 2009
Location: Caputh, Brandenburg
Gross floor area: 301 m^2
Number of bedrooms: 2
Main materials / structure: concrete, wood, glass / precast concrete, timber frame construction
Ecological features: wooden building, geothermal heat pump

House W is located on a hillside property in Caputh with a view of the Schwielowsee lake. The ground plan follows the longitudinal expansion of the property and the building is constituted from cubes built offset to each other. They expand over three levels with terraces respectively allocated to them. Room-high glazings extend the interior to the outside over the terraces into the garden.

Exposed concrete, wood, glass and steel characterize the building from the outside. The horizontal formwork of the upper floor and the surface of the terraces follow the alignment of the building. They stand out from the tall pine trees on the property.

The flooring on the basement as well as on the ground floor is seamlessly coated with polyurethane. On the upper floor, however, white oiled parquet flooring is installed. The built-in furniture is made from composite wood and coated white as well. A geothermal heat pump is used for heating and provides warm water.

4

5

6

1 Exterior view from south
2 Exterior view from east
3 Exterior view from west

4 Kitchen area
5 Living area
6 Dining area
7 Studio

7

1

2

3

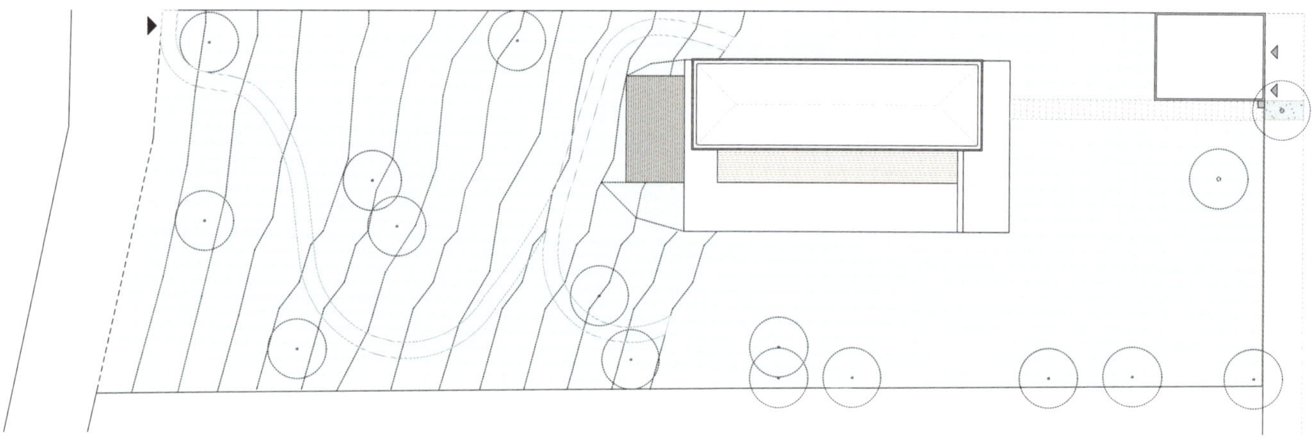

4

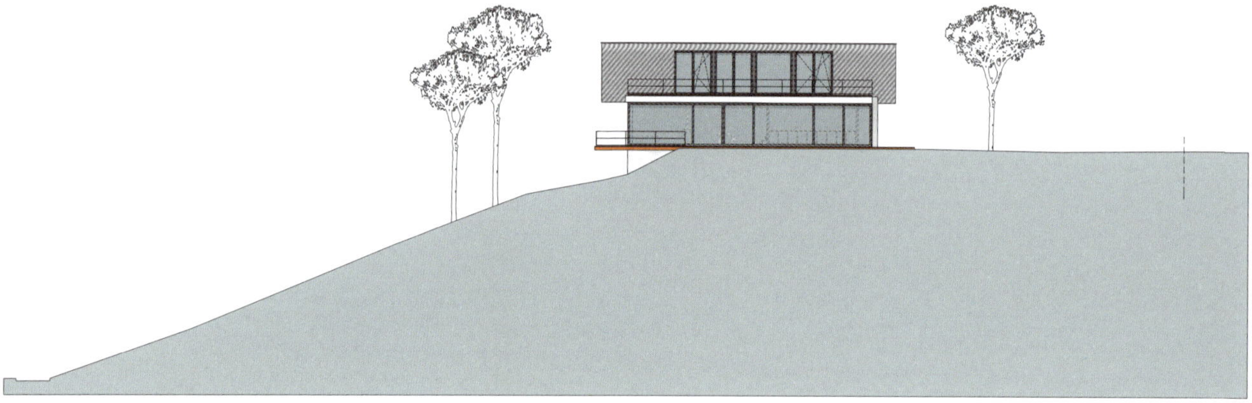

1 Bathroom
2 Gallery with studio
3 Site plan
4 Terrain section from south
5 First floor plan
6 Ground floor plan
7 Basement floor plan

5

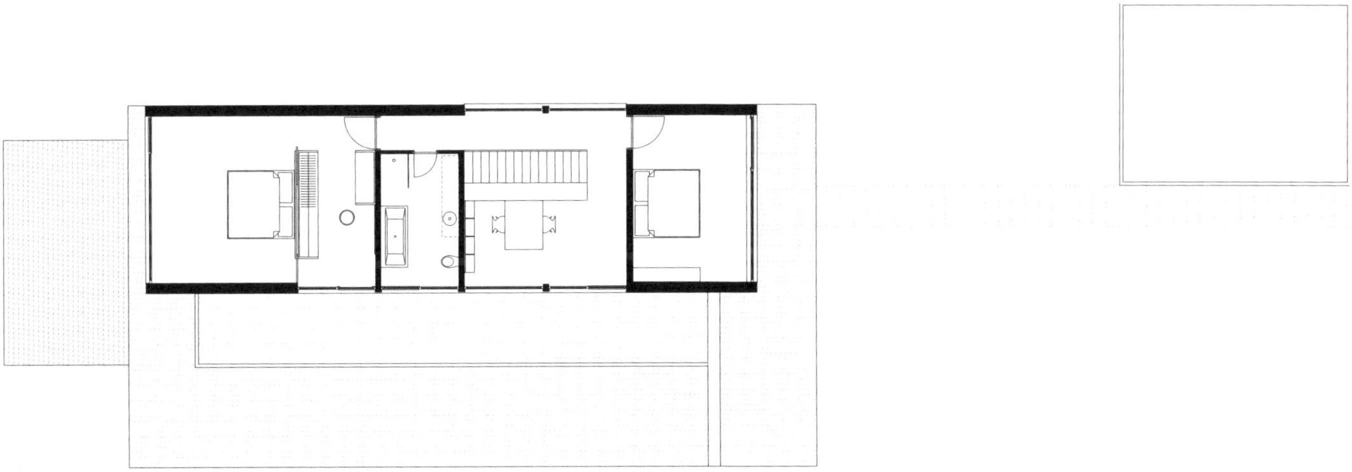

6

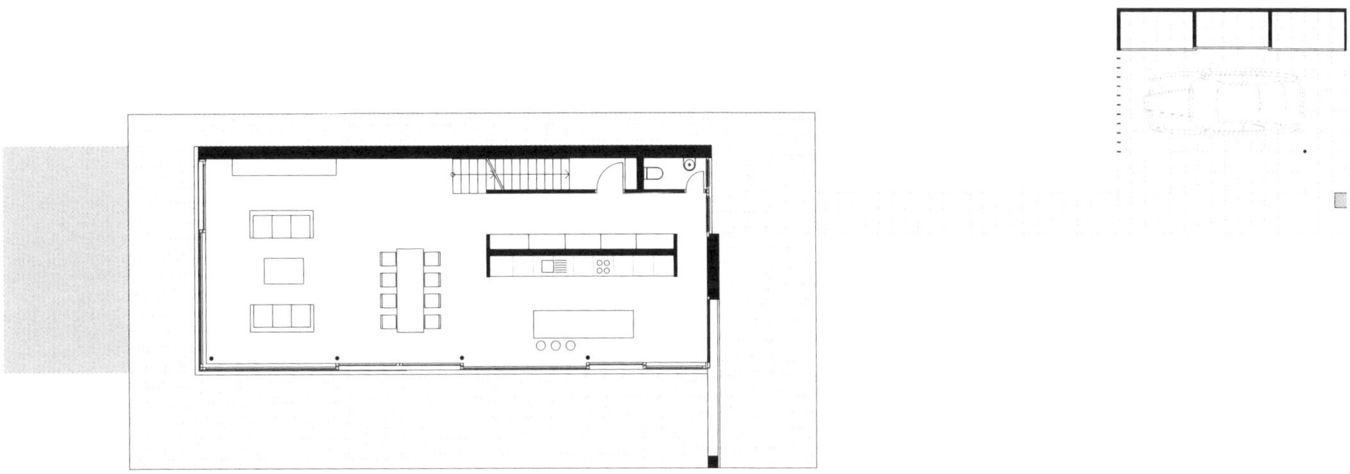

7

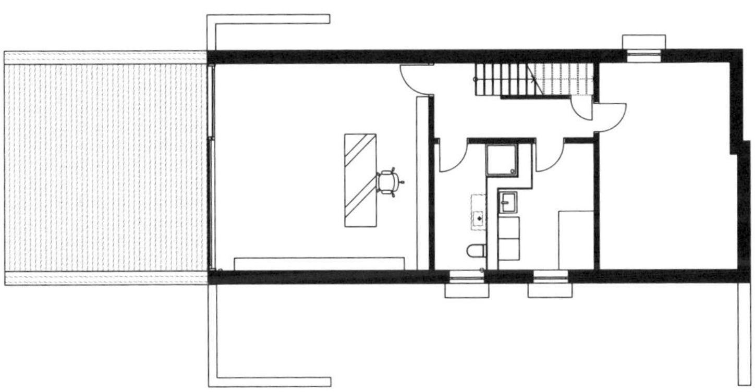

HOUSE WILDNER

1

2

Architects: castello feisthauer weber – cfw architekten
Year of completion: 2018
Location: Thomm, Rhineland-Palatinate
Gross floor area: 364 m²
Number of bedrooms: 5
Main materials / structure: pumice, concrete, wood / masonry
Ecological features: low-energy house, photovoltaics, geothermal heat pump, heat recovery ventilation system

The building ensemble with a garage towards the street is typical of the region and adapts to the trapezoidal hillside property in a small village. Its peripheral location results in a far reaching view and provides space for a family of five and a granny flat in the basement, with direct access due to the hillside terrain. The division of the building can be seen in the axis of the ridge on the façade as well as inside. Classic patterns have been implemented unconventionally to satisfy the high demand of the client in a contemporary manner. The house is energy-efficient due to the installing of photovaltaics, a heat pump, and an air ventilation system. The technical equipment also provides comfort for the inhabitants. The grounds support the design of the building and utilize the hillside terrain with associated shelters, terraces, and access roads.

3

4

1 Exterior view from northeast
2 Exterior view from southwest

3 Staircase in exposed concrete
4 Kitchen with void
5 Corridor on the first floor
6 Bathroom on the first floor

5, 6

1

2

1 View on the gable
2 Detail view on the vanity

3 Southwest elevation
4 Northwest elevation
5 Northeast elevation
6 Southeast elevation
7 Ground floor plan
8 First floor plan
9 Basement floor plan

3

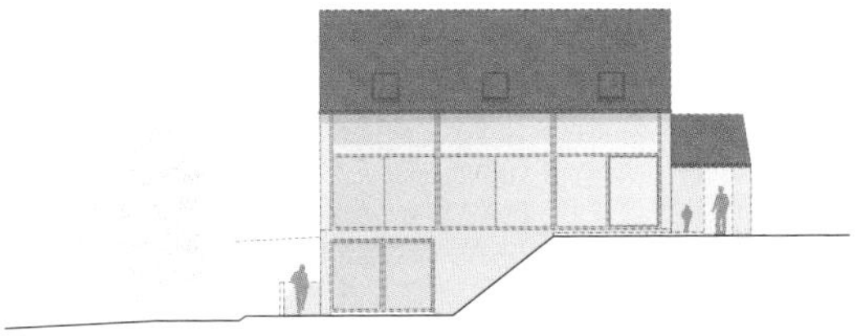

4

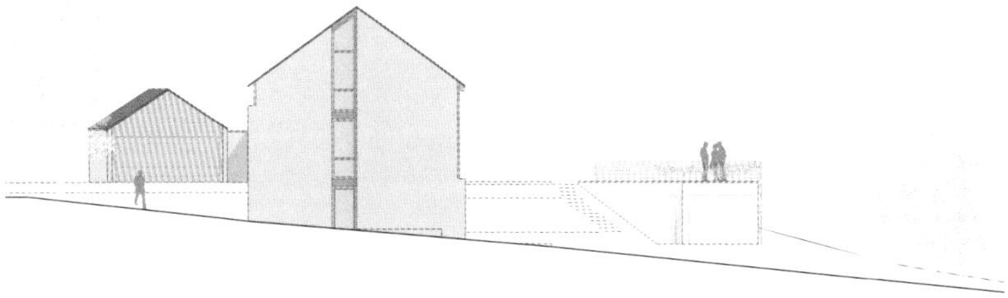

5

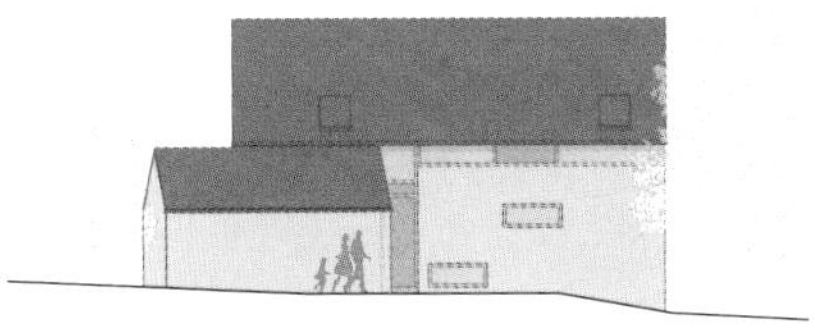

6

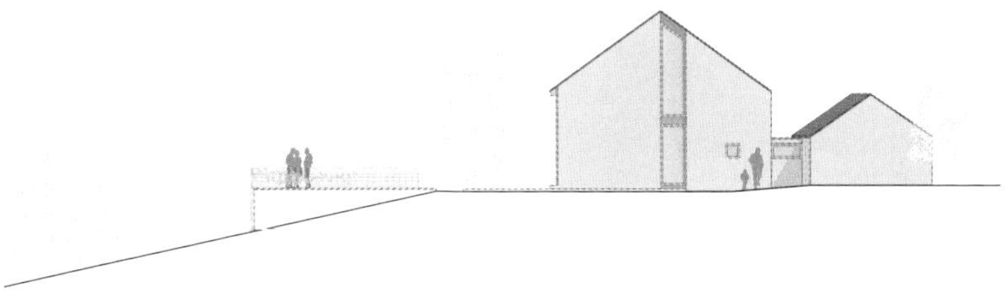

7

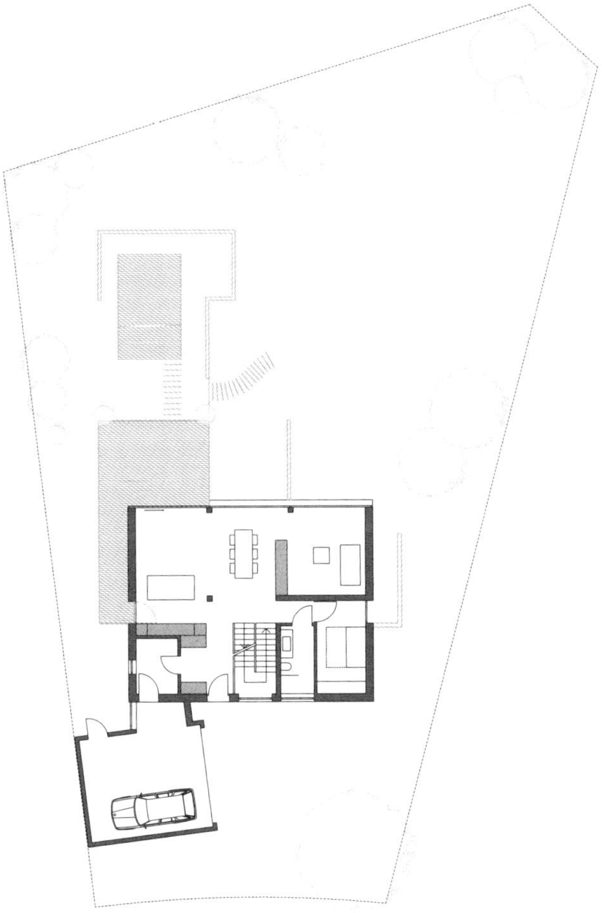

8

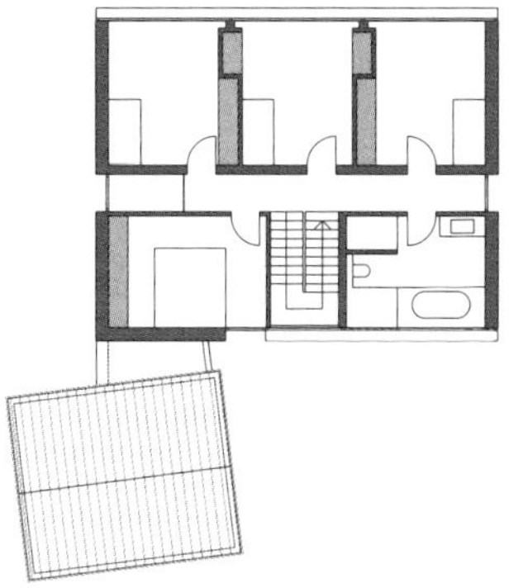

9

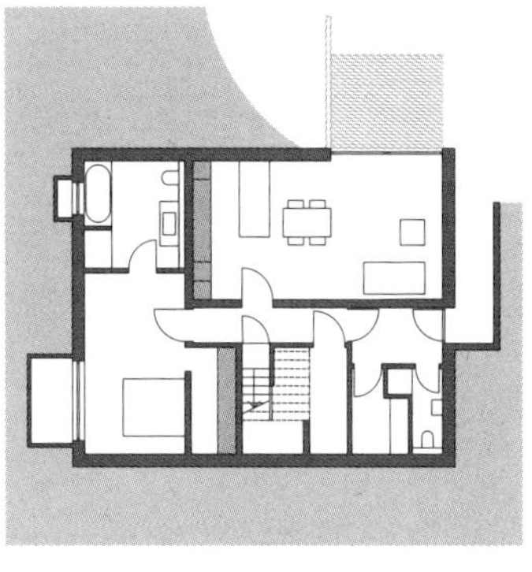

HOUSE WALTER GÖBEL

1

2, 3

Architects: banz + riecks dipl.-ing., architekten
Year of completion: 2013
Location: Bochum, North Rhine-Westphalia
Gross floor area: 445 m^2
Number of bedrooms: 3
Main materials / structure: reinforced concrete, wood / timber frame and solid hybrid construction
Ecological features: 40 % under demands of EnEv, total energy consumption 15.5 $kWh/m^2 a$

The spatial concept of the house is structured through its offset build-up and the client's library, being the center of the privat and intellectual life. The central, laterally glazed staircase connects the stories and the library wall. This structure provides substance and vitality to the building as a whole.

The house is accessible via a square cut-out. It is tied to the corridor and the staircase to make the entrance situation seamless and directly perceptible.

Its structural counterpart is the entrance area diagonally opposite towards the garden. A wind-protected outdoor reading area has been created here, which is accessed via an inner two-story reading room. The open living and dining area as well as the kitchen have been aligned with the garden. On the north side there is a work space with a separate bathroom. This area can be used for home care purposes as well, is accesibly designed and therefore suitable for multi-generational living.

4

5

6

1 Garden view
2 Access area
3 Glass façade

4 Library room accessing the first floor
5 Library room accessing the ground floor
6 Library room with view into the garden

1

2

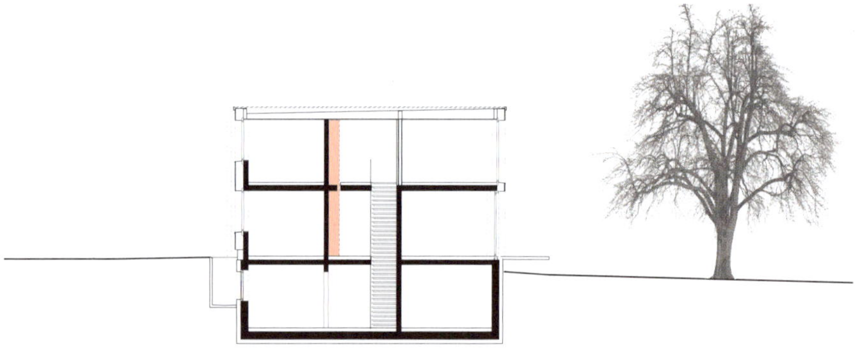

3

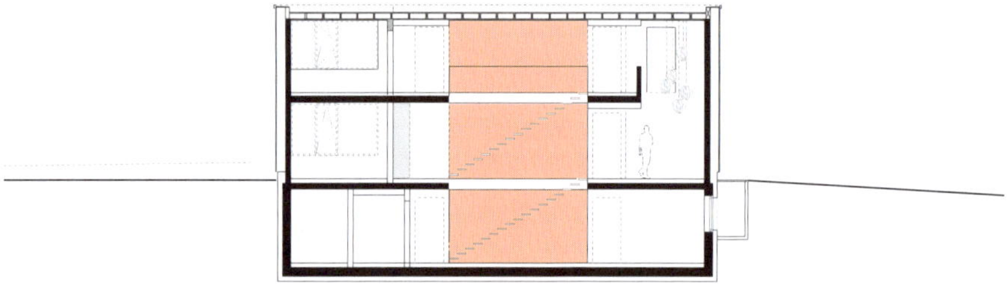

1 Site plan
2 Cross section
3 Longitudinal section

4 First floor plan
5 Ground floor plan
6 Basement floor plan

4

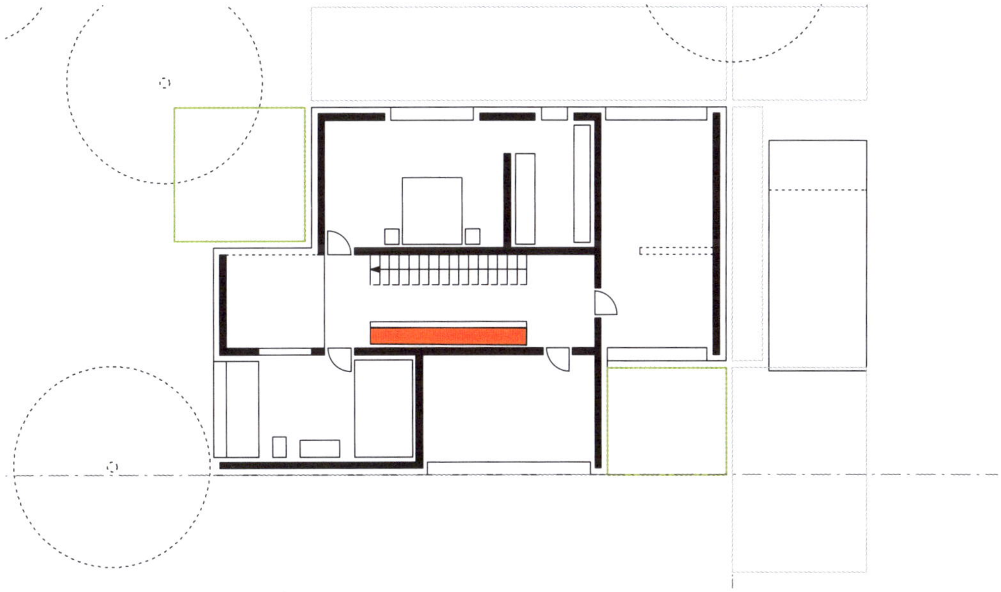

5

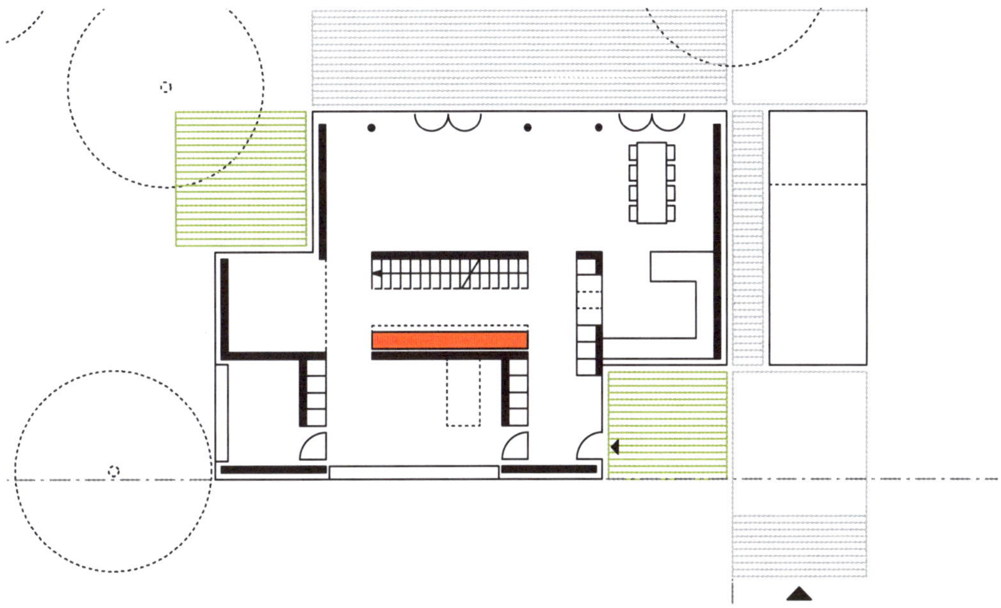

6

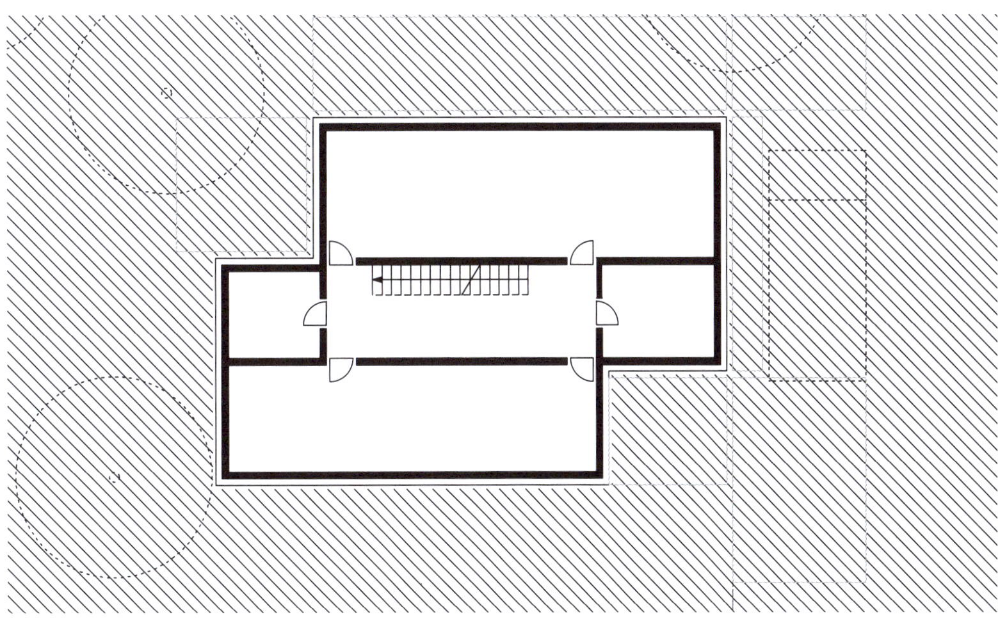

HOUSE FER

1

2, 3

Architects: Nehse & Gerstein Architekten
Year of completion: 2015
Location: Neustadt am Rübenberge, Lower Saxony
Gross floor area: 105 m^2
Number of bedrooms: 2
Main materials / structure: wood / mixed construction

This newly constructed building serves as a weekend home and is located in Mardorf at the Steinhuder Meer. The plot slopes slightly from the road to the south towards the garden and is surrounded by a dense stock of bushes and trees on all sides. The house was placed in the northern area of the plot and the complex contains not only the areas for living but also a roofed entrance and a boathouse. The entrance area functions as an incision, for the building appears closed to the street side. White wooden slats provide additional weather protection and privacy. The façade on the garden side is characterized by striking dormer and large window cases.

The corridor serves as a central distribution unit and provides access to the guest room, bathroom, the upper floor, and the living and dining area. Furthermore, the course of the terrain is also visible in the interior. Corridor and living area are offset to each other through different levels on the ground floor. The living area therefore is separated and opens generously to the garden through room-high windows. The dormer on the upper floor houses the bedroom and a second bathroom for enhanced privacy.

4

5

6

1 Front view
2 Exterior view with entrance area
3 Back view

4 Terrace
5 View into the living area
6 Kitchen, dining and living area

1

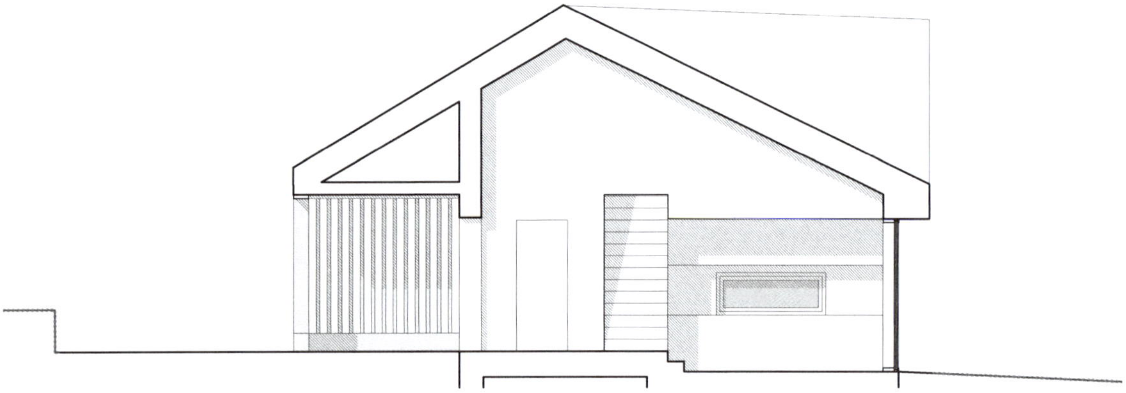

2

3

1 Garden side elevation
2 Sketch exterior
3 Sketch interior

4 First floor plan
5 Ground floor plan

4

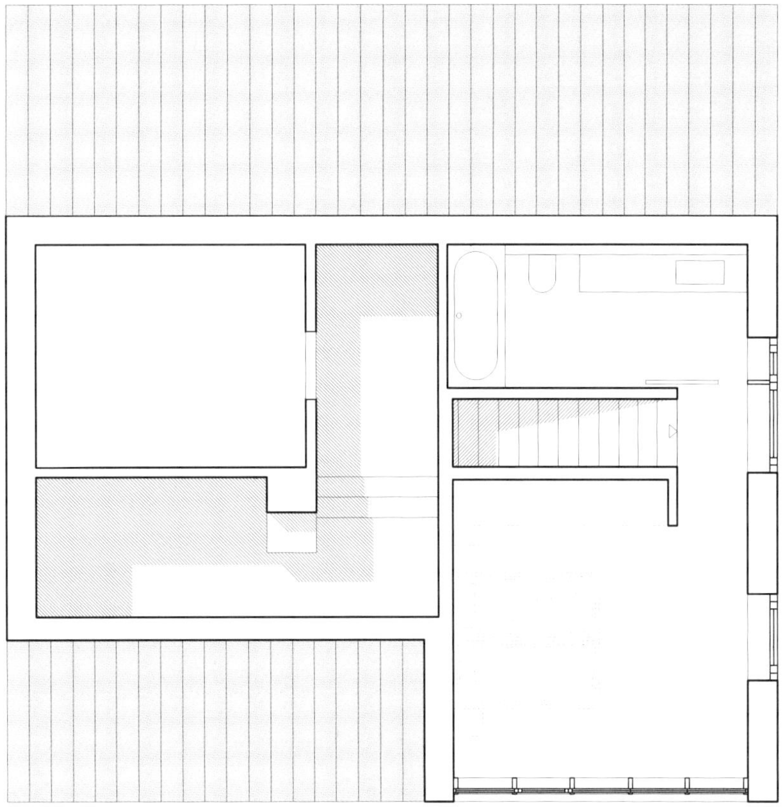

5

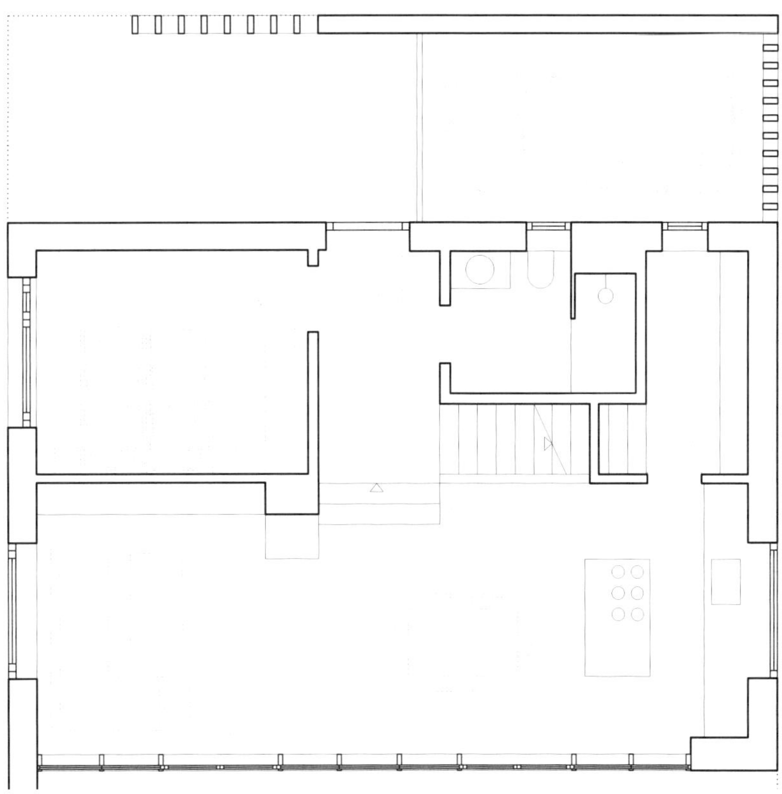

HOUSE 3 – GRAULESHOF

1

2

Architects: Liebel / Architekten
Year of completion: 2018
Location: Aalen, Baden-Württemberg
Gross floor area: 326.8 m^2
Number of bedrooms: 3
Main materials / structure: plastered concrete, wooden floor / solid construction
Ecological features: solar system, use of passive solar energy through southern glazing, high insulation standard

3

The two-story house on a hillside opens with its living areas completely to the south and offers a view into the landscape. On the street side, on the other hand, the house has a single story and is almost closed. The building concept is flexible and future-oriented: The fully accessible entrance level with dining, living, and private areas can be used as a separate unit after the children have moved out. Depending on the requirements, part of the sloping floor could be occupied by a nursing person or separated off as a granny flat.

4

An essential component of the architectural concept is the atrium, which provides optimal lighting for the living area. Cooking and dining areas as central lounges thus benefit from two-sided, all-day lighting – on the one hand via the large south-facing terrace with a view of the open countryside, and on the other hand via the atrium sheltered from the wind, which gets into the house through the atmospheric evening sun. The bedroom on the street side, which is closed to the north, also receives sufficient daylight from the atrium, as does the bathroom area, which is additionally illuminated by a skylight. On hot days, the introverted atrium is an ideal retreat.

1 Exterior view from the north
2 Exterior view from the south

3 Open cooking and dining area
4 Living area with three-sided glazing
5 Atrium providing daylight
6 Garden access from the atrium

5

6

1

2

3

1 Kitchen with view to the south into the greenery
2 Staircase to the hillside floor and open living area
3 Dining area and atrium in the evening sun

4 Site plan
5 First floor plan

4

5

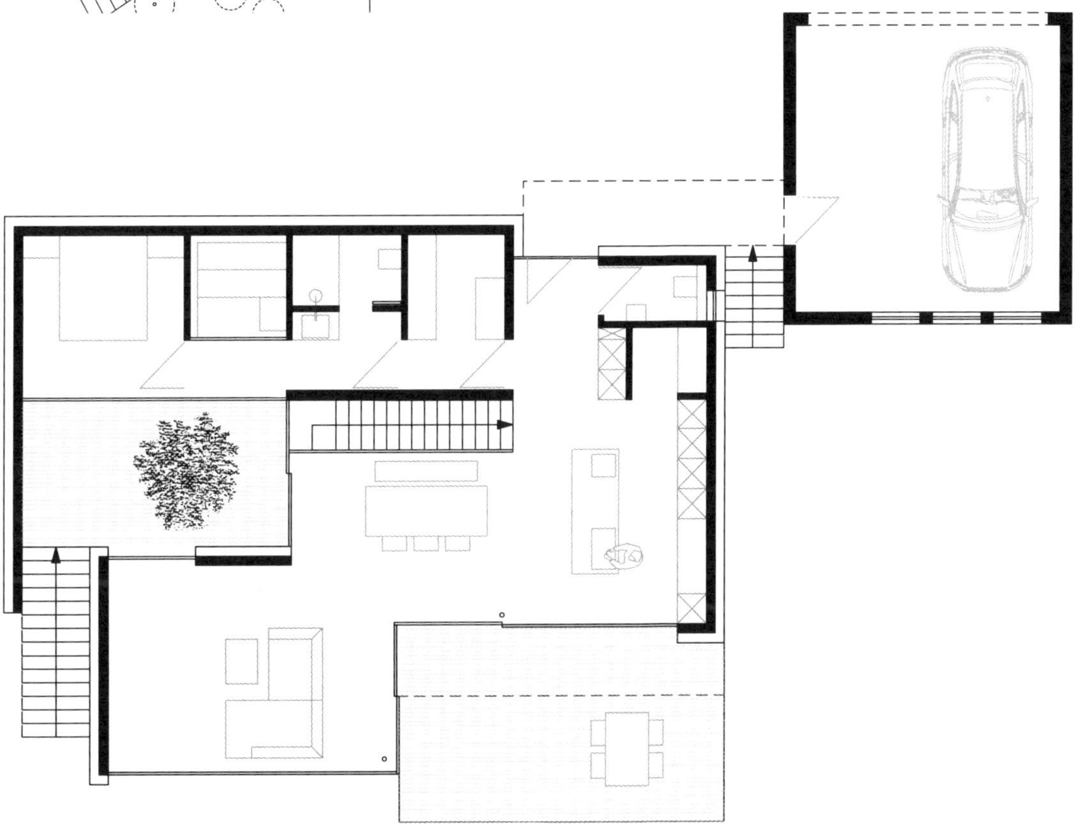

R8

1

2

1 Exterior view from northwest
2 Northwestern façade at dawn

3 First floor plan
4 Ground floor plan
5 Basement plan
6 View into living area and garden
7 Living area extending towards the garden
8 Bedroom

The new building is located in a residential area on the outskirts of Munich, characterized by single- and two-family houses. It was built in the second row in a spacious garden with old trees. On the outside the building appears as a monolithic, white cube seeming to grow directly out of the ground. A few large openings are oriented towards south and west, allowing a glimpse onto the groups of trees.

The entrance area extending over two stories, the open staircase, and the corridors are equipped minimalistic and only lit via skylights. Inside, the materials have been reduced to exposed concrete walls and cement floors to stimulate the visitor's awareness. Furthermore, they draw attention to the layout and allocation of the rooms. The rooms retain a minimalistic character, but are – in terms of material – designed in a more homey way. White walls and local oak extend the material repertoire. Large, massive windows with deep oak casings provide a sheltered view into the garden and can be used as a cozy recess. Through the reduction of materials, and the decorative fitting a calm and pleasant atmosphere is created.

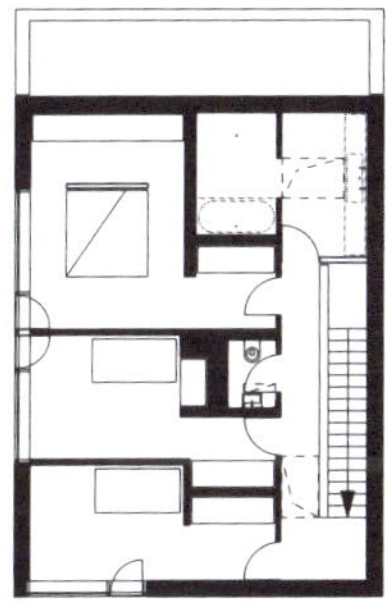
3

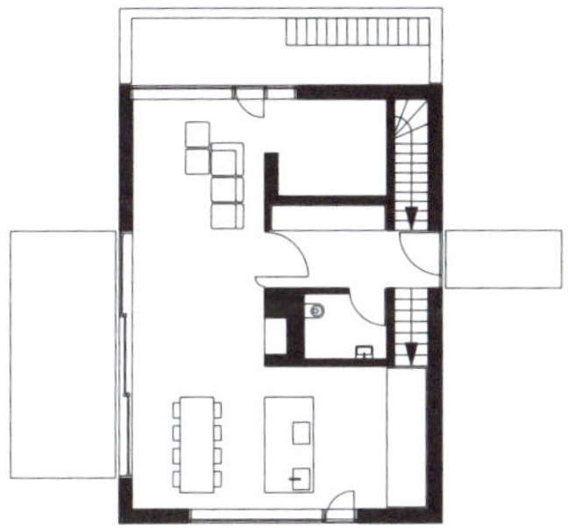
4

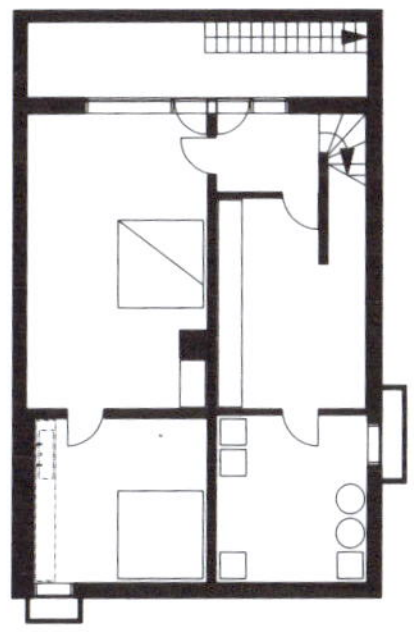
5

Architects: Neutard Schneider Architekten Partnerschaft mbB
Year of completion: 2010
Location: Munich, Bavaria
Gross floor area: 300 m^2
Number of bedrooms: 3
Main materials / structure: concrete, oak / solid construction
Ecological features: geothermal heat pump

6

7

8

EXTENSION T276

1

2

Architects: keenco3 UG – Planungsgesellschaft für Holzbau
Year of completion: 2017
Location: Hamburg
Gross floor area: 125 m^2
Number of bedrooms: 1
Main materials / structure: timber frame construction (walls), plywood planks (ceiling)
Ecological features: conservation of existing living space, use of sustainable resources, solarthermics

A cubic extension constructed in wood enlarges the living space of a family of four by replacing a small garage. It offers space for a generous living room, a study, and a guest room. The garage has been shifted halfway into the ground. The charming existing building from the 1920s remains largely untouched, only the ground floor has been reorganized. The extension distinguishes itself in terms of materials, volume, and structural design, while being respectful to the existing building. The timber frame construction is clad with a Douglas fir form work reflecting the pattern of the existing clinker brick.

The interior is characterized by white walls and polished screed. The undersides of the plywood ceilings are visible and match the white-oiled wooden staircase. The living area draws its unique character from the peculiar design of the staircase, and the different floor levels. A single brick wall of the existing building contrasts with predominantly white colors, emphasizing the building's rustic features. Existing masonry thus is integrated into modern space design. A rectangular window was embedded into the brick wall to loosen up the structure, to open up the living area, and to connect the interiors with each other. In addition, large glass doors offer a view into the garden, thus enlarging the visual space.

3

1 Exterior view from north
2 Exterior view from east

3 Staircase to the workspace
4 Living with clinker brick wall

4

1

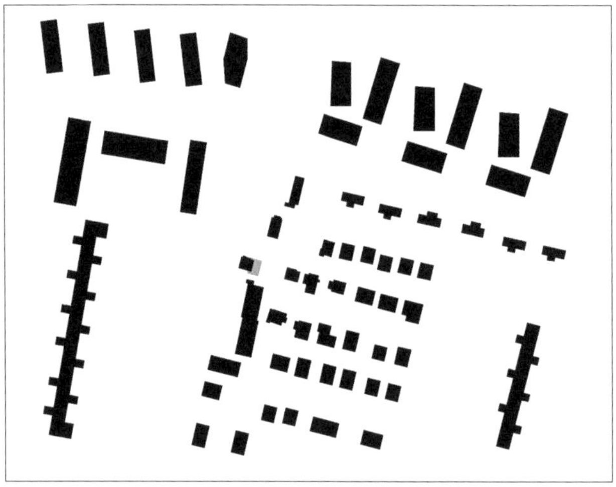

2

3

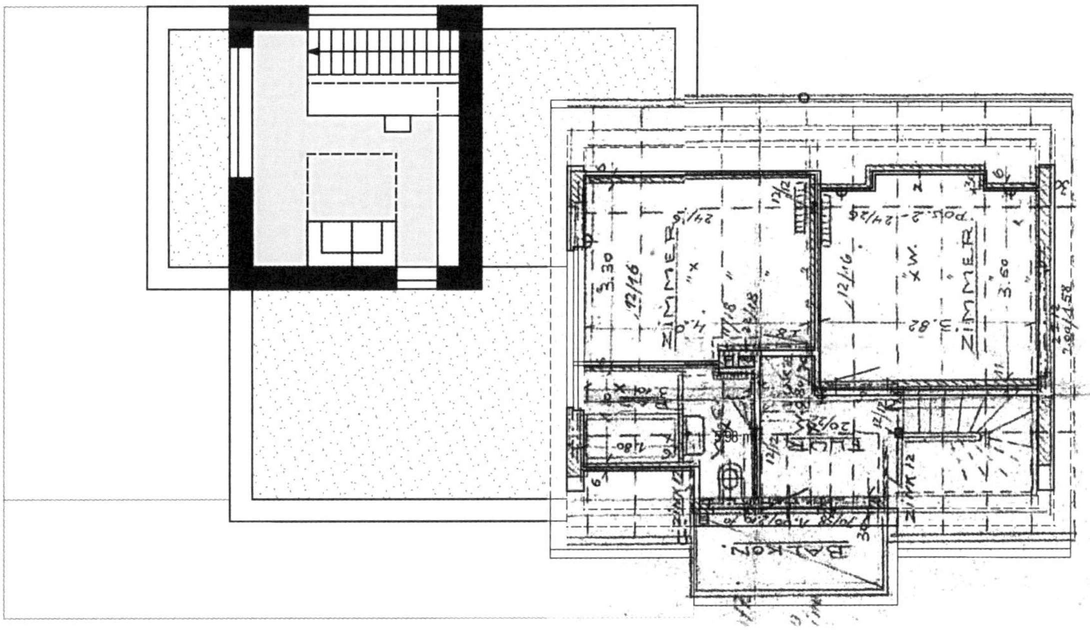

4

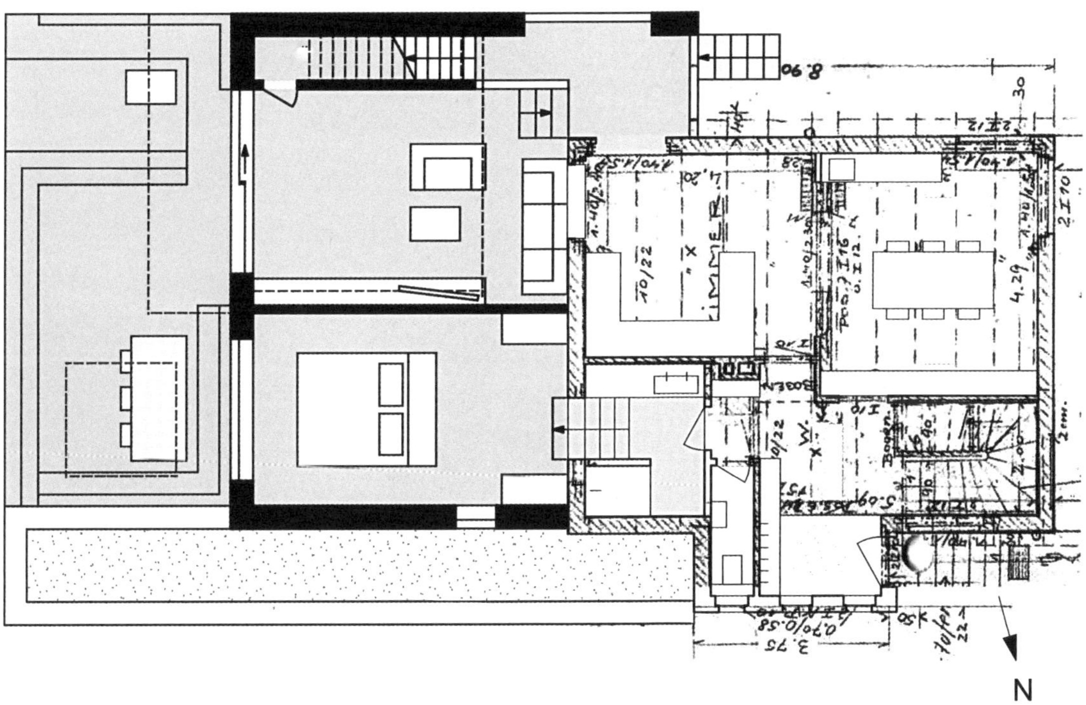

1 Site plan
2 Axonometry of the whole ensemble
3 Attic floor plan
4 Ground floor plan

SMALL HOUSE IN SOLINGEN

1

Architects: kirschnick architektur
Year of completion: 2013
Location: Solingen, North Rhine-Westphalia
Gross floor area: 166 m²
Number of bedrooms: 3
Main materials / features: exposed concrete, porcelain stoneware / solid construction

2

98

Budget-friendly constructing by reducing the unnecessary to its essentials was a substantial part of the concept. The small in house in Solingen lives up to these principles and implements them consistently and straight.

The structure with a gable roof spanning over two stories shows the regional building tradition. The L-shaped floor plan is derived directly from the plot and allows for a simple zoning of the floors. This enables the separation of kitchen, living and dining area, and implements the terrace in a new spatially interesting way.

A double staircase discreetly placed in the entrance hall leads to the upper floor. Three private rooms and a full bathroom are located underneath the gable; each of them is aligned to the proportions of the façade and optimized according to its individual function. They are equipped with fixed glazing. The solitary gray building adapts to the Solingen tradition of slate façades, while avoiding to imitate them too closely. Furthermore, the windowcases with their smoothly plastered white scuncheons reinforce the distinct proportions of the windows and the building as a whole.

Exposed concrete ceilings and porcelain stoneware shape the raw aesthetics of the ground floor. This rough style is taken up again on the upper floor: Surfaces smoothly plastered in white create huge, light-flooded rooms and continue the color design in a logical and comprehensible way.

A distinct, minimalist architecture lacking selfishness and competitiveness has been created, combining regional tradition with contemporary interpretations.

3

1 Exterior view terrace
2 Front view

3 Exterior view with open box gutter
4 Kitchen with view into the garden
5 View from the living area into the corridor
6 View into the living area

4, 5

6

1

2

3

4

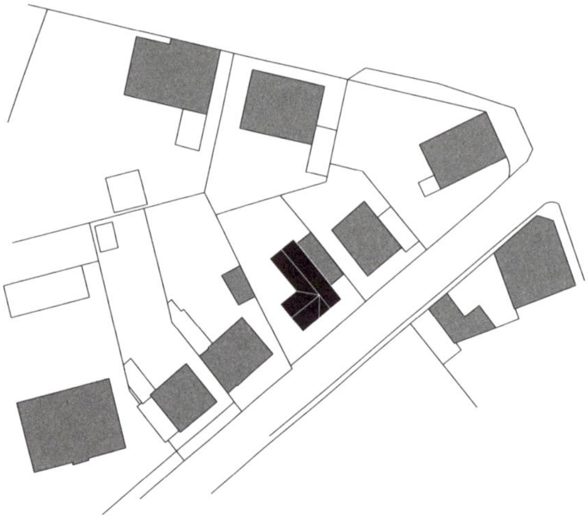

1 Exterior view with greening
2 Open box gutter
3 Section
4 Site plan

5 First floor plan
6 Ground floor plan

5

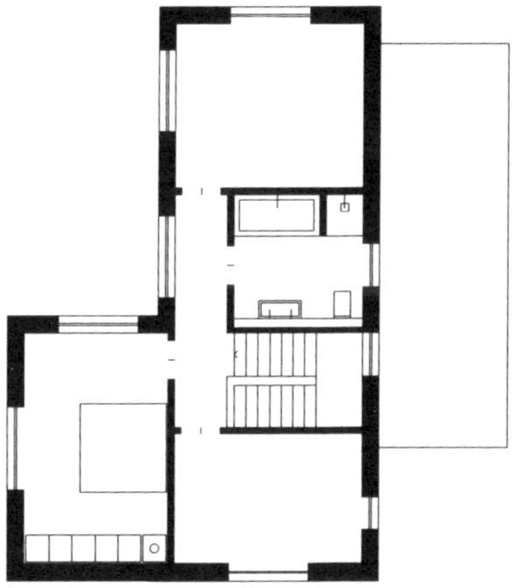

6

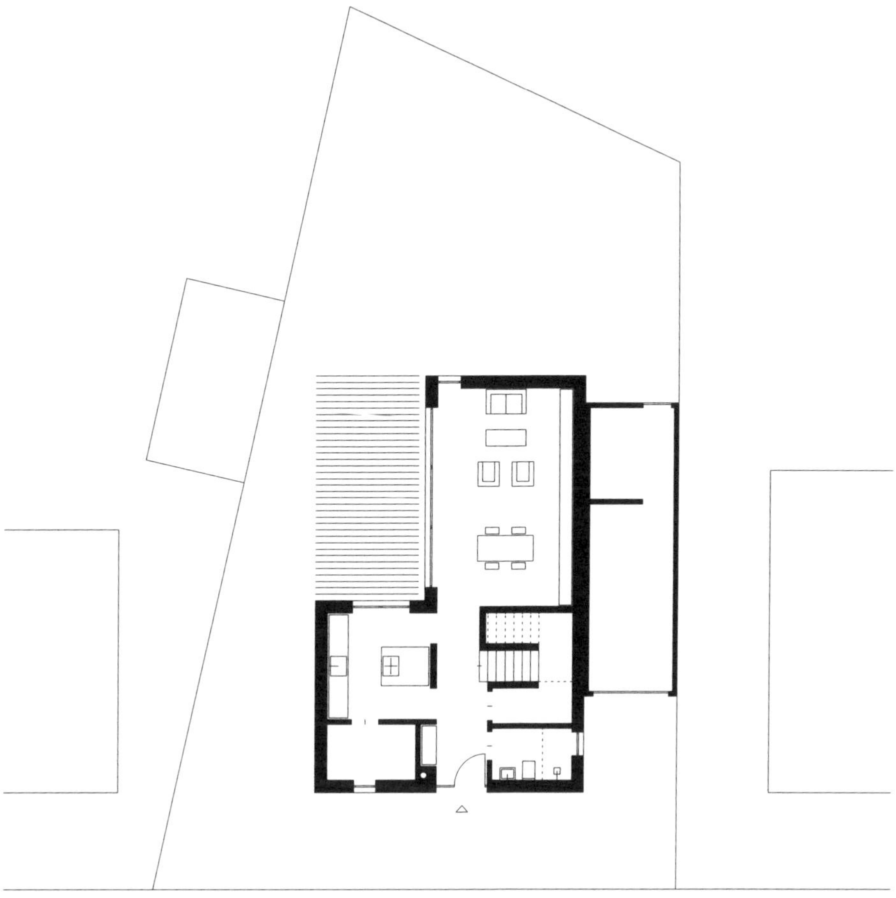

HOUSE WLG

1

2

3

Architects: nbundm* Architekten und Stadtplaner
Year of completion: 2017
Location: Zuchering, Bavaria
Gross floor area: 280 m²
Number of bedrooms: 3
Main materials / structure: insulating bricks, mineral plaster, massive oak / monolithic massiv construction
Ecological features: air-water heat pump, no exterior insulation finishing system, sustainable building materials

House WLG is located right in the center of a new housing complex. It was built around a square plan and is flanked by two wooden supplementary buildings. Living area, bedrooms, and study are housed on three floors, sheltered by a large, asymmetrical roof. A transverse gable on the southwestern edge marks the children's bedroom, eventually shaping the form of the whole building. Every window case was placed axially symmetrically in the wall of the room behind them. Their size is measured according to their respective use, creating four punctuated façades. The rooms are grouped around a concrete stair tower. While four, sometimes large, sliding doors subdivide the ground floor, the bedrooms and bathrooms on the upper floor are accessible from the staircase via revolving doors. The building was constructed in brickwork as a monolith. During the process robust and durable materials were used, whose natural surfaces show a harmonious play of colors.

4

5

1 Exterior view from east
2 Context of the settlement
3 Transverse gable

4 Exterior view from west
5 Living area
6 Entrance area
7 Wardrobe and library

6, 7

1

1 Dining table

2 Attic floor plan
3 First floor plan
4 Ground floor plan
5 Section through dining area and gallery

2

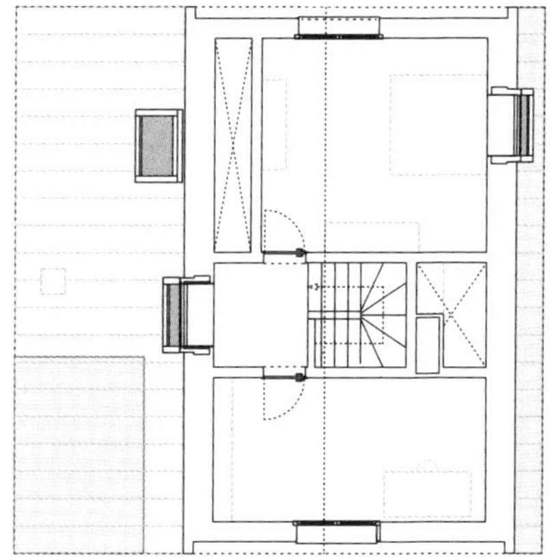

3

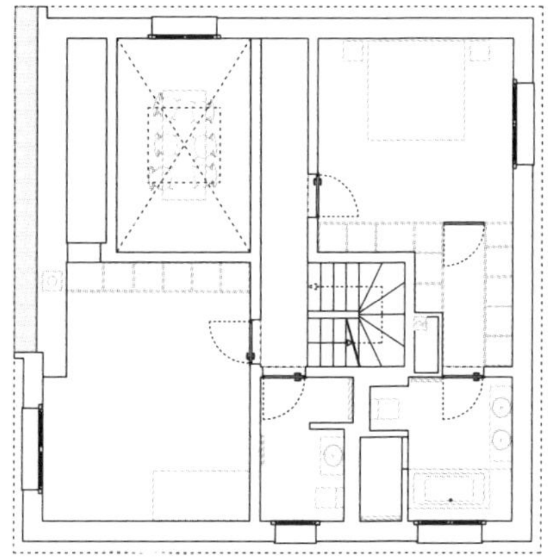

4

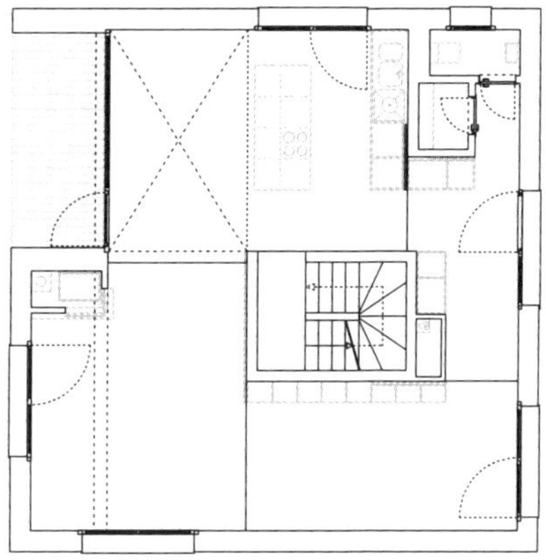

5

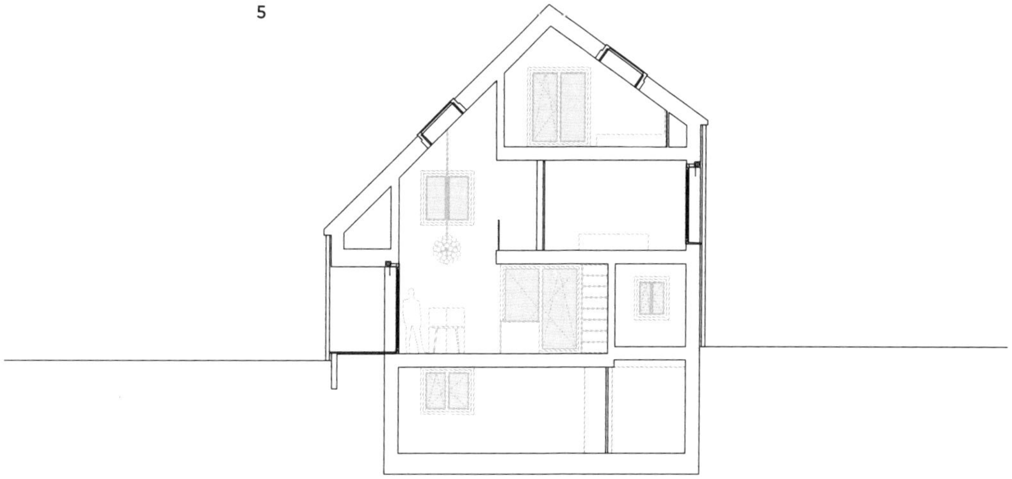

EASTERN SWABIAN JURA HOUSE

1

2

Architects: Schiller Architektur
Year of completion: 2015
Location: Ostalb District, Baden-Württemberg
Gross floor area: 210 m^2
Number of bedrooms: 3
Main materials / structure: concrete, brickwork / solid construction

This project is influenced directly by its topographic surroundings. The plot is situated on a slope, resulting in a minimalist building offering privacy as well as a view of the eastern Swabian Jura. The house is located slightly offset in the rear part of the plot. This position on the edge of the slope required the living layer to be moved by the height of half a story above the garden level. An access path along the garage passes through the garden to the entrance area. The zoning situation reminds of a courtyard. The retaining wall along the access path forms the transition to the higher neighboring property and offers an additional area for a children's playground.

A stair landing accesses the living layer, consisting of an open living, dining, and cooking area with adjacent terrace. The significantly elevated position above street level provides a better view on one hand and more privacy on the other hand. Openings in the façade create beautiful, protected views and interesting lighting. Despite its offset position, the garden is well accessible from the terrace via a large open staircase with seating steps.

Private rooms, such as bedrooms and children's rooms, are located on the upper floor. It also houses a study with windows on the north side looking out on the landscape. The children's rooms are extending through large windows towards the Swabian Jura. Bedroom and bathroom are rather introverted, only equipped with smaller windows.

The exterior is characterized through projections of the rooms and roofs as well as the matching opening in the façade. The minimalist impression is completed by the reduced use of materials, such as visible cement screed and painted plaster.

3

1 Exterior view front side
2 Exterior view hillside perspective

3 Kitchen and dining area
4 Exterior view back side
5 Living area

4, 5

1

2

3

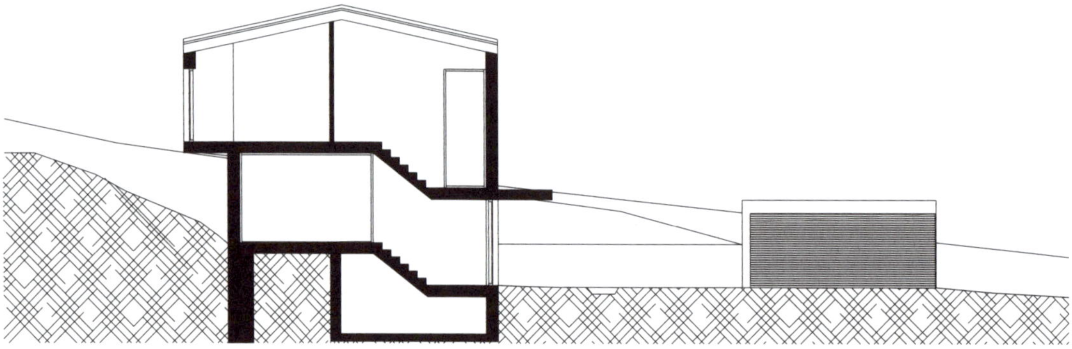

1 Study
2 Children's room
3 Longitudinal section

4 First floor plan
5 Ground floor plan

4

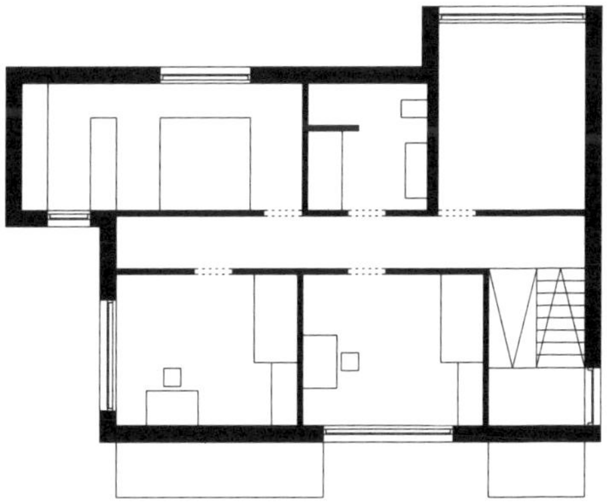

5

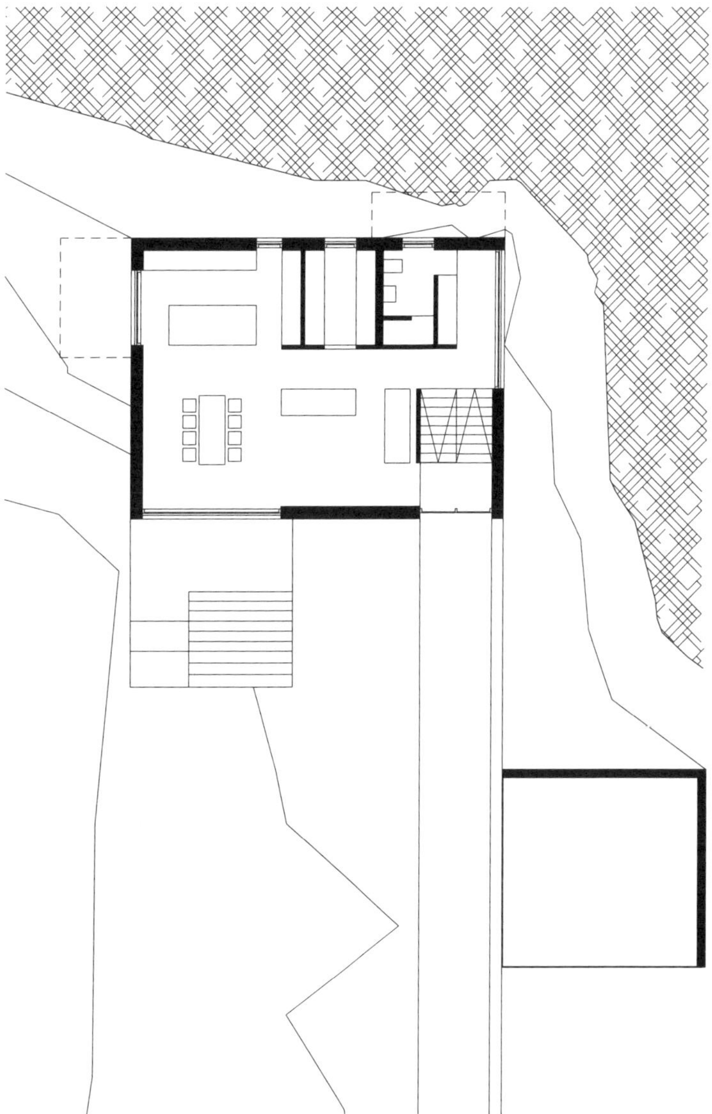

HOUSE S. IN BAD GODESBERG

1

2

Architects: Architekturbüro Bolle Licker
Year of completion: 2015
Location: Bonn, North Rhine-Westphalia
Gross floor area: 365 m^2
Number of bedrooms: 4
Main materials / structure: plaster, exposed concrete in the interior; porous brickwork in the exterior / solid construction
Ecological aspects: geothermal heat pump

The site is noble, but has no special qualities having any impact on the design of the building. There are no special topographic features, no distinct developement style, no dominant building material, and no distinct local architecture as well. The narrow plot predetermined the compact, longitudinal structure of the two-story building. The floor plan was organized crosswise with a central entrance in the northeast, and a staircase.

The central entrance hall directs the view to the two stories tall dining area, being in the center of the living area. It extends to the left towards the kitchen, offering a glimpse of the front yard and the street. To the right there follows the living area leading to the terrace and the garden. This division is continued on upper floor as a floor plan.

The owner wished for an ecological production. Plastered porous brickwork has been unused in combination with sequences in exposed concrete. Underfloor heating with a geothermal heat pump achieves energetic advantages.

The building is distinctively structured and maintains the necessary intimacy to the outside despite the openness in the interior. It appears calm and blends into the existing environment while remaining esthetically independent.

3

4

1 Street view
2 Garden view

3 Staircase
4 Entrance area
5 Living area

5

1

2

3
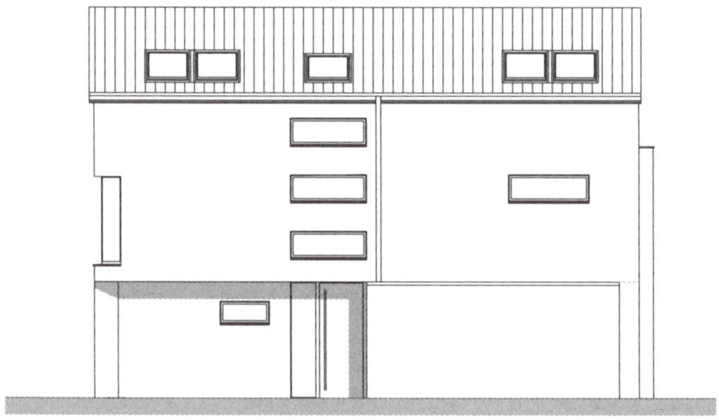

4
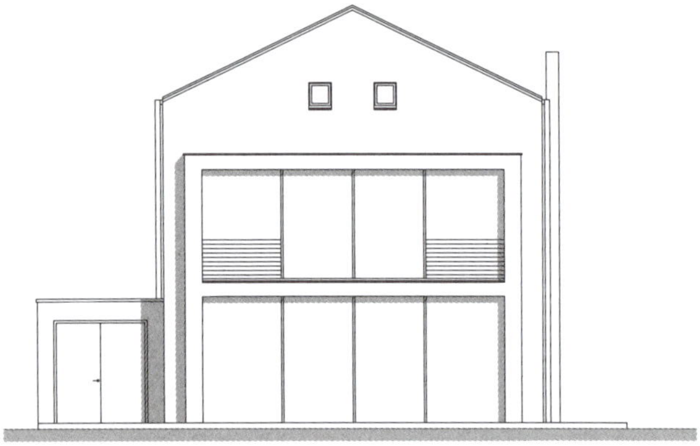

5

1 Void
2 Bathroom
3 Northeast elevation
4 Northwest elevation
5 Southeast elevation

6 First floor plan
7 Attic floor plan
8 Ground floor plan

6

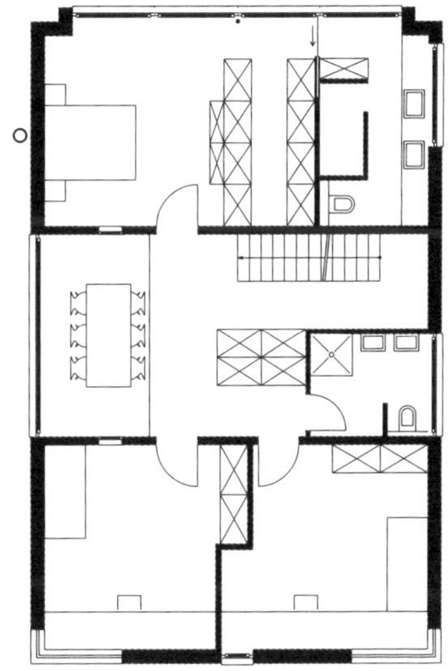

7

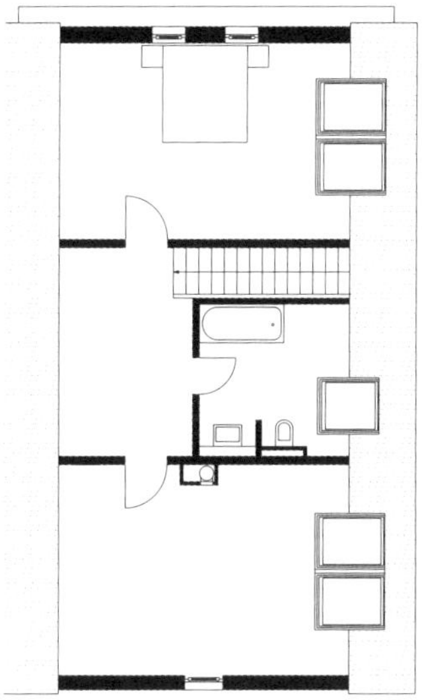

8

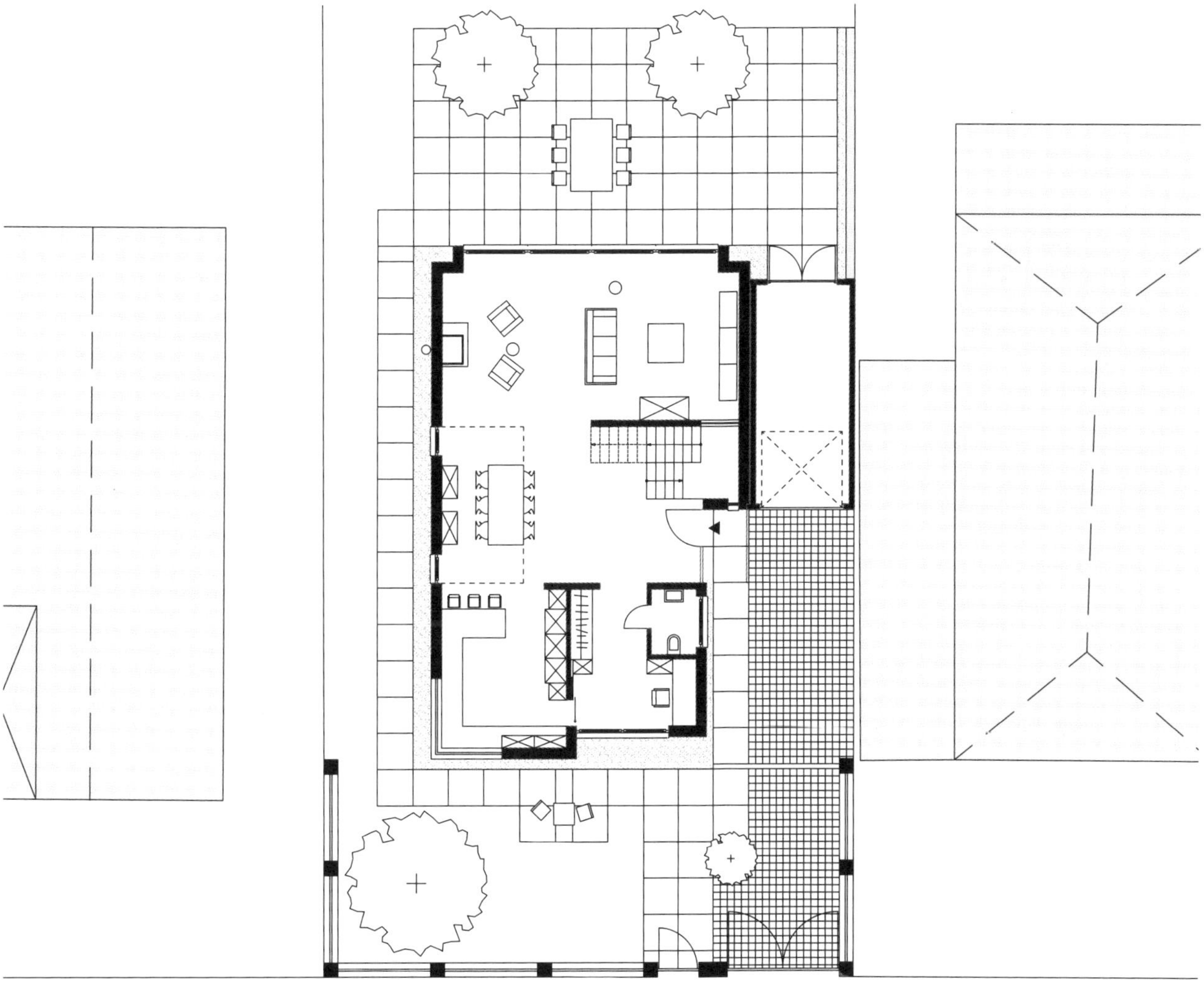

ENERGY-EFFICIENT HOUSE

1

2, 3

Architects: pier7 architekten
Year of completion: 2013
Location: Meerbusch, North Rhine-Westphalia
Gross floor area: 210 m^2
Number of bedrooms: 3
Main materials / structure: masonry, reinforced concrete, exposed screed / solid construction without cellar
Ecological features: energy-efficient house (KfW 70), geothermal energy, controlled ventilation of living space

The energy-efficient house was erected on a former parking lot on the outskirts of the village to the open landscape. A single-story house with an inclined roof and fixed eaves height was planned on the narrow plot. Within this framework, the new building was created as an interpretation of the building regulations. Despite the specifications, the house has a ground floor and an upper floor. A basement was deliberately omitted. On the ground floor there is a large, open living area. The way to the upper floor runs via the generous air space of the steel staircase, along the work gallery to the individual rooms. The façade is plastered in white, large-format joint incisions divide the views and draw the openings together into a common façade image. The building developed its concise, monolithic cubature from the building regulations. The unobtrusive details with internal rain gutter support the minimalist appearance. The generous roof window construction creates additional air space on the upper floor. The building is constructed according to the KfW 70 standard. Three near-surface geothermal boreholes ensure the heat requirements and offer additional cooling comfort in summer. Triple glazing, external sun protection, and a high standard of thermal insulation have been consistently implemented together with energy-saving heating technology.

4

5

1 Exterior view from southwest with carport
2 Front view from south
3 Back view from north at dawn

4 Work gallery in front of the airspace
5 Cooking and dining area
6 Living area

6

1 Shower with glass partition
2 Detailed view of the staircase
3 Bathroom with large wall cabinet

4 Ground floor plan
5 First floor plan
6 Site plan

4

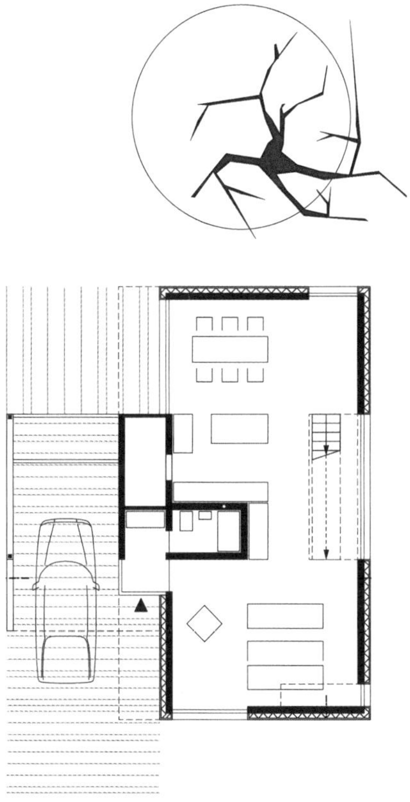

5

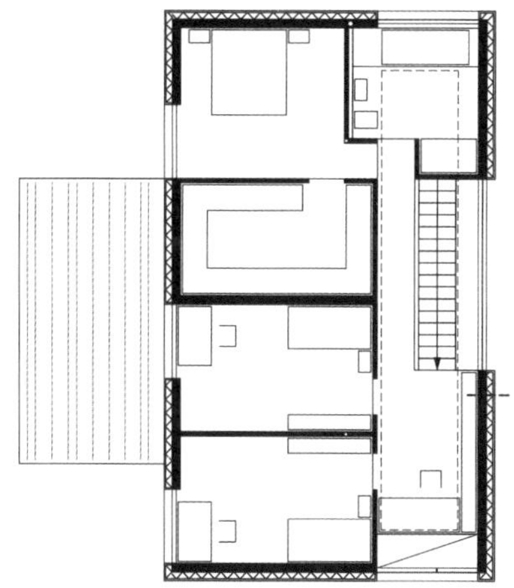

6

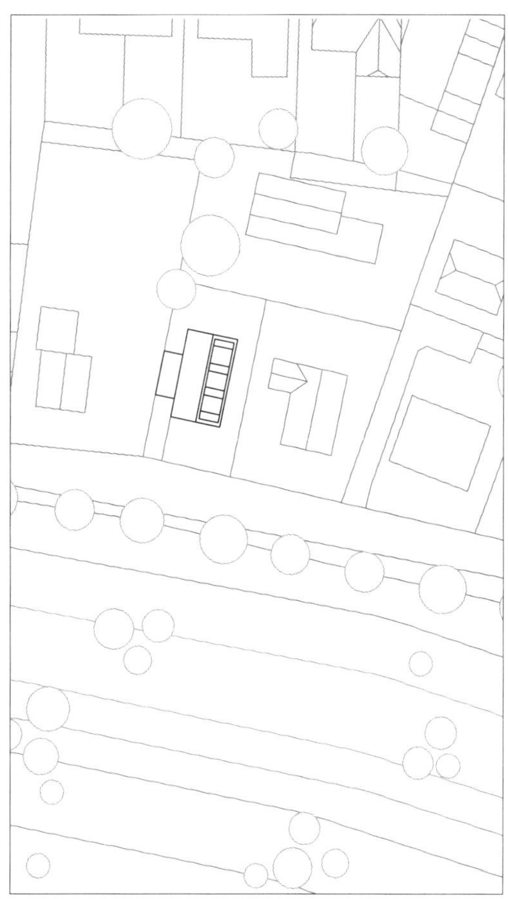

HOUSE KFW55

1

2, 3

Architects: DBW Architekten
Year of completion: 2014
Location: Lauingen, Bavaria
Gross floor area: 300 m^2
Number of bedrooms: 4
Main materials / structure: bricks / solid construction
Ecological features: heat recovery, wood, solar, regenerative heat supply

This new construction demonstrates a possible option of a contemporary single-family house with a modern architectural vocabulary. An almost central, bearing wall divides the structure into a garden-faced and a street-faced section. The glazing, partially spreading over two stories, enlarges the living space visually and floods it with lots of natural light. On the outside, the façade is structured by horizontal and vertical as well as by smaller and larger openings. The variety of forms breaks up the surface. By following the outer structure, the arrangement of forms helps developing the modern appearance of the building.

An ecologically sustainable construction was important during the process. Single-layered, solid brick components were used. A central ventilation system with heat recovery reduces the consumption of energy. The fireplace is suitable for heating purposes and is supported by a large solarthermic system. Thus, sustainable and renewable energy is provided for the entire house.

4

5

6

1 Entry perspective
2 Garden view
3 View from the garden

4 Gallery view
5 View from the garden onto the house
6 Street side at twilight

1

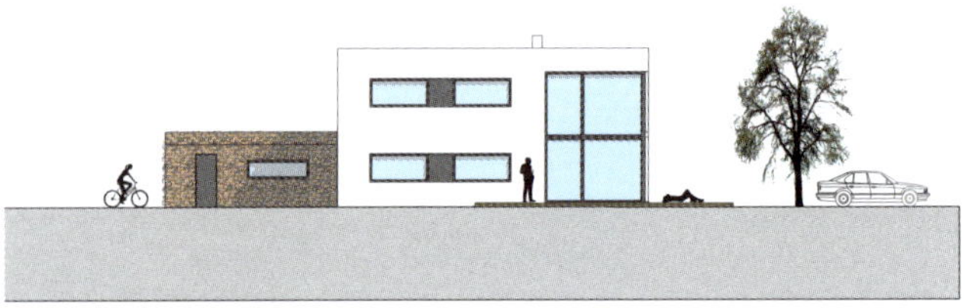

2

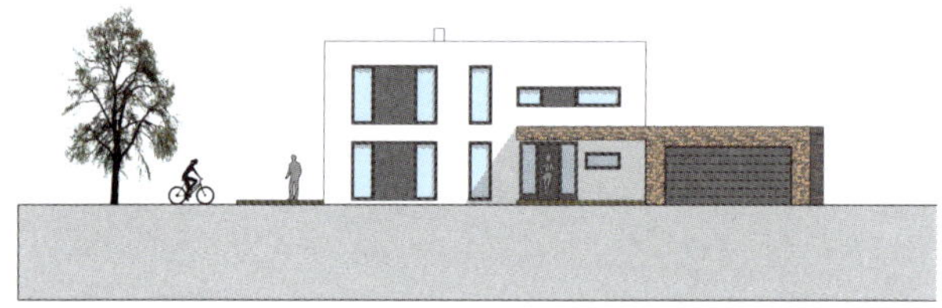

3

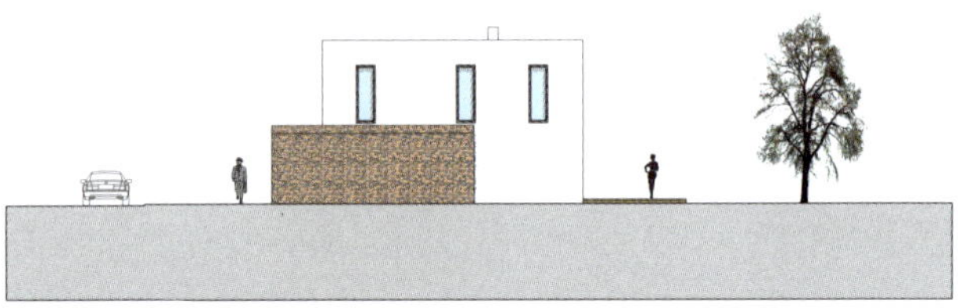

4

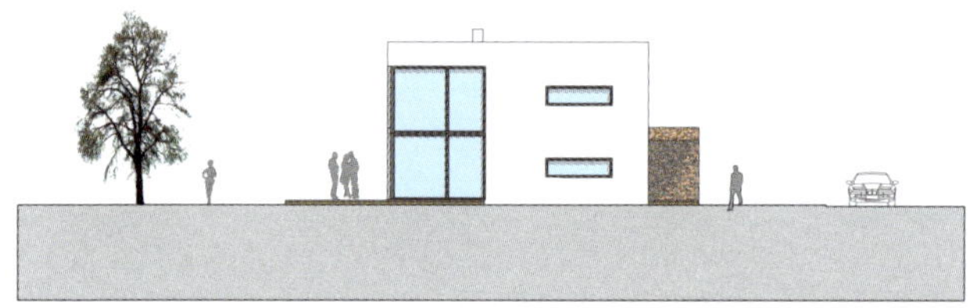

5

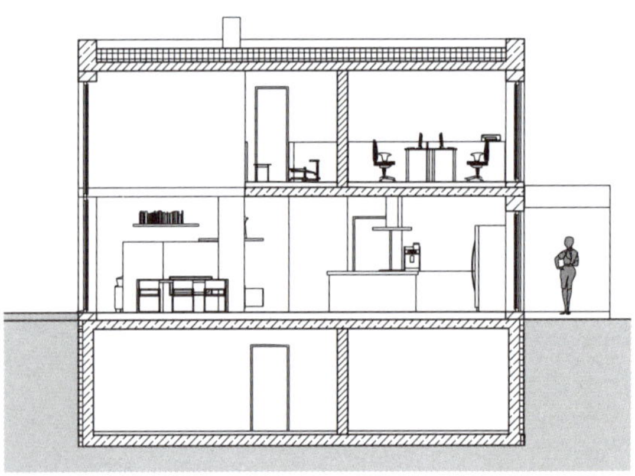

6

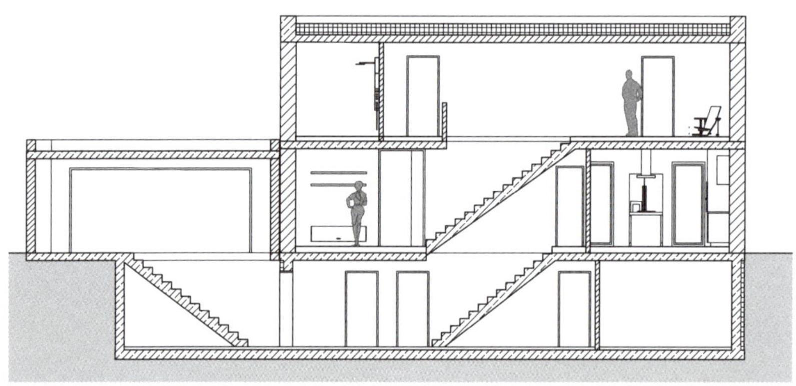

1 Southwest elevation
2 Northeast elevation
3 Northwest elevation
4 Southeast elevation
5 Cross section
6 Longitudinal section

7 First floor plan
8 Ground floor plan
9 Basement floor plan

7

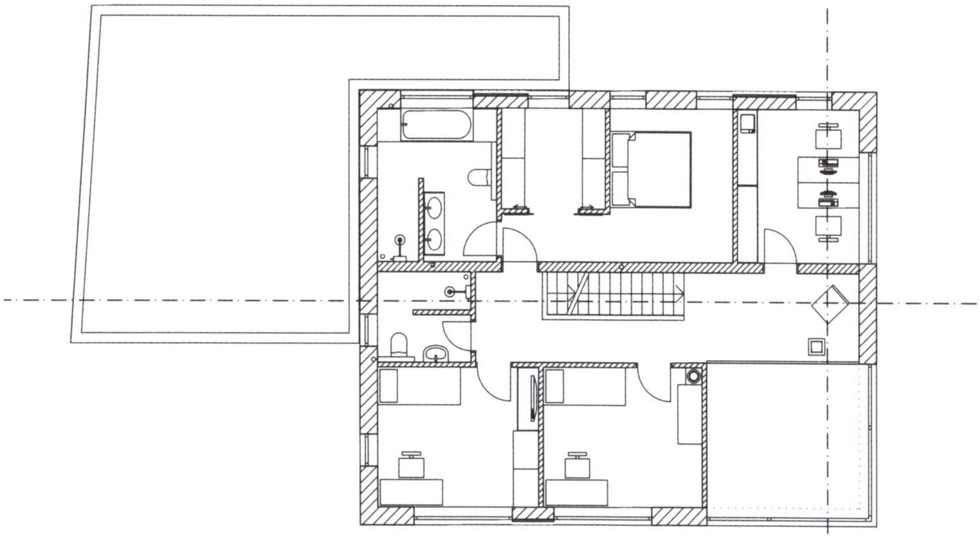

8

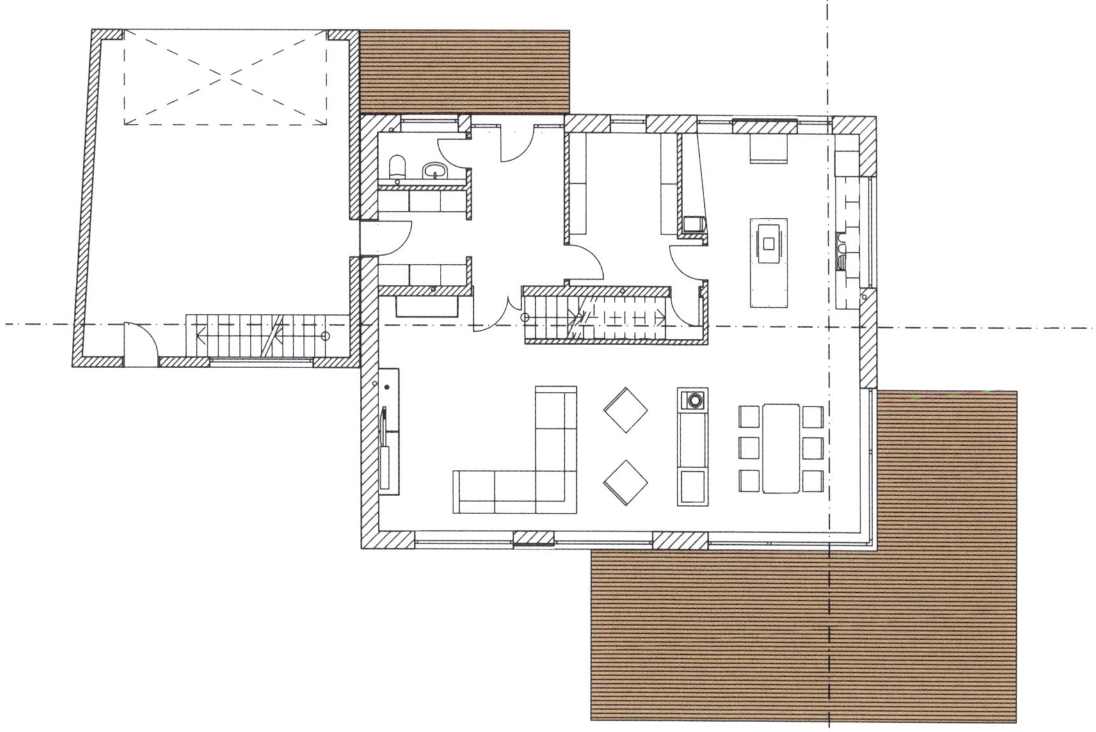

9

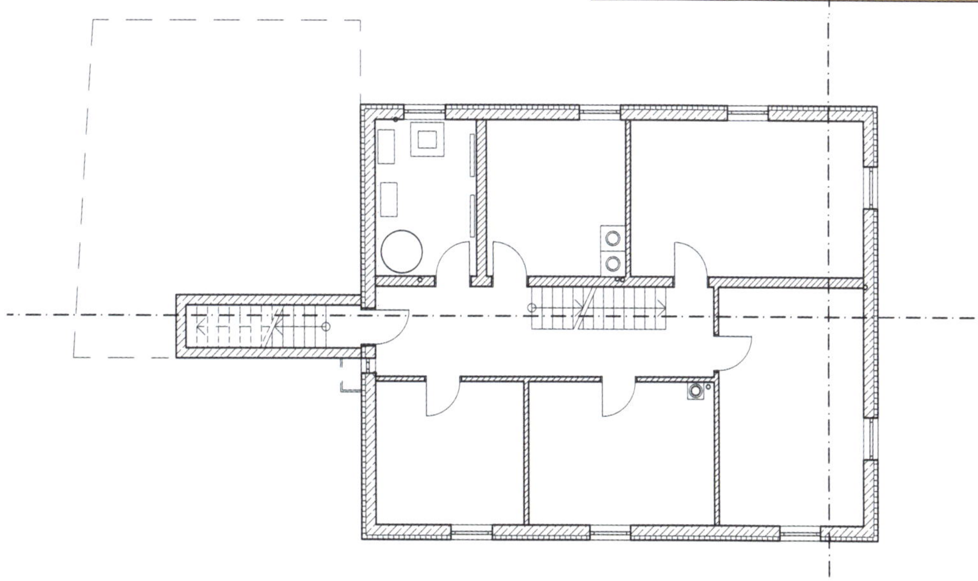

HOUSE DN

1, 2

3

4

Architects: Henecka Architekten
Year of completion: 2016
Location: Bruchsal, Baden-Württemberg
Gross floor area: 294 m^2
Number of bedrooms: 1
Main materials / structure: exterior insulation finishing system, oak wood claddings / solid construction
Ecological features: compact design, closed façade towards the northern side, expansive windowcases towards the southern side

This single-family house was built for a young couple and finished in 2016. Situated on a hillside and on the edge of a field, the compact building structure appears to be reserved when approached from the the street. Garage door, entrance, letter box, and intercom are built seamlessly into the curtain wall made from vertical oaken strips.

From the entrance area in the basement there leads a narrow staircase equipped with a curved ceiling and a light dome upwards to the living area. The façade expands generously to the garden with bright windows. Widely cantilevering eaves provide shadow on hot days and shelter from the rain.

The interior of the building astonishes with light-flooded rooms and open spaces. The visible screed laid throughout the house underlines the merging of the room zones. The extensive glazing provides a view of the garden and terrace.

5

6

1 Garden view from southwest
2 Garden view from east at dawn
3 Cantilevered roof above terrace
4 Street view from the northwest

5 Bedroom
6 Fireplace with garden view
7 Staircase
8 Bathroom with glass divider

7

8

1

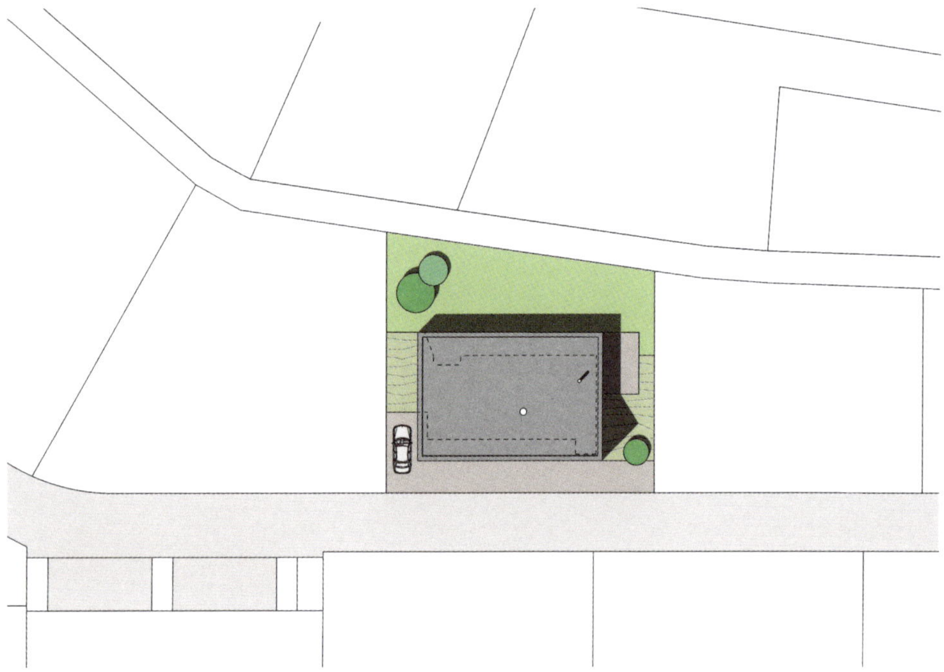

2

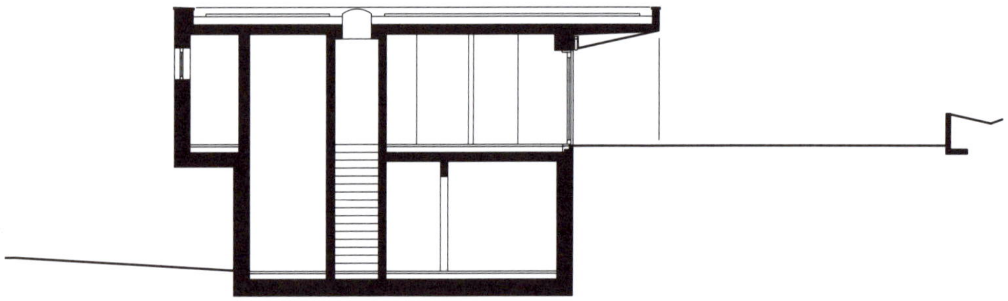

3

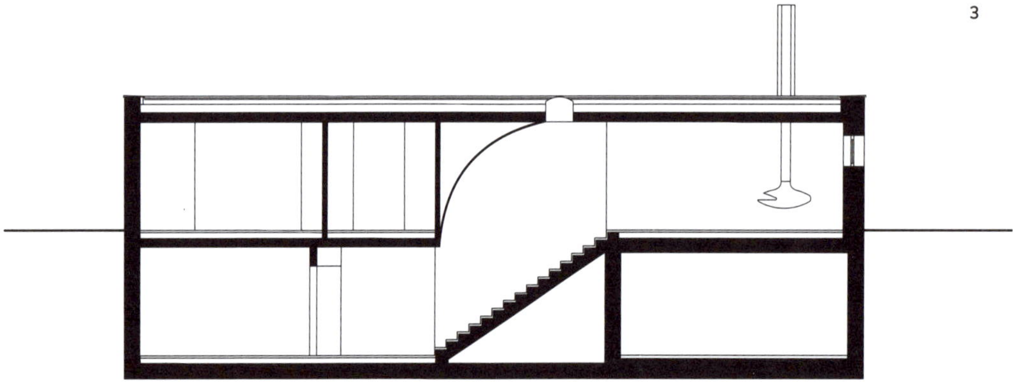

4

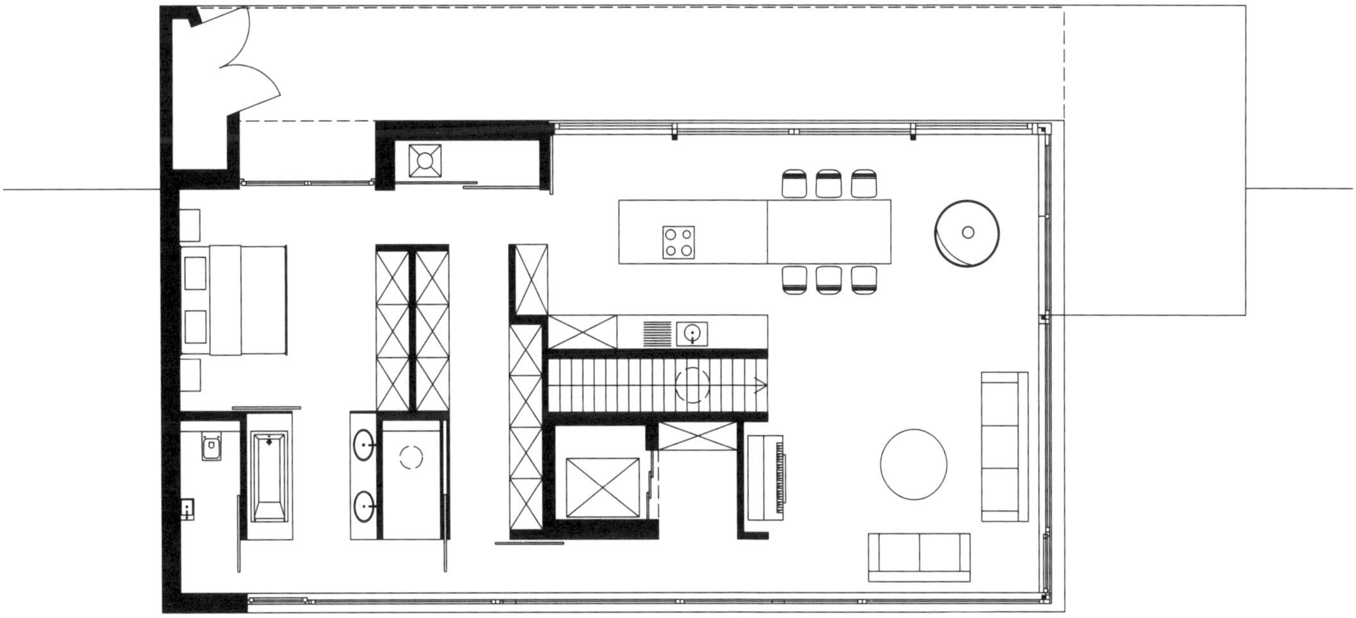

5

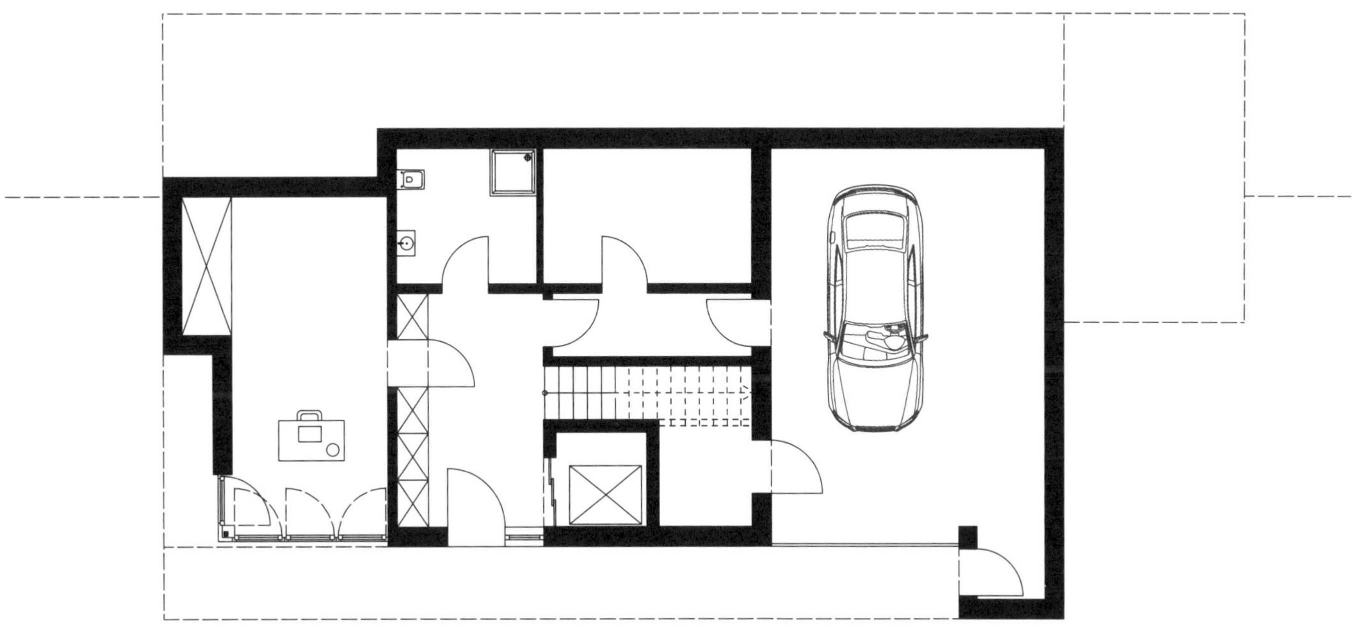

1 Site plan
2 Cross section
3 Longitudinal section
4 Ground floor plan
5 Basement floor plan

ONE-TO-TWO-FAMILY HOUSE

1

2

Architects: MS Planwerk · Möller Eickenberg Architekten
Year of completion: 2016
Location: Langenfeld, North Rhine-Westphalia
Gross floor area: 590 m^2
Number of bedrooms: 3
Main materials / structure: sand-lime brick, mineral wool insulation, mineral plaster, wooden strip cladding
Ecological features: air-water heat pump, underfloor heating, controlled ventilation, photovoltaics, passive house, energy-surplus building

126

The new construction of a one- to two-family house at Kurfürstenweg 40a in Langenfeld is a passive or energy-surplus building. This is characterized by the fact that it requires hardly any heating energy in conventional form (electricity, gas or oil). Due to above-average insulation, special multiple-glazed windows and a ventilation system that recovers heat from the room air for heating purposes, the consumption of conventional energy is extremely low. In addition, a large photovoltaic system generates solar energy and is used to support the heating and hot water heating system. The building thus generates more energy than it needs for heating and hot water generation.

The following is worth mentioning about the architecture and the integration into the surroundings: The gable house was built according to the specifications of the development plan and adapted to the surrounding buildings as a clearly contoured, minimalist building. The bright, light-flooded rooms combine with the generously designed outdoor facilities to form a harmonious unit. A roofed terrace area offers shade and protection from rain. From there the green garden can be overlooked, which offers numerous seating possibilities for relaxing. The projecting main entrance area is designed as a windbreak and gives the building character as an architectural means.

The ground floor plan includes a hallway between the porch and the living area, from which the upper floor is accessed by a double staircase. Conversion into a two-family house is easy if this hallway is divided in the middle. On the ground floor this will create a self-contained two-room apartment with a spacious living and dining area, bedroom, bathroom, and central corridor.

3

1 Street view from northeast
2 Garden view from southwest

3 Staircase
4 Living area with kitchen and fireplace

4

1

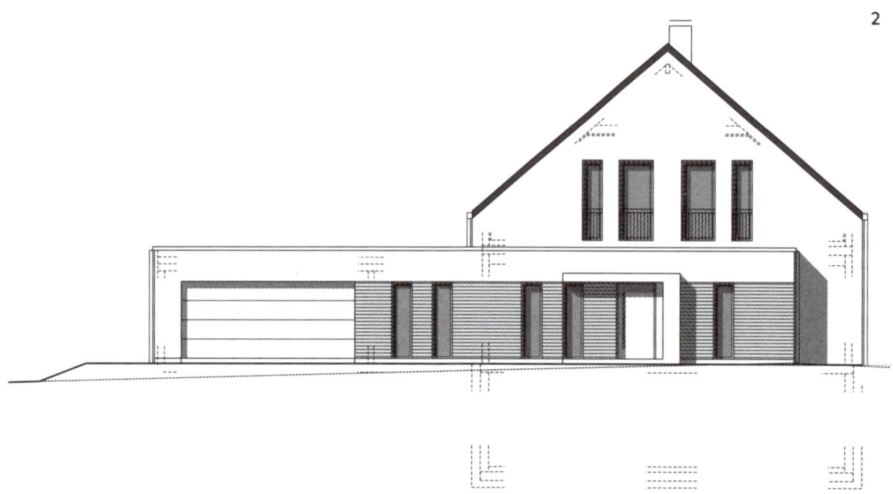

2

1 Ground floor plan with exterior area
2 Northeast elevation

3 Draft floor plan with outdoor facilities
4 Intermediate status of general garden planning
5 Sketch of the entrance area

3

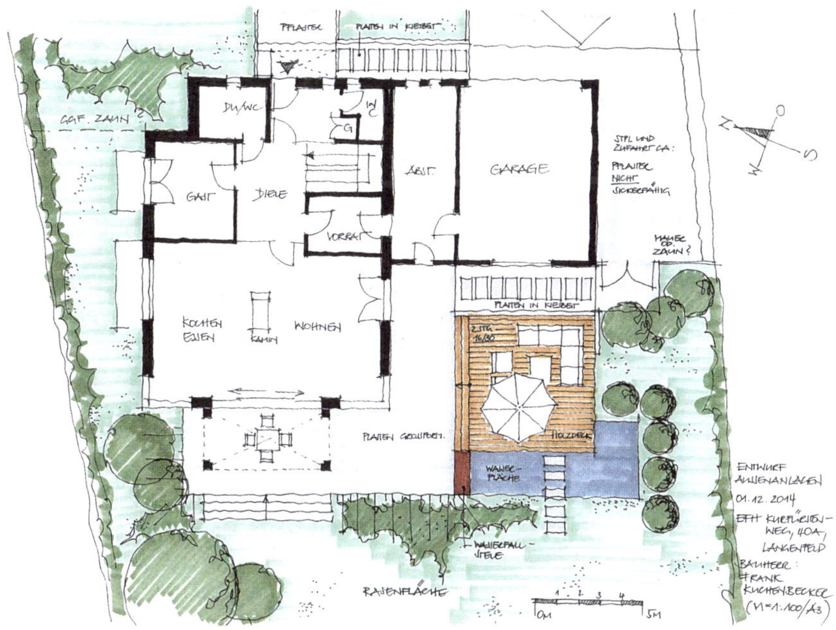
PFLASTER
PLATTEN IN KIESBETT
GGF. ZAUN
DU/WC
WC
GAST
DIELE
VORRAT
GAST
GARAGE
KÜCHEN ESSEN
KAMIN
WOHNEN
PLATTEN GROSSFORM.
HOLZDECK
STPL UND ZUFAHRT GA: PFLASTER NICHT SICKERFÄHIG
MAUER OD. ZAUN?
ENTWURF AUSSENANLAGEN
01.12.2014
EFH KURFÜRSTENWEG, 40A, LANGENFELD
BAUHERR: FRANK KUCHENBECKER
(M=1:100/A3)
RASENFLÄCHE
0M
5M

4

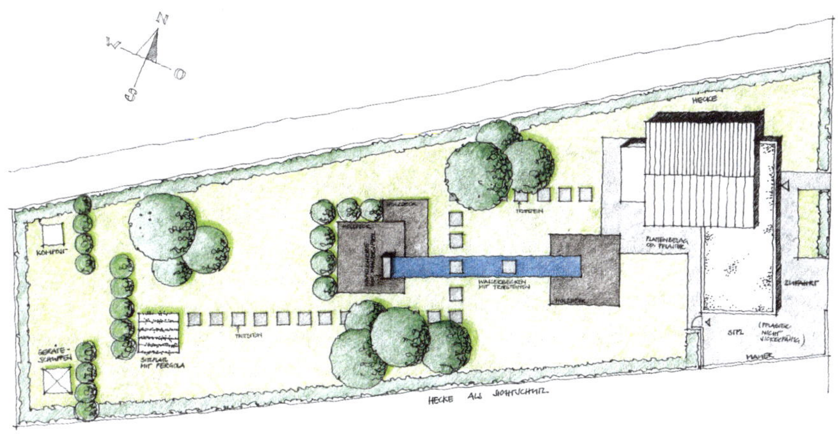

5

HOUSE V

1

Architects: Viktor Filimonow Architekt
Year of completion: 2013
Location: Waldkraiburg, Bavaria
Gross floor area: 240 m^2
Number of bedrooms: 4
Main materials / structure: insulated bricks, concrete, wood / solid construction
Ecological features: simple technical equipment, thermal component activation on the first floor

2

The plot is located in a small district surrounded by dense forest. Its environment is characterized by a conservative single-family house settlement as well as an experimental housing construction of the 1990s. The newly built, contemporary single-family house stands out independently from its context. Towards the garden it opens generously, while remaining largely closed to the street. Nevertheless, its cubature is differentiated and thus inviting. The main building is whitewashed – a reminiscence to the style of Bavarian farms with barns. In this sense the garage with its wooden façade works as a contrasting counterpart.

The inner structure of the house is centered around the wishes of the owners for open and spacious rooms. The ground floor is structured by the staircase. Coming from the entrance, it seals off the living spaces for strangers, from the other side it acts as a shield for the peripheral areas. The void above the dining area removes the traditional boundaries of the two stories, making the house perceptible as a single unit. The gallery becomes an extended, multifunctional space, usable as a music bunk, reading corner, or as a guest room. Its functions are flexible and adatable to the needs of its inhabitants, making it a lively place in the house.

The architect and the client deliberately weighed the necessities, wishes, and qualities, resulting in an individual and expressive single-family home that the young family inhabits with pride.

3

1 Street view
2 Garden view with terrace pavilion

3 Entrance area
4 Wooden façade of the outbuilding

4

1 

 2

3 

4

1 Gallery
2 Kitchen as a central family space
3 Fireplace in the living area
4 Cross section

5 First floor plan
6 Ground floor plan

5

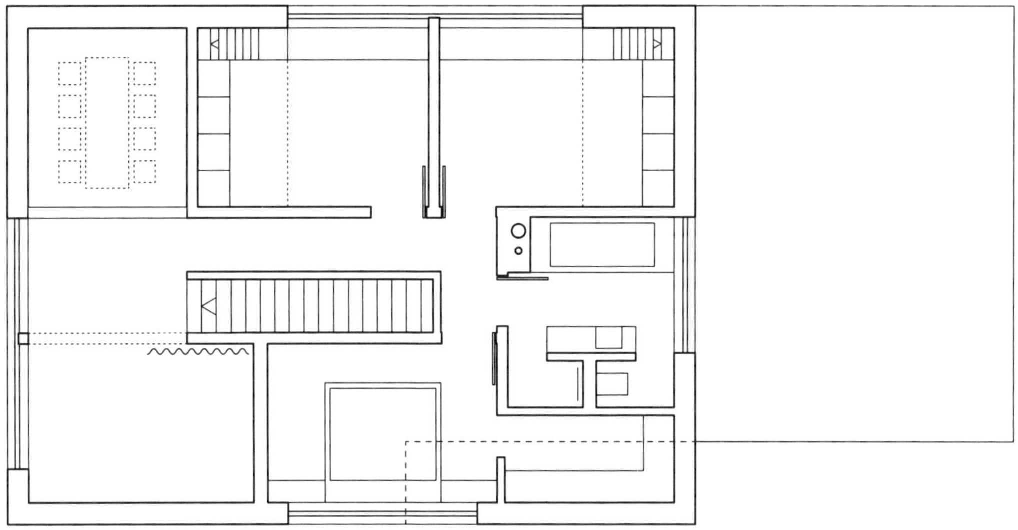

6

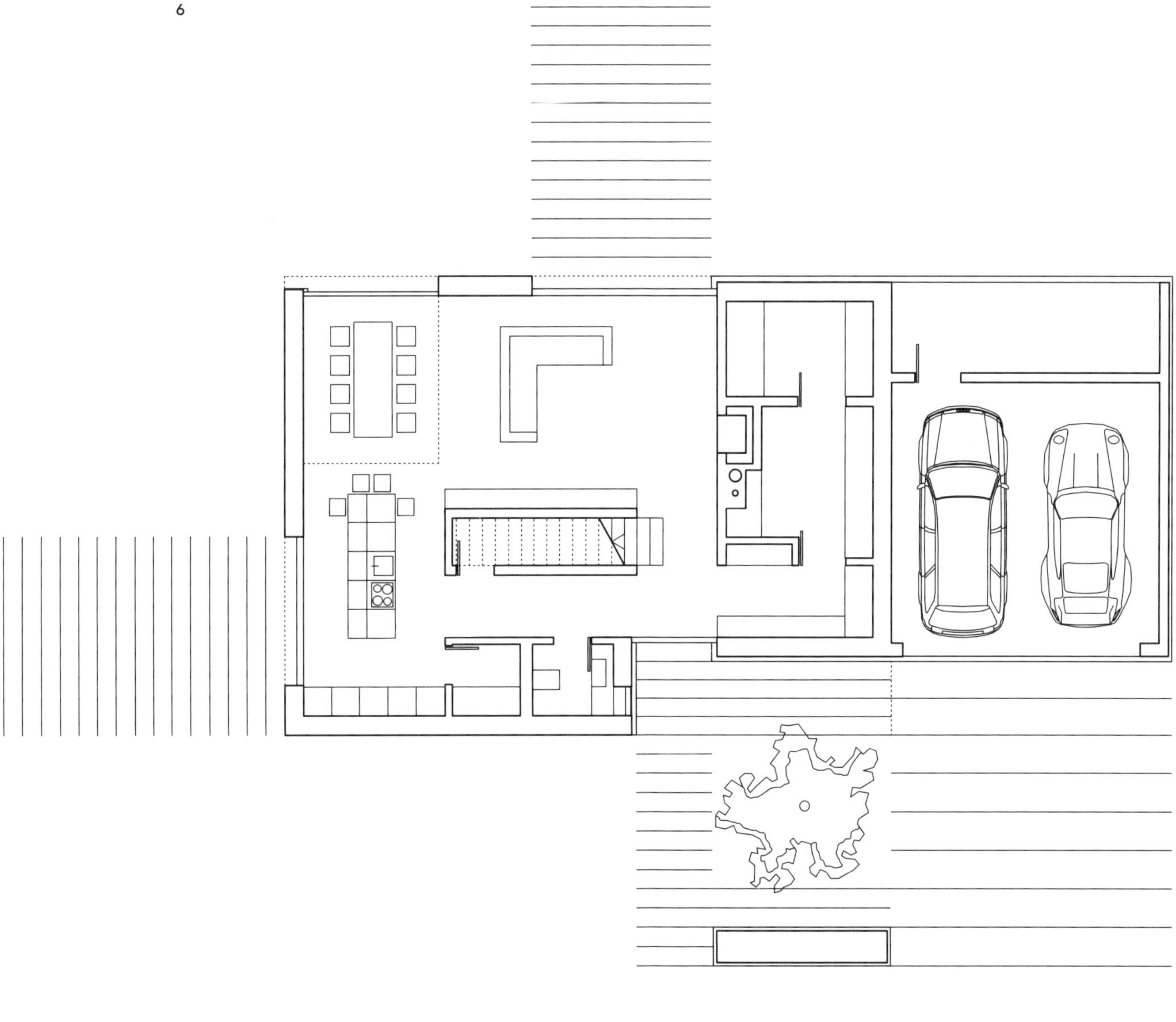

HOUSE IN CONTEXT

1, 2

3

Architects: Architekten Lenzstrasse Dreizehn
Year of completion: 2017
Location: Linkenheim, Baden-Württemberg
Gross floor area: 300 m^2
Number of bedrooms: 3
Main materials / structure: concrete, wood, steel / solid construction
Ecological features: use of sustainable materials

Initially, the plans were to preserve the stock. However, a comparison of investment and possible benefit showed that the old house was to be demolished in order to create more living space. The urban integration of the new building into the general picture was primarily important. Thus, the street front had to be continued with gabled houses. The new building was given a maximum cubature. A one-and-a-half-story settlement house was replaced by a two-and-a-half-story residential building. The clear outer edges of the house were loosened up on the ground floor by projections and recesses of the façade. The jumps in the façade create outdoor areas with a wide variety of functions and recreational qualities. A roofed parking space, which also marks the entrance area of the building, adjoins the house. An east terrace along the long side of the house offers a private outdoor retreat with a connection to the spacious terrace facing the garden. The used materials, concrete, wood and steel, run like a golden thread through the entire building and can be found both in the construction and exterior design as well as in the interior fittings and furnishings.

4

5

1 Kitchen with cooking island
2 Bathroom
3 Exterior view of the façade

4 Staircase to the attic floor
5 Staircase to the ground floor
6 Staircase to the first floor
7 Sloping roof with window row

6, 7

1

1 Exterior view of the eastern terrace

2 First floor plan
3 Ground floor plan
4 Cross section

2

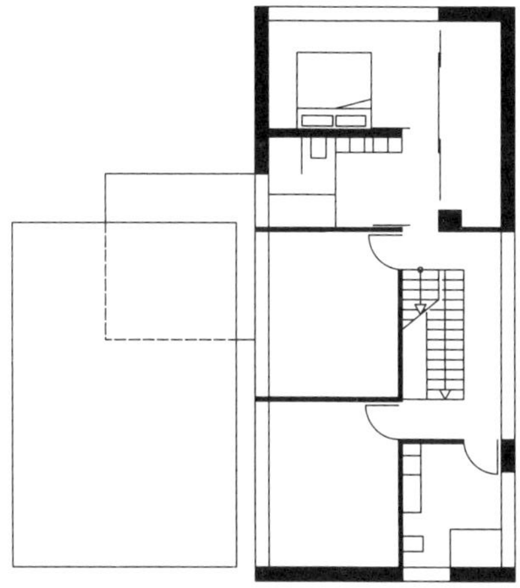

3

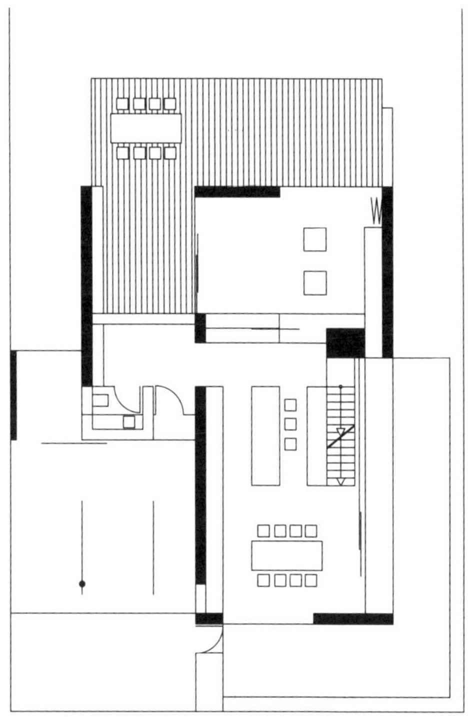

4

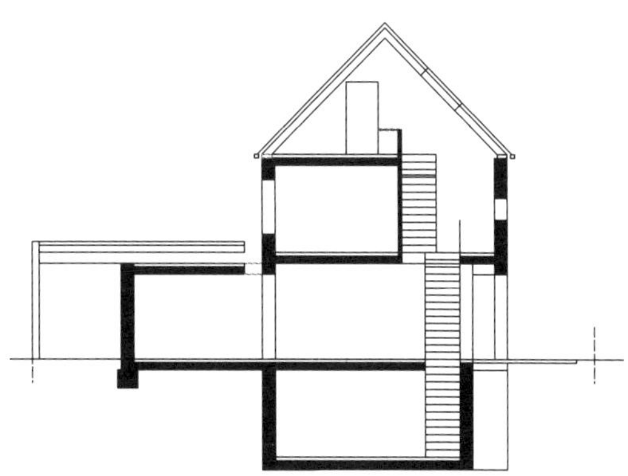

LIFE ON TOP

1

Architects: Architekten Spiekermann
Year of completion: 2016
Location: Oelde, North Rhine-Westphalia
Gross floor area: 208 m^2 and 45 m^2 roof terrace
Number of bedrooms: 2
Main materials: wooden panels

2

The base is a white cube on the ground floor. The larger, central building structure swings above - partly free-floating, partly resting on the cube. The entire façade of this building, including roof areas and roof terrace, was designed as a sculptural unit from one material. The slope on the ground floor runs parallel to the roof slope. The free-floating part of the building, with its sloping course, also forms the roofed entrance area together with the car parking space. The house entrance was also positioned in the adjacent narrow side of the white cube, which guarantees comfortable access to the house. A further detail is the wall running out of the white cube, which welcomes the residents with open arms.

The façade, roof and the large roof terrace opening to the back garden are clad with cement-bonded wood fiber panels. Neither down pipes nor rain pipes disturb the perfect unit, as they were integrated into the curtain wall technology as internal drainage. The outer form of the building reflects the inner functions. Behind the sloping entrance canopy is the staircase to the upper floor. Inside, the traditional room layout is reversed. On the ground floor there is an office, bedroom with dressing room and bathroom as well as a guest room. On the upper floor, under the ridge, a spacious, open-plan living and cooking area opens up with access to the roof terrace and a guest bathroom. In the bathrooms a noble lime marble plaster provides for an appearance, which radiates pleasant peace with an almost sacral impression. The single-family house is perfectly coordinated with all shapes, materials and colors.

3

4

1 Exterior view with entrance area
2 Side view

3 Front view
4 Garden view
5 Interior and exterior perspective
6 First floor staircase
7 Ground floor staircase

5, 6

7

1

2

1 View onto roof and terrace
2 Detail of panels

3 First floor plan
4 Ground floor plan

3

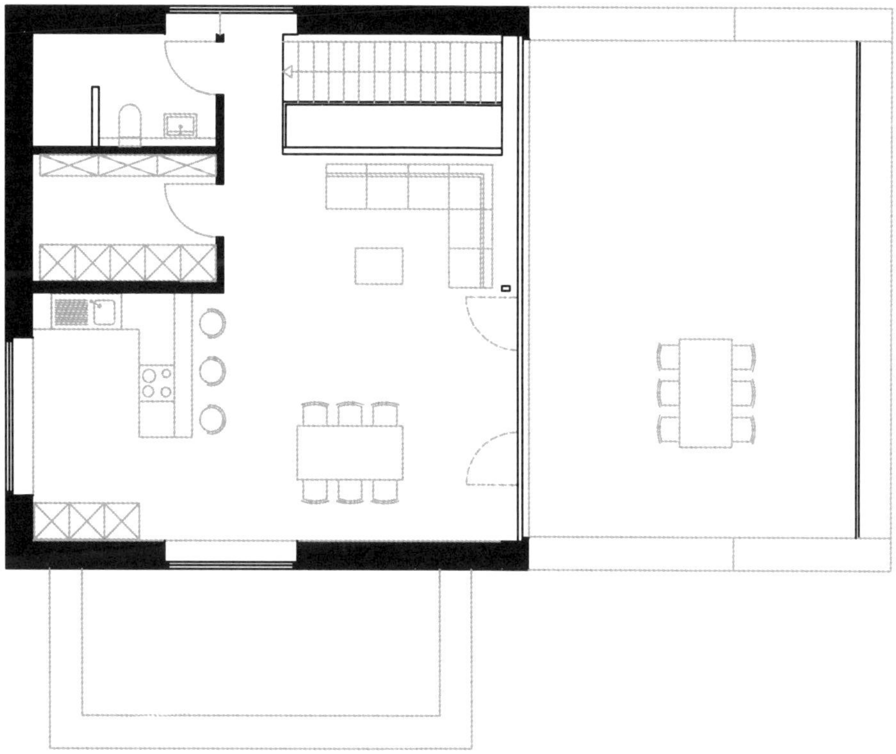

4

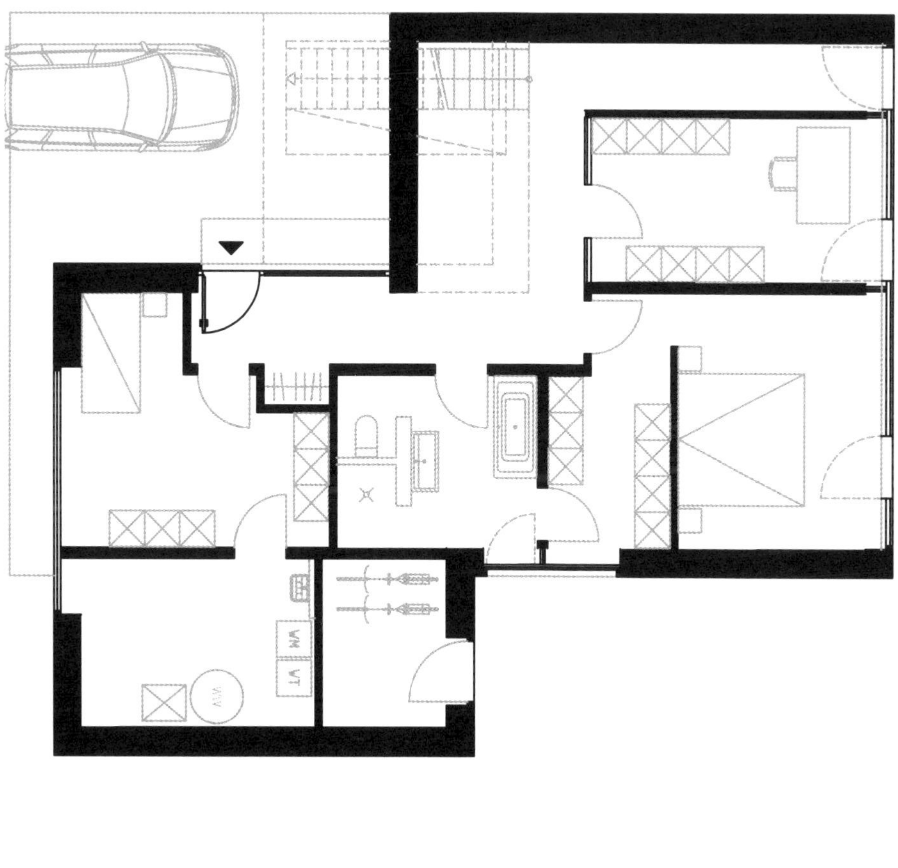

SUN-HOUSE

1

2

Architects: Sprenger Architekten und Partner
Energy conception: Sonnenhaus Huber & Schelling
Year of completion: 2012
Location: Hechingen, Baden-Württemberg
Gross floor area: 165,7 m^2
Number of bedrooms: 2
Main materials / structure: wood / timber frame construction, wooden plank stack ceiling
Ecological features: wood as renewable material, recyclable insulation, solar hot water supply and photovoltaics for CO_2-neutral operation

The building's appearance blends in with the rural surroundings, adopting the formal language of the building's surroundings and partly reinterpreting them. The rectangular building is arranged orthogonally to the existing house and thus becomes accessible via a courtyard situation. The north, east and west façades are largely closed due to a consistent southern orientation. Ancillary rooms and bedrooms are located in the north, common rooms are oriented towards the south. A compact volume minimizes heat loss in winter. By optimizing the ancillary rooms and two-story living areas, a generous feeling of space is nevertheless achieved. On the ground floor there is a bedroom with bathroom in addition to the living area. The upper floor accommodates a differently usable bedroom as well as a gallery.

The building design was based on a flexible floor plan. The building, which is designed as a holiday home, is also conceivable as a two-person household, a barrier-free retirement home or the home of a family of four. Despite the ambitious energy concept, the project had a tight budget. Large parts were built by the client himself.

An optimized timber construction forms the core of the supporting structure. The exterior façade and parts of the interior cladding are also made of wood. Recycling insulation enables a high standard of insulation.

The principle of the solar house is based on covering as much of the heating and hot water supply as possible with solar energy. The south-facing hot water collectors, with their vertical arrangement, offer optimum light output in winter, and the reflections of the pond support this effect. The heat gained supplies a hot water tank which can also bridge periods of bad weather. For extreme weather conditions, a pellet stove is used for additional heating. A ventilation system with heat recovery minimises heat losses and supplies the building with fresh air. With the electricity production of the photovoltaic system, CO_2-neutral building operation can be achieved. The architecture picks up on the elements of this innovative concept and makes them visible in the building design.

1 Exterior view from south
2 Exterior view from north

3 Living area
4 Staircase with view onto the terrace

3

4

1

2

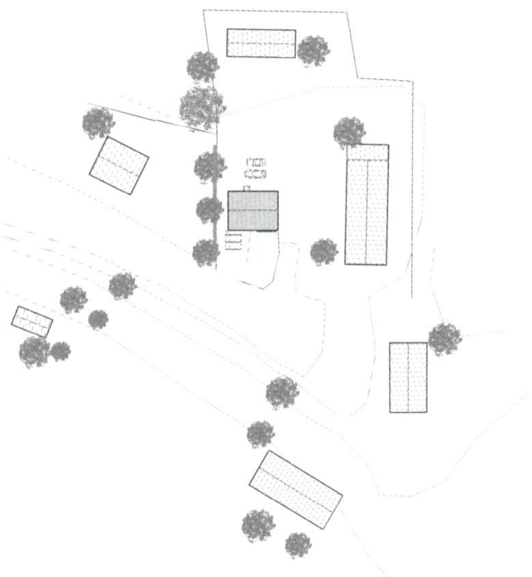

3

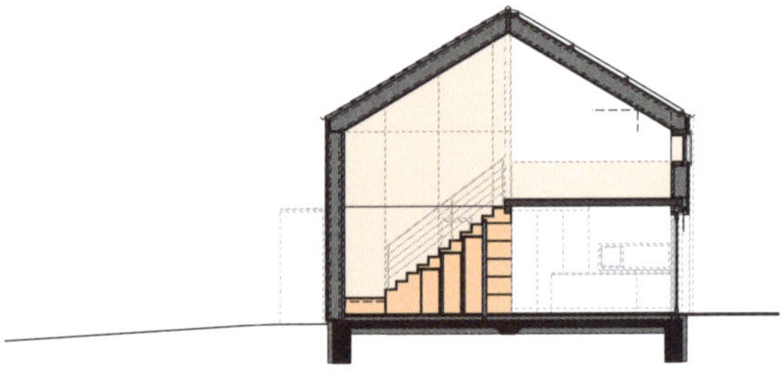

4

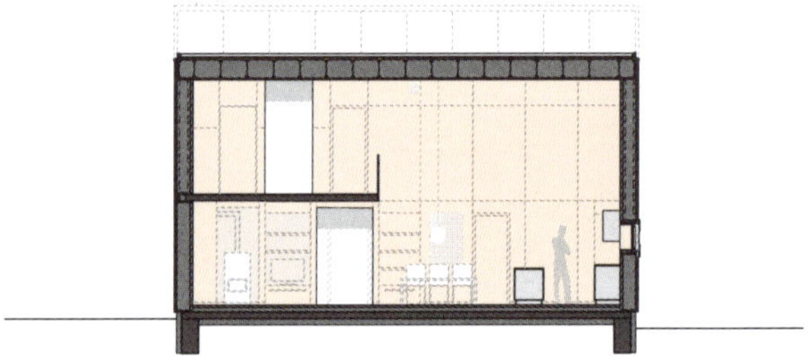

5

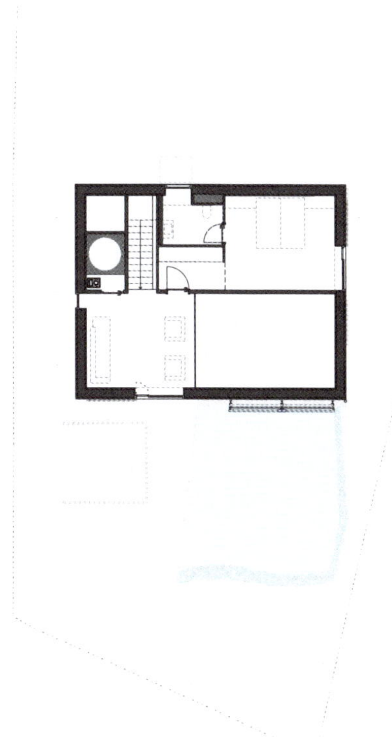

6

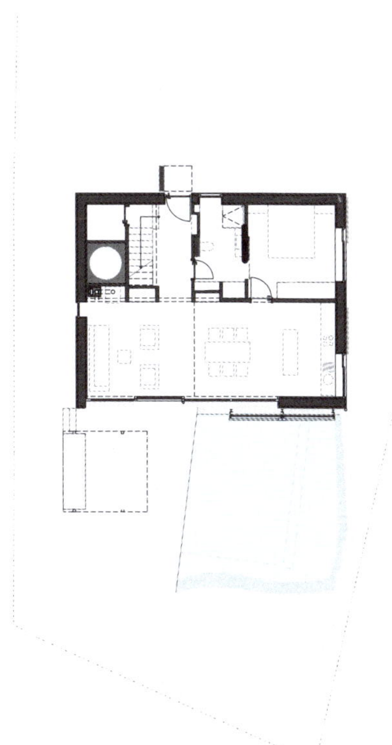

1 Terrace with photovoltaics and collectors
2 Site plan
3 Cross section
4 Longitudinal section

5 First floor plan
6 Ground floor plan

HOUSE H IN BURGHAUSEN

1, 2

3

Architects: Viktor Filimonow Architekt
Year of completion: 2014
Location: Burghausen, Bavaria
Gross floor area: 400 m^2
Number of bedrooms: 3
Main materials / structure: bricks, concrete, wood / solid construction
Ecological features: ventilation system with heat recovery

This single-family house was built in a new development area. Situated on a marginal plot and on a slope, if offers an impressive view of the landscape and a river. Despite the building activity in the neighborhood, a maximum amount of privacy was aimed for the realization of this project.

Two squat cubes of the house are stacked rectangular. Each of the cubes fulfils its own funktions. The brace on the ground floor protects the precious private interior of the property from curious onlookers, the cube above reaches into the depth of the property and zonates the area into their respective functioning purposes, being the large lawn, or the intimate pool in the corner.

4

5

1 Street side view
2 Exterior view with rooftop terrace
3 Garden side view

4 Covered terrace
5 Pool with visual protection
6 View into the garden

6

1

2

3

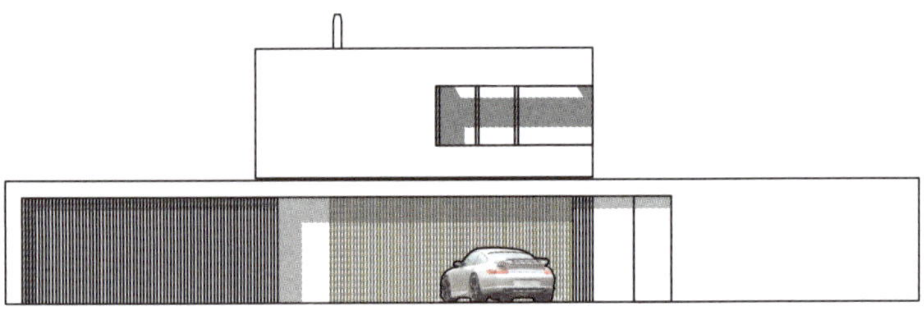

4

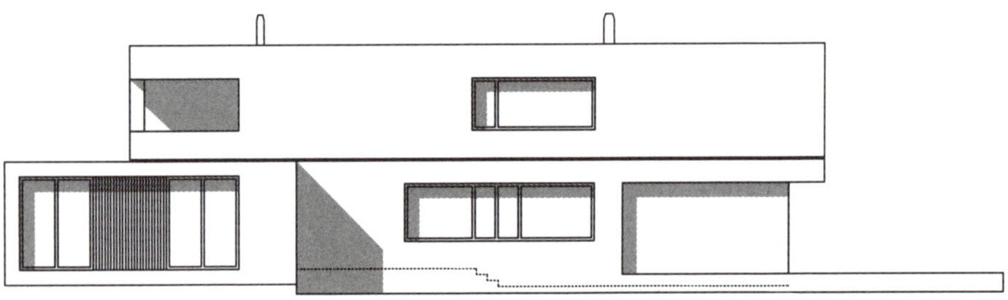

5

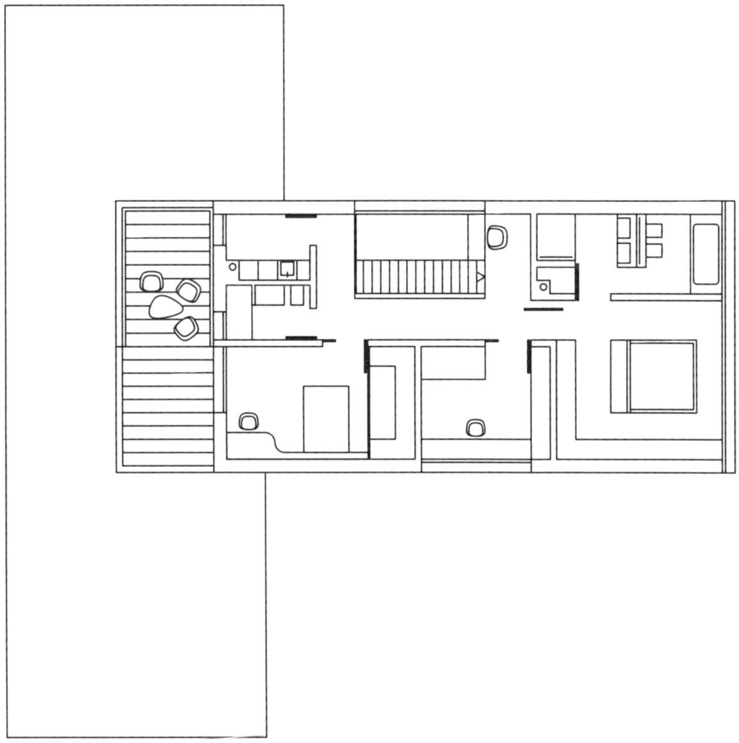

6

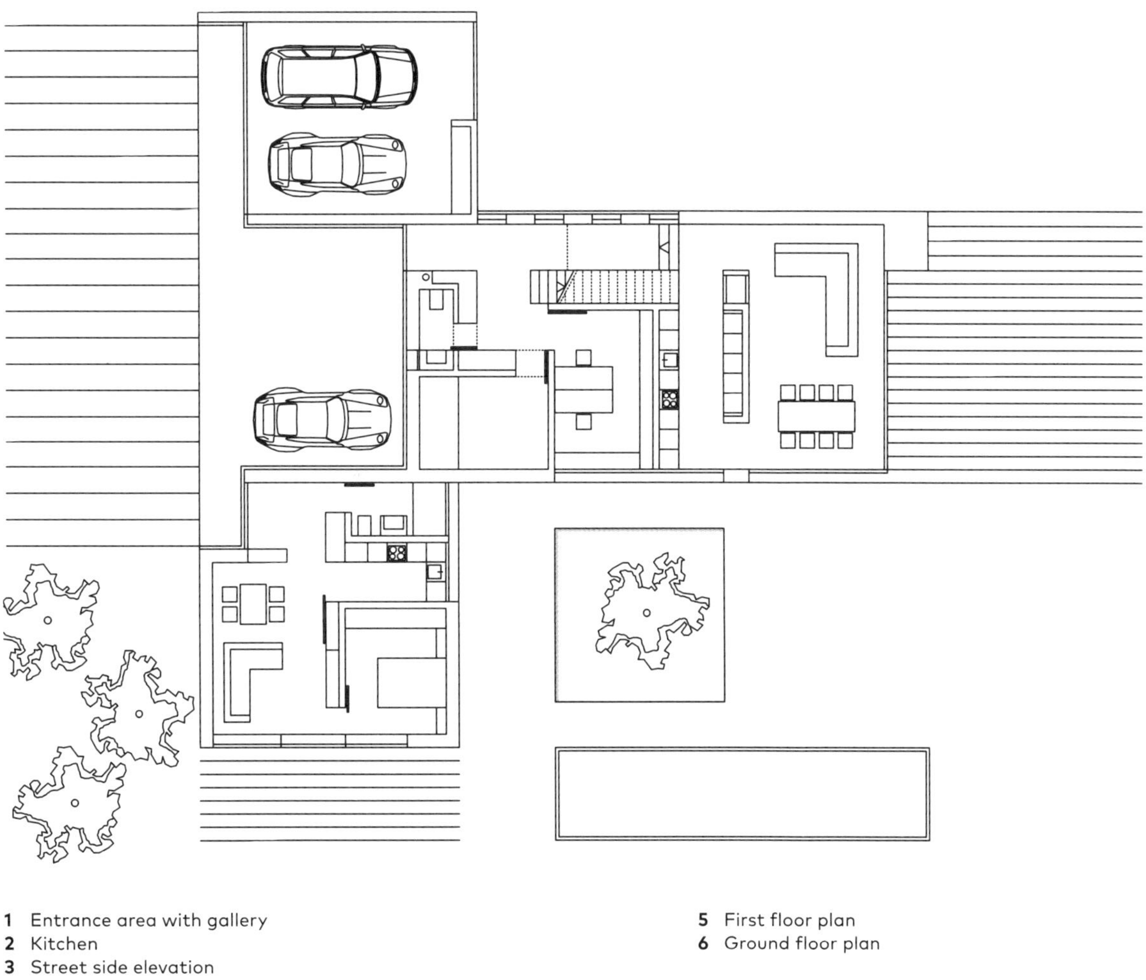

1 Entrance area with gallery
2 Kitchen
3 Street side elevation
4 Garden side elevation
5 First floor plan
6 Ground floor plan

1+1=2 GENERATIONS

1

2

Architects: hausfreunde Architekten
Year of completion: 2016
Location: Deggendorf, Bavaria
Gross floor area: 194 m^2
Number of bedrooms: 2
Main materials / structure: wood, chisel concrete, shell limestone / brickwork

The client's requirements included a house for two people with an open floor plan and an offset elevation, fitted with a certain amount of flexibility. Additionally, a granny flat, optionally usable as a rental property, was desired for the mother. In consequence, the design idea arose to construct the main house and the granny flat as independent, separate objects. Areas as for building services, wardrobe, and guest bathroom have been placed into a low building connected to the main body.

The granny flat appears to be closed to the street side. Its extended exterior wall shields and protects the whole private area. Only on the garden side the ensemble opens up generously. The staggered floor plans of the buildings create an entrance area that leads to the interior, enabling a pleasant and protected transition from the outside to the inside. Following the topography the living area could be designed with a generous room height. Cooking, dining, and living area are additionally subdivided by the different levels of the terrain, while the chisel concrete wall prevents direct views of the safe haven.

A staircase leads to the gallery, which serves as a workplace and can also accommodate guests as required. Installations are provided here in such a way that they can be divided into two separate rooms without great effort. The building is connected with its environment through views of the local steeple and the Danube basin. The bedroom is connected to the living room and gallery through an internal window and is thus included in the open floor plan. The bathroom is adjoined by a spacious dressing room. The open concept allows interesting views from all rooms and connects the interior and exterior space.

3

1 Garden view
2 Street view

3 Entrance area
4 Spacious staircase towards the dining area

4

1

2

3
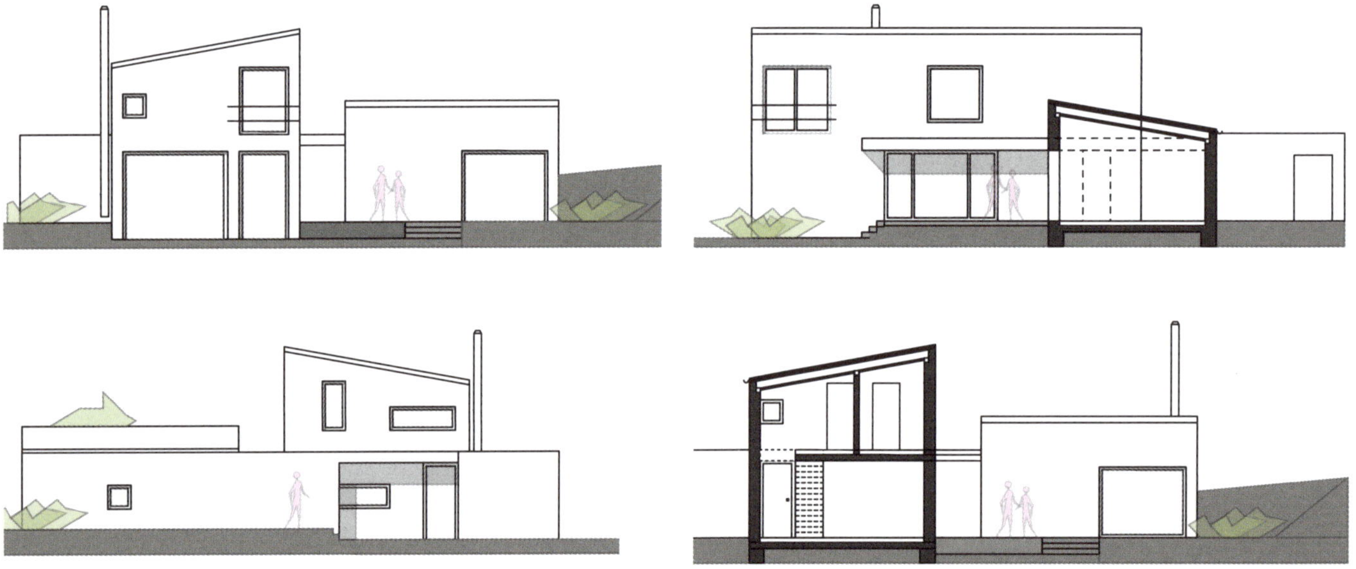

1 Gallery
2 Dining and living area
3 Elevations and sections

4 First floor plan
5 Ground floor plan
6 Site plan

4

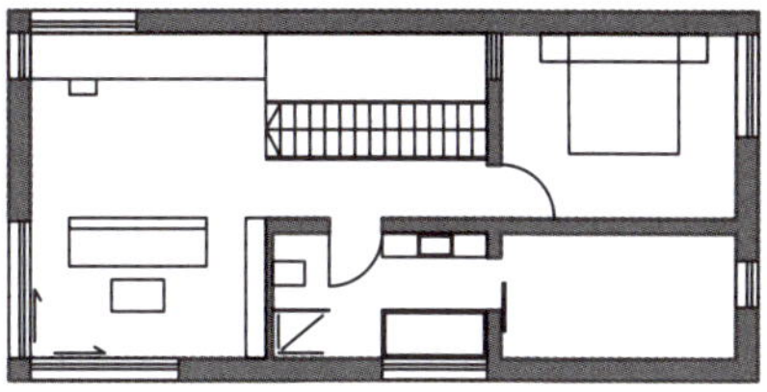

5

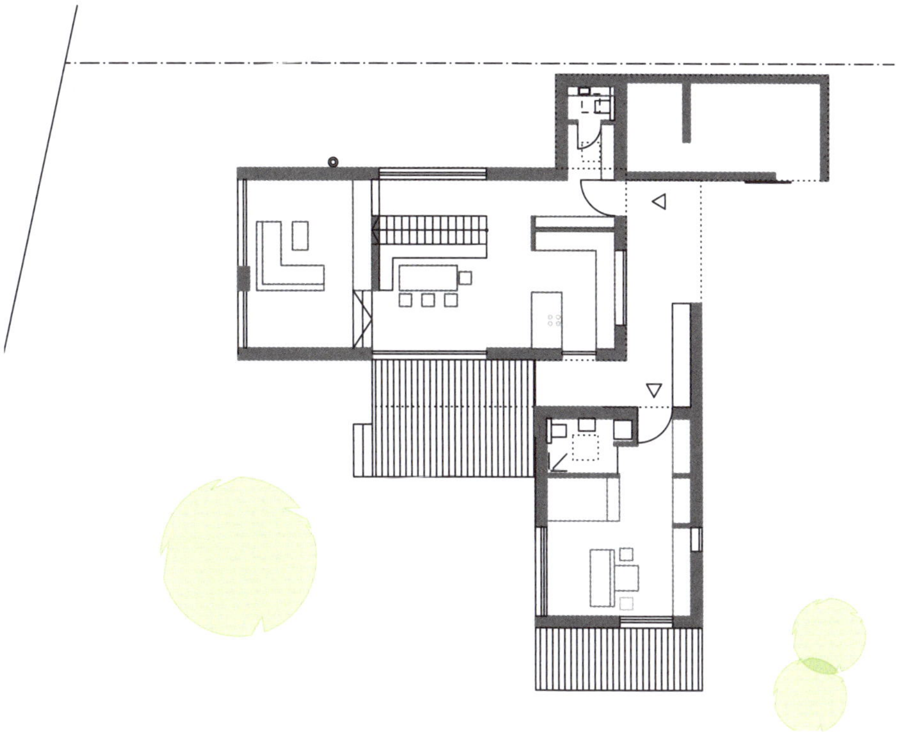

6

HOUSE GIGLER

1

2

Architects: CBA Clemens Bachmann Architekten
Year of completion: 2013
Location: Neubeuern, Bavaria
Gross floor area: 297 m^2
Number of bedrooms: 4
Main materials / structure: larch shingles / timber frame construction

The building is based on a distinct design concept, the client wanted a maximum opening of the visual axis to the opposite Wendelstein mountains. As the building is exentsively surrounded by fields, almost all of the rooms offer an impressive view of the mountain range. The entire southwest façade is designed as sliding glass façade. The large, frameless sliding elements extend the living space into the outside area and guide the view towards the surrounding nature. Only the back side with just a few windows is predominantly closed.

The timber frame construction was clad with split larch shingles on the outside. A concrete garage slides into the main house as a contrasting volume. House Gigler was awarded the Rosenheim prize of wood construction in 2016.

3

1 Side view
2 Front view

3 Detail of the façade
4 Entrance area

4

1

2

3

4

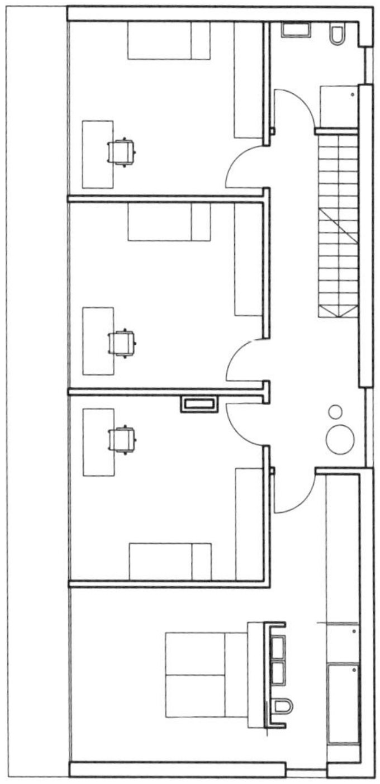

5

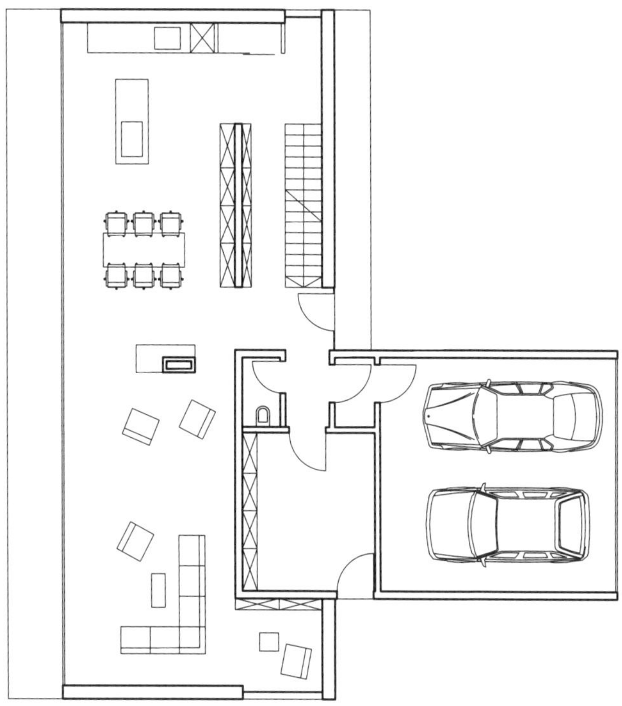

1 Detail of the façade with larch shingles
2 Side view with closed back side
3 Garage sliding into the main body

4 First floor plan
5 Ground floor plan

HOUSE F IN HALTERN AM SEE

1

2, 3

4

Architects: quadrat + architektengesellschaft mbH
Year of completion: 2014
Location: Haltern am See, North Rhine-Westphalia
Gross floor area: 255 m²
Number of bedrooms: 4
Main materials / structure: clinker, exposed concrete, oak parquet / solid construction
Ecological features: KfW 55

The deliberately simple and minimalist building contrasts with the usual saddle roof structures of the surroundings. Choosing brick as the main building material, on the other hand, creates a link to the traditional architecture of the Münsterland region. The absence of conventional details such as attic panels and window sills focuses the brick in its original character.

The archaic and protective impression of the building from the outside is reversed in the interior. Through the open floor plan and the connected living, dining, and cooking areas with their generous glazings with views of the garden achieve a light and lively expanse. Bed and children's rooms are accessed via a gallery flooded with light by skylights.

The reduction and the play in the choice of materials, such as the anthracite-colored screed in the bathrooms, the massive oak floorboards or the raw exposed concrete ceiling, make the interiors comfortable and exciting.

5

6

1 Southeast view with carport
2 Northeast view with access area
3 Garden view
4 Street view

5 Entrance area
6 Living and dining area
7 Detail flush fitted door
8 Gallery

7, 8

1

2

3

1 Gallery
2 Kitchen
3 Open living, dining, and cooking area

4 Ground floor plan
5 First floor plan
6 Cross section
7 Longitudinal section
8 South elevation
9 East elevation
10 West elevation
11 North elevation

4

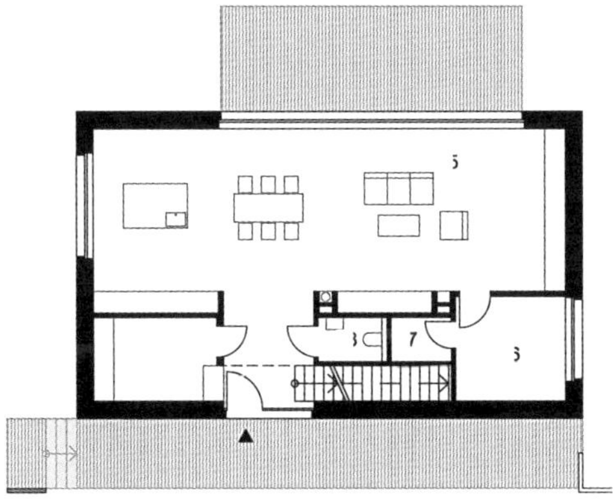

5

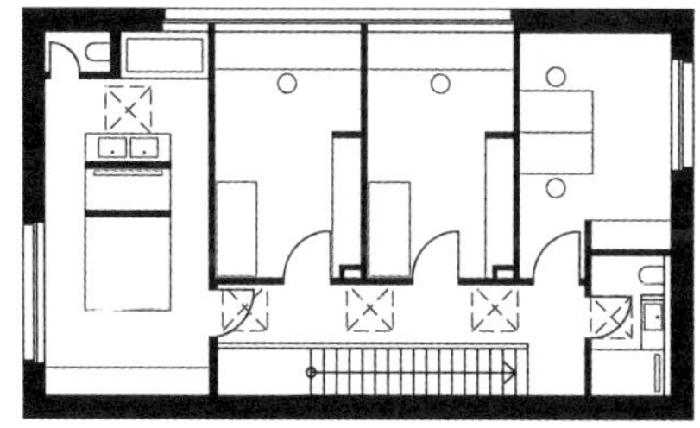

6

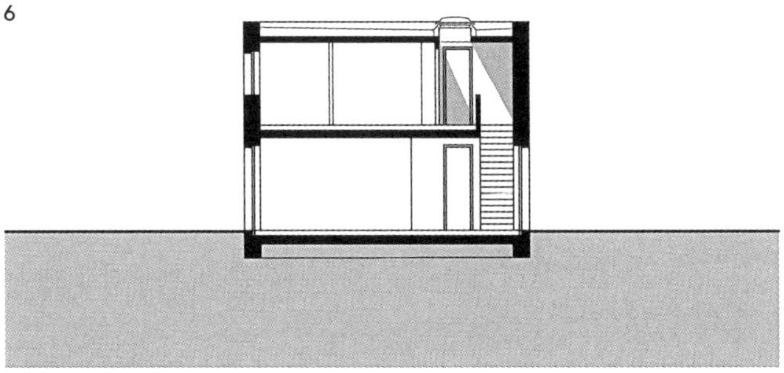

7

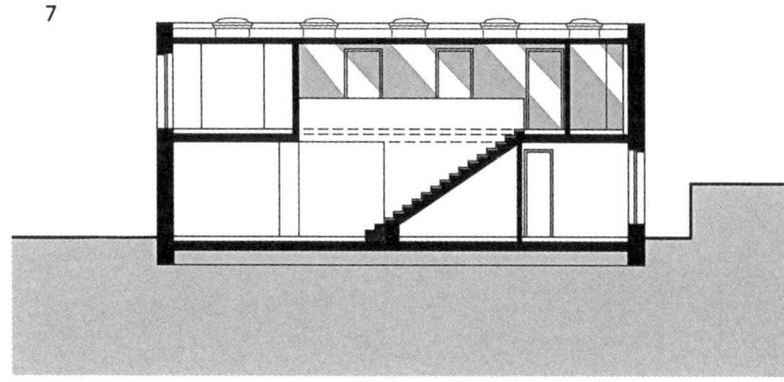

8

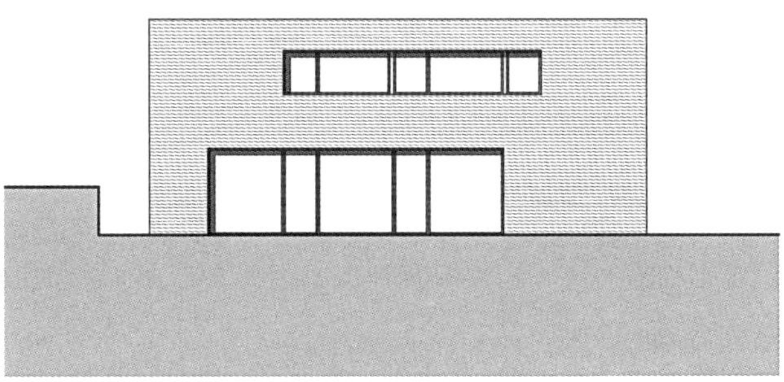

9

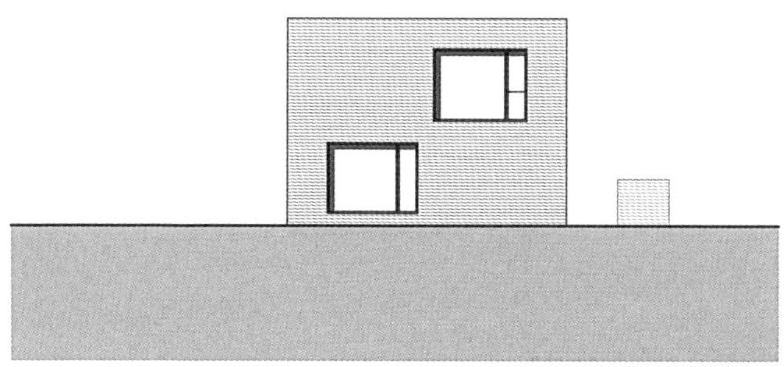

10

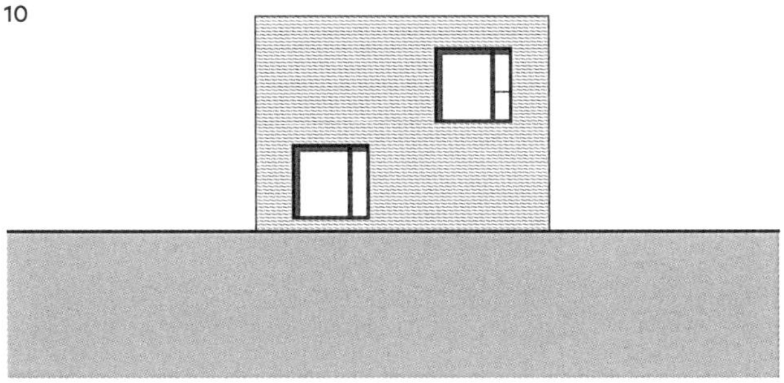

11

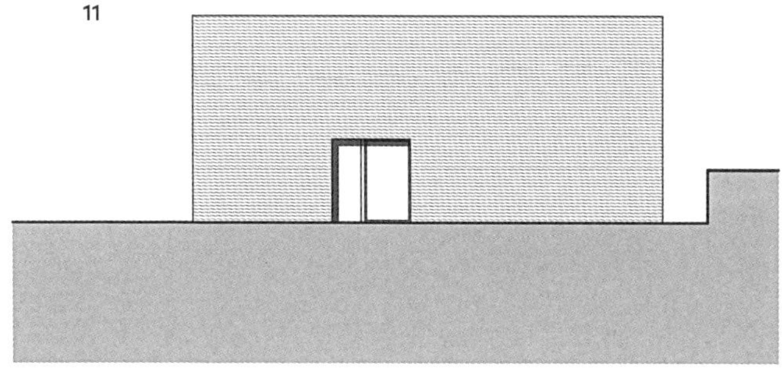

HOUSE AT KUR-PROMENADE

1

2

Architects: wolff:architekten gesellschaft von architekten
Year of completion: 2019
Location: Berlin
Gross floor area: 155 m²
Number of bedrooms: 2
Main materials / structure: plastered solid construction
Ecological features: subsidiary solarthermics for heating and warm water

At the end of the avenue-like "Seekorso" lies the property of the single-family and office building. The area is part of the former villa colony "Luxusbad Cladow-Glienick" and oriented towards the Groß Glienicker See lake. The design principle was to harmoniously incorporate the office of the client, self-employed in the media industry, into a single-family house. A void, expanding two stories and spanned by a bridge-like gallery, builds the core of the house and separates the sleeping and office areas. In its center there is an old olive tree, the plant pot is integrated into the kitchen block. The austere cube is cantilevered to the street side and rests on two bright clinker brick walls, which are offset against each other in the entrance area. Inside, two exposed concrete staircases running in opposite directions interlock to provide independent access to the bedroom and office areas. The latter is oriented towards the street on the upper floor with almost frameless glazing. The entrance is located under the cantilevered cube of the upper floor and is protected from rain and weather. In addition to a collector system on the flat roof, the gas condensing boiler is supported by a heating circuit of the inner chimney in the living area.

3

4

5

1 Garden view from south
2 Exterior view from west

3 Cooking area with olive tree
4 Two-story void
5 Bridge-like gallery

1

2

3

1 Street view from southeast
2 Cooking area with two-story void
3 Bathroom on the first floor

4 First floor plan
5 Ground floor plan
6 Longitudinal section

4

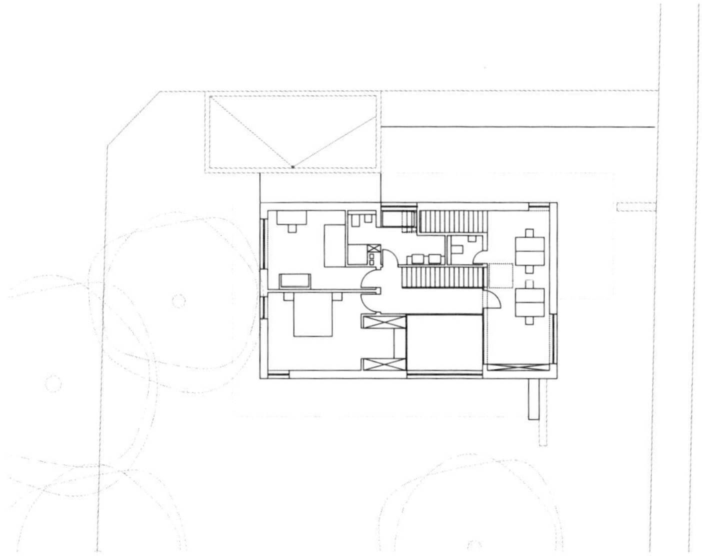

5

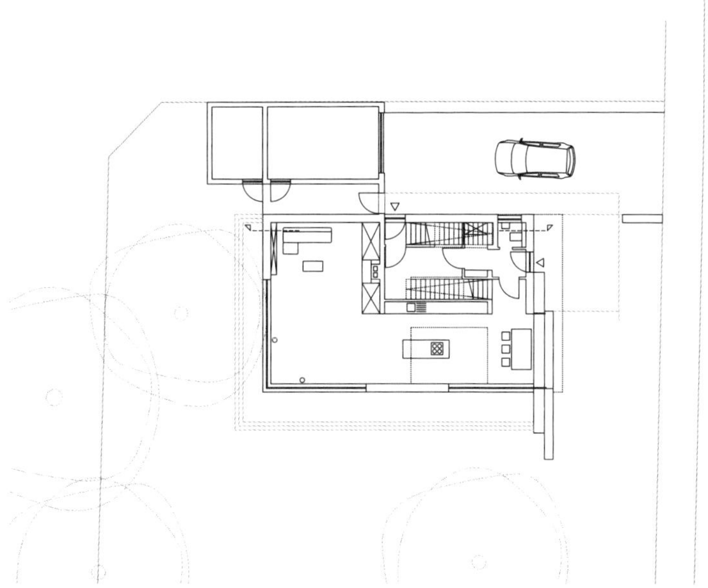

6

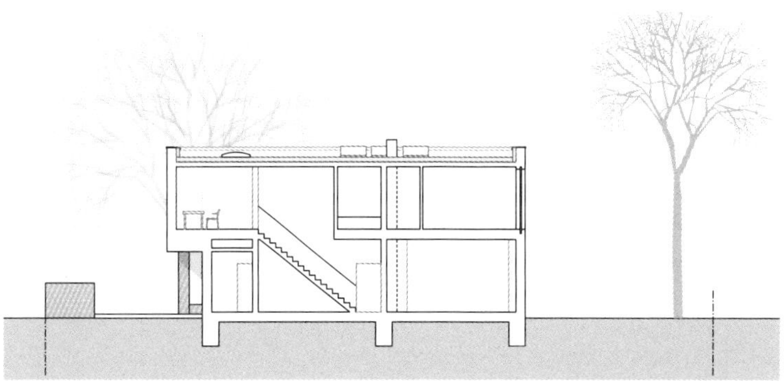

HOUSE IN THE BLACK FOREST

1

2, 3

Architects: Schneider | Architekten Partnerschaft
Year of completion: 2013
Location: Königsfeld, Baden-Württemberg
Gross floor area: 325 m^2
Number of bedrooms: 3
Main materials / structure: timber frame construction
Ecological features: KfW 70, greened flat roof on the outbuilding

The property is flat with a slight slope to the east side, the main building aligned towards the south-east side. It is horizontally wood-clad and has a gabled roof without an overhang. It is restricted to the westside neighbor through a one-story out-building with a flat roof and fiber cement paneling. The building is accessed via a protected entrance niche in the outbuilding. In the open living area with kitchen and dining table, a mullion-transom glazing extends over the southeast corner in front of the terrace. A double staircase accesses the attic floor with the sleeping area and a bathroom. A dressing room has been integrated into the parents' bedroom and an open gallery into the attic of the two children's rooms. A study and a large cellar are located in the basement, which can be lit naturally due to the embankment through a ribbon window. The timber frames of the building are insulated completely with wood fiber and equipped with a rain protection sheet. The building is heated by an air-water heat pump with underfloor heating. In addition, a ventilation system was installed.

4

5

6

1 Exterior view from southwest with entrance
2 Exterior view from southeast at dawn
3 Exterior view from south

4 View from the staircase to the dining area
5 Dining and living area
6 Open living and dining area with kitchen

1

2

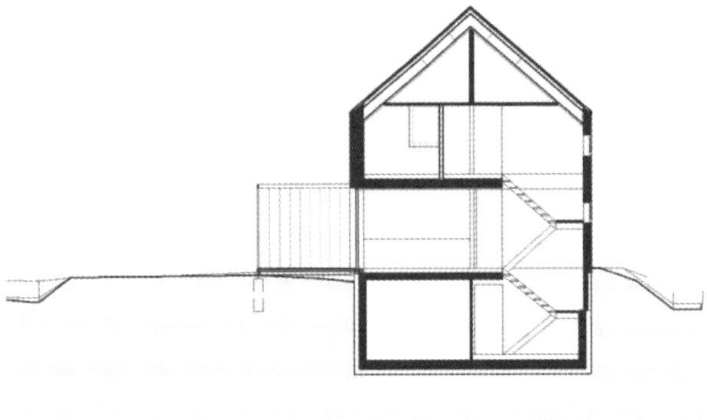

1 Site plan
2 Cross section

3 First floor plan
4 Ground floor plan

3

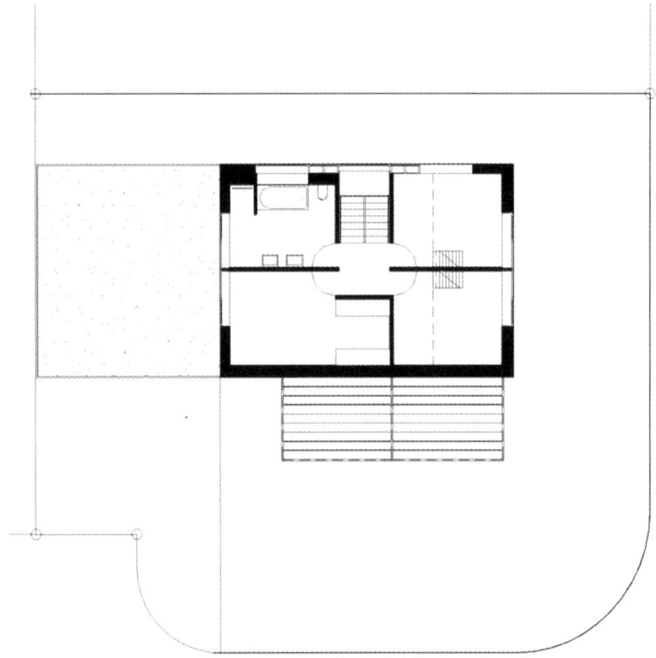

4

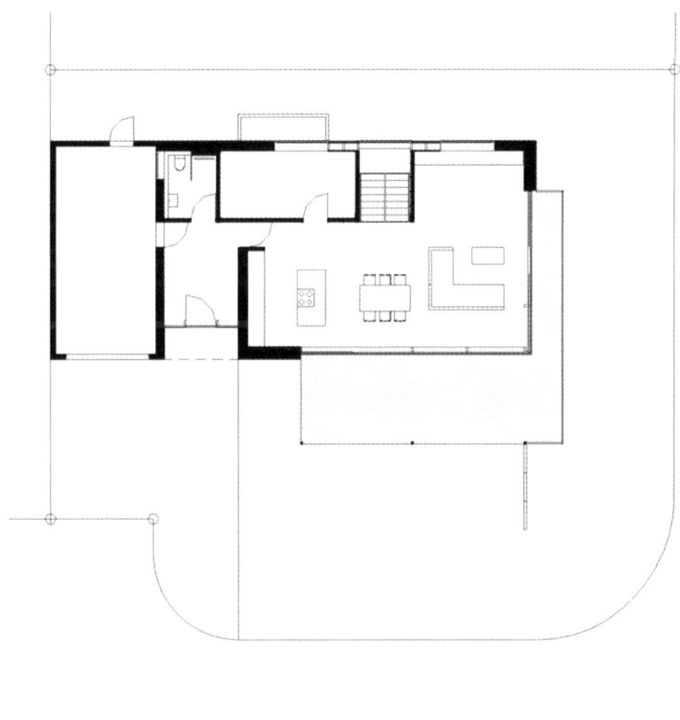

ON THE EDGE OF A FOREST

1

2, 3

Architects: bauer architektur
Year of completion: 2016
Location: Weimar, Thuringia
Gross floor area: 236 m^2
Number of bedrooms: 1
Main materials / structure: masonry, reinforced concrete
Ecological features: geothermal heat pump, ventilation system with heat recovery, rooftop greening

The specifications of the development plan in the residential area Am Schießhaus, situated to the east of the city, are particularly interesting, especially for the demanded height and shape of the structure. The villa on the edge of the forest shows every aspect of these special features in its street façade. An elevated upper floor transforms the legal requirements into light through large windows and glass patio doors.

Newly set interior heights create exclusive rooms on the living floor, blending into the adjacent forest. Urban character and nature interact with each other through the extensive glazing. A rooftop terrace provides sunny as well as shady areas and connects living space and outside world. The public living area is located on the ground floor, widely flanking the garden and terraces.

4

5

1 Front façade from south
2 View of the rooftop terrace
3 Street view from southeast

4 View of the ground floor terrace
5 View to the rooftop terrace
6 Garden view from north
7 View from the staircase

6, 7

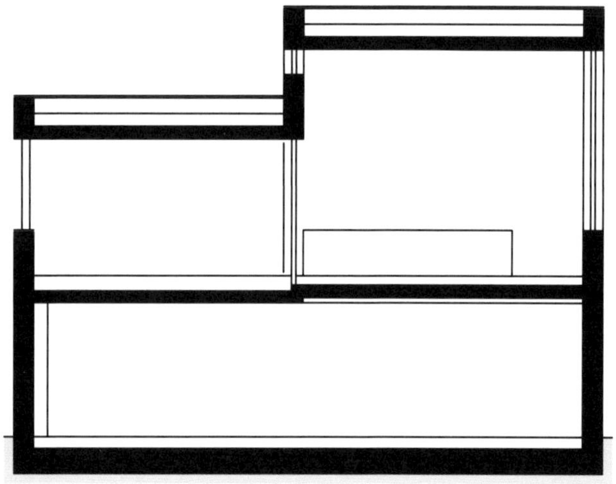

1

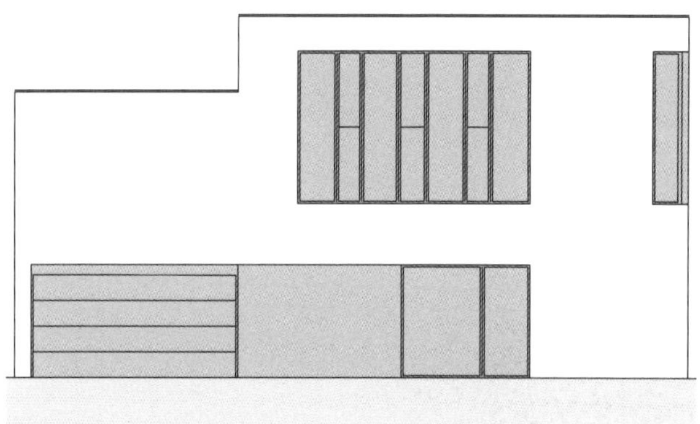

2

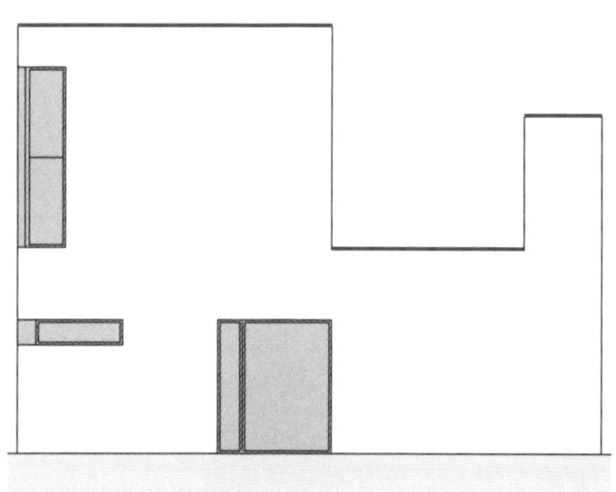

3

1 Cross section
2 South elevation
3 East elevation

4 Site plan
5 First floor plan
6 Ground floor plan

4

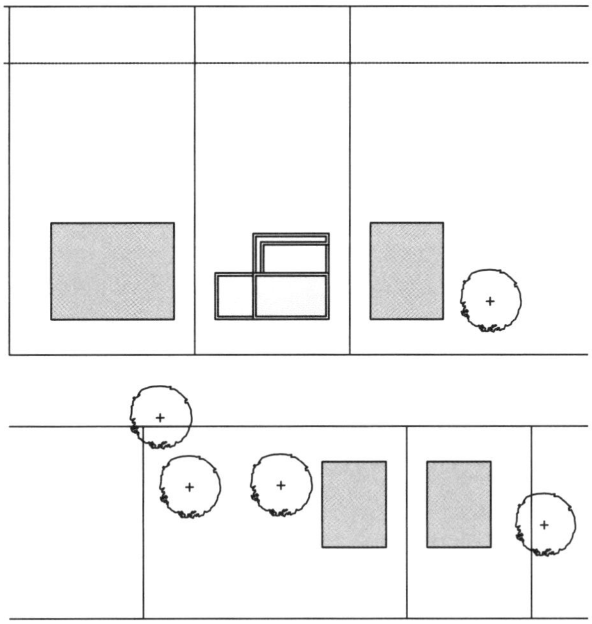

5

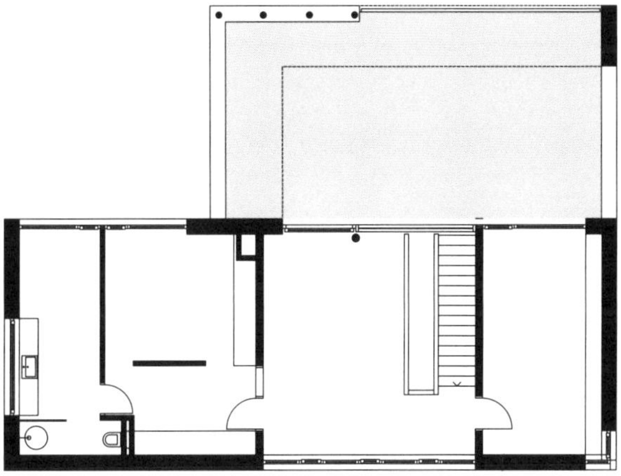

6

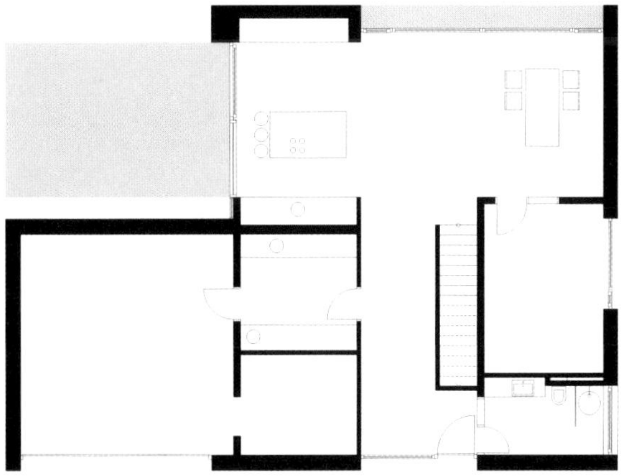

TINY WOODEN HOUSE

1

2

Architects: ARCHITEKTanBORD
Year of completion: 2013
Location: Horgau, Bavaria
Gross floor area: 123 m^2
Number of bedrooms: 2
Main materials / structure: reinforced concrete base plate with driven piles / timber frame construction with ventilated façade
Ecological features: prefabricated elements, energy consumption 22 % below EnEV

174

This unusual slender single-family house with a solid wood façade is located in Horgau near Augsburg. The plot is located in a flood-prone area, therefore a pile foundation was chosen due to the prevailing soil conditions. In order to meet the specified cost and time frame, the construction was implemented in a prefabricated timber frame structure.

The building has two floors with a living space of 99 square meters and offers enough space for a family with one child. On the ground floor there are the publicly accessible rooms, such as the kitchen and living room, the private bedrooms are located on the upper floor.

Wood is also present in the interior as one of the most important building materials in the form of natural ceiling beams. The floor slab and a single interior wall were made of reinforced concrete. This media wall reinforces the building, divides the living and dining areas, stores heat and offers numerous electrical connection options.

Window openings supply the rooms with the necessary daylight. They follow a strict grid, which is also reflected on the ventilated wooden cladding, and direct the view from the inside to the outside. The building was built energy-efficient according to the EnEv 2012 and surpasses the standards by 22 percent. As soon as the floor slab had hardened, the building could be handed over ready to move in within 20 working days.

3

1 Exterior view from southwest
2 Exterior view with surrounding landscape

3 Living area with sitting accomodations
4 Living area with dresser

4

1

2

3

4

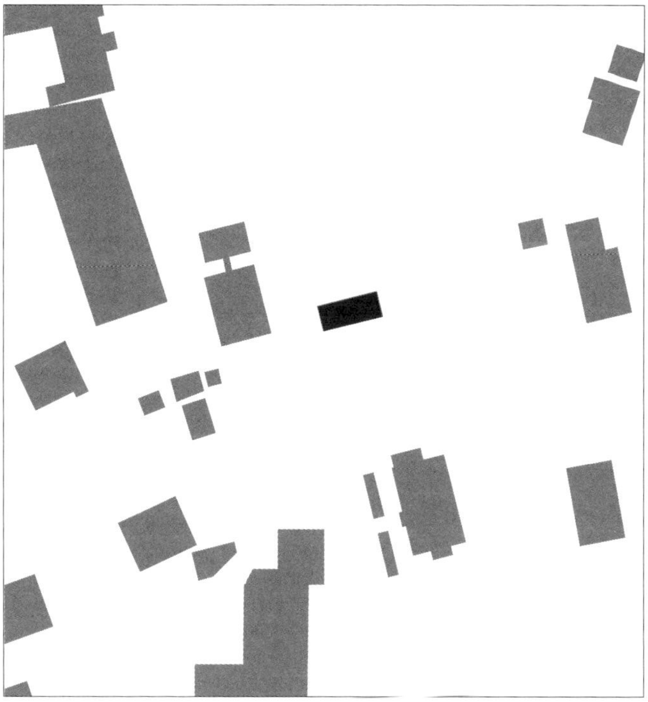

5

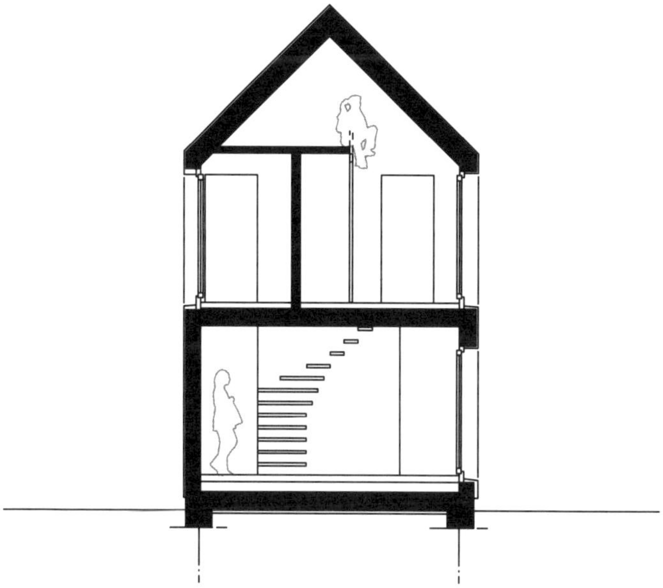

6

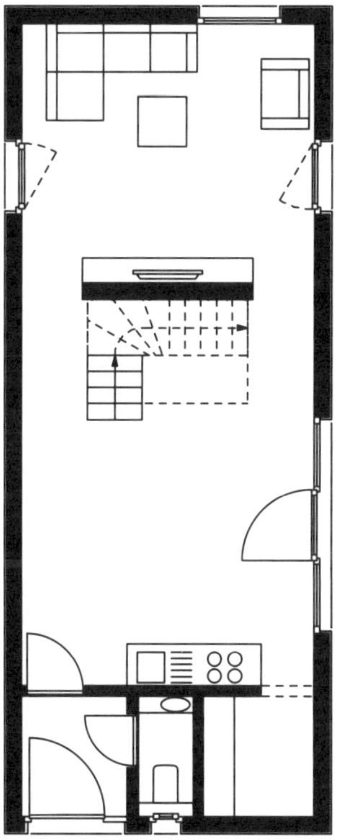

7

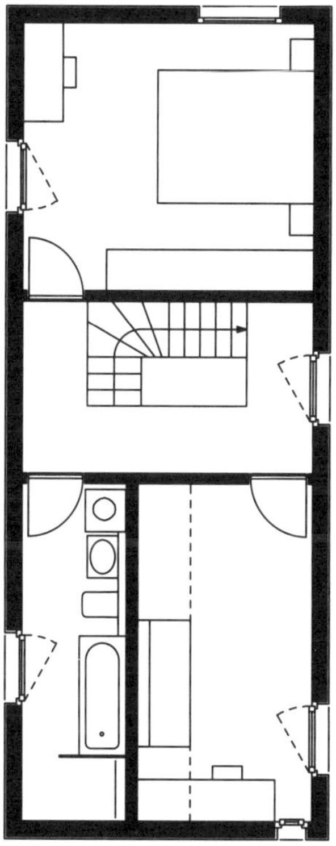

1 Exterior view from west with entrance area
2 Exterior view from east
3 Detail of the façade

4 Site plan
5 Cross ection
6 Ground floor plan
7 First floor plan

SLANT 13

1

Architects: oxen architekten
Year of completion: 2017
Location: Rösrath, North Rhine-Westphalia
Gross floor area: 275 m²
Number of bedrooms: 2
Main materials / structure: concrete, wood / solid construction
Ecological features: geothermal energy

2

The building located at the outskirts of a mountain range in the Bergisches Land has an asymmetrical gable and is clad with a vertical wooden casing. This accommodates parking spaces for garages, bicycles and motor scooters directly accessible from the street by a driveway. The garage with its adjoining rooms looks like a building pushed underneath above the wooden superstructure and thus recedes in its appearance. The entrance to the house is protected from the weather by a pergola-like corridor. Only at its end does the function of daily living become readable through the single-story modern, white plastered latch. Generous window areas and openings as well as a square window seat niche allow views into the adjoining landscape. The surrounding open spaces are designed simply and close to nature in the style of a farmer's garden. In the attic there are study rooms and an apartment as a granny apartment for the daughter. The building itself meets ecological requirements and is heated by means of a geothermal heat pump. Summer heat insulation is guaranteed by external Venetian blinds.

3

1 Courtyard view from northwest
2 Façade section

3 Weather-protected isle towards entrance
4 Gable view from north
5 Window recess with seating area
6 Living area with view

4, 5

6

1

2

3

1 Garden view from south
2 Entrance courtyard from west
3 Street view from northwest

4 First floor plan
5 Ground floor plan
6 Site plan
7 Cross section

4

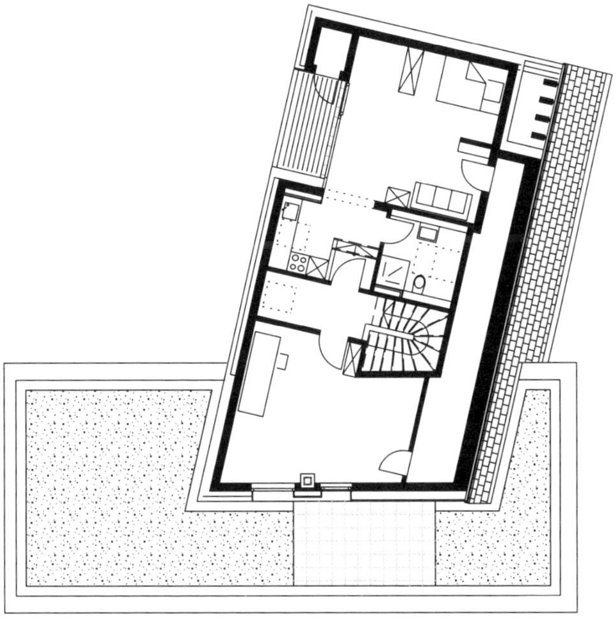

5

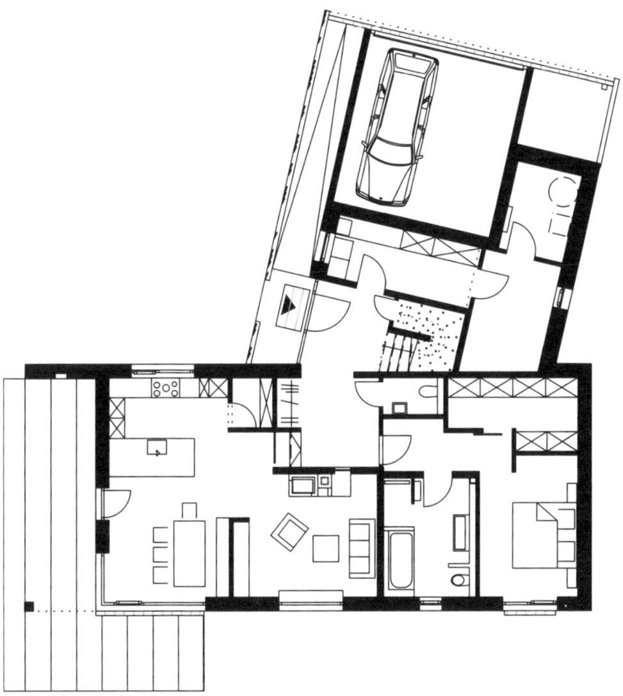

6

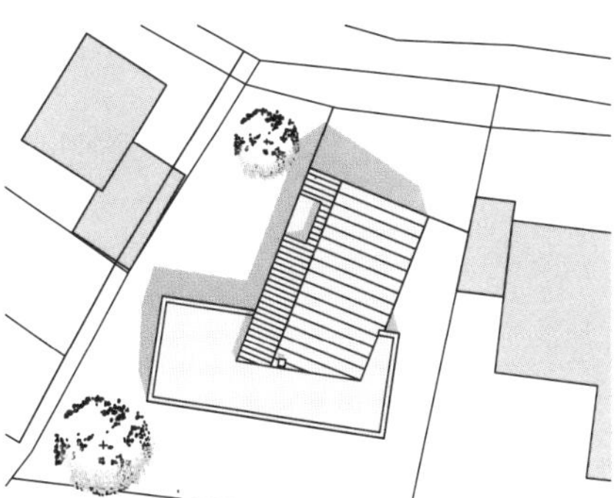

7

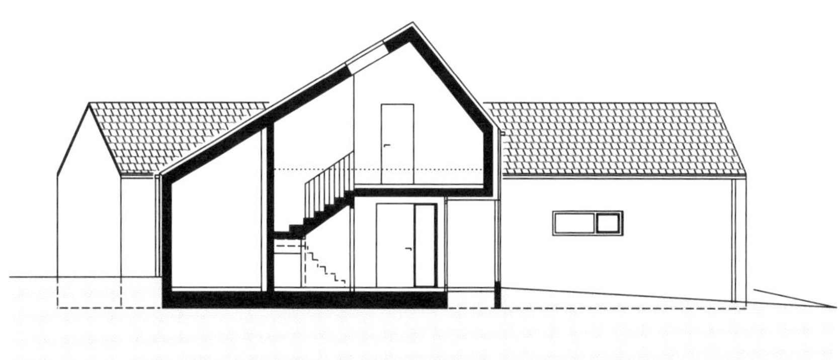

COTTAGE AMMERSEE

1

2

Architects: moosmang architekten
Year of completion: 2012
Location: Schondorf am Ammersee, Bavaria
Gross floor area: 211 m²
Number of bedrooms: 3
Main materials / structure: wood / timber frame construction
Ecological features: highly insulated wooden components, heat generation through south glazing and photovoltaic system

The cottage is situated on the edge of a mansion site, on a northern slope. A plinth floor spans the difference in terrain between the street and the garden level, so that the two holiday flats at the top are orientated to the garden. The building was erected as a timber frame construction on a massive basement floor. The weather formwork consists of glazed spruce wood and has been left sawed rough. The planners and the timber construction company Fichtl from Hechenwang worked closely together and in coordination with the architect the work planning was finally developed into a workshop planning. The use of machines in the workshop made it possible to manufacture the components precisely and accurately. The resulting large panels with the complete external planking made it possible to assemble the shell within a few days. After the installation of the building service lines, the installation cavity was closed with the finished planking on the room side and the rest of the interior work was completed. The highly insulated wooden components, the solar heat gains from the southern glazing and the photovoltaic system on the roof ensure high energy efficiency.

3

1 Exterior view from southwest
2 Exterior view from south

3 Exterior view from northeast
4 Kitchen
5 Living room

4

5

1

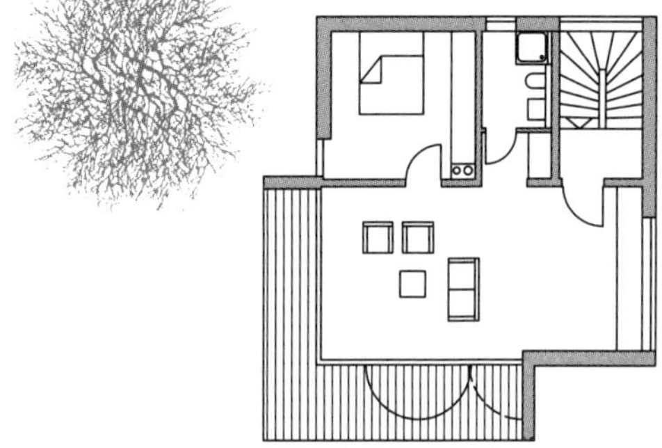

2

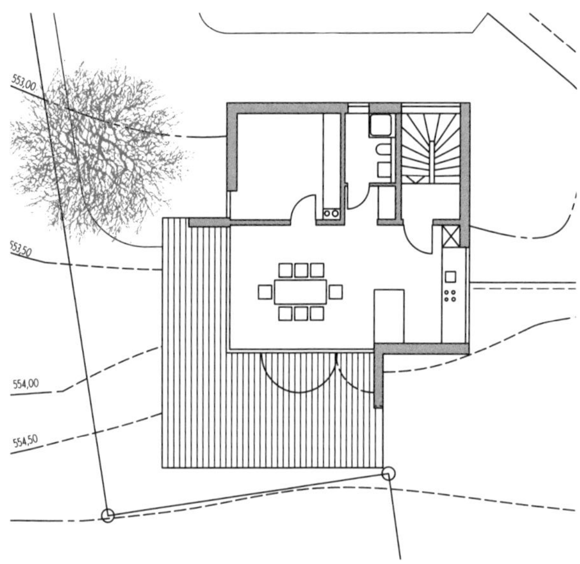

3

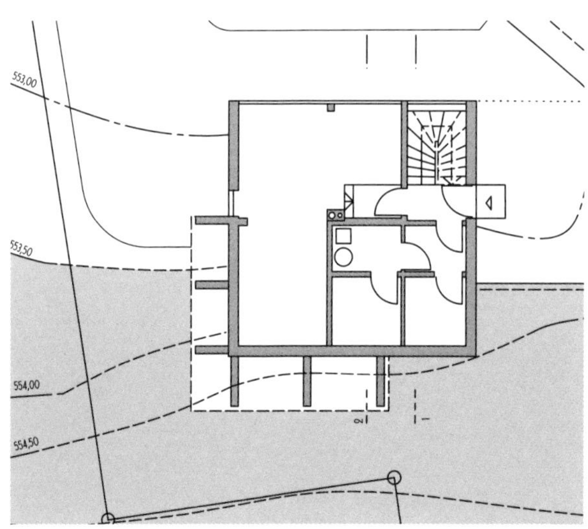

1 First floor plan
2 Ground floor plan
3 Basement floor plan
4 Cross section
5 South elevation
6 East elevation

4

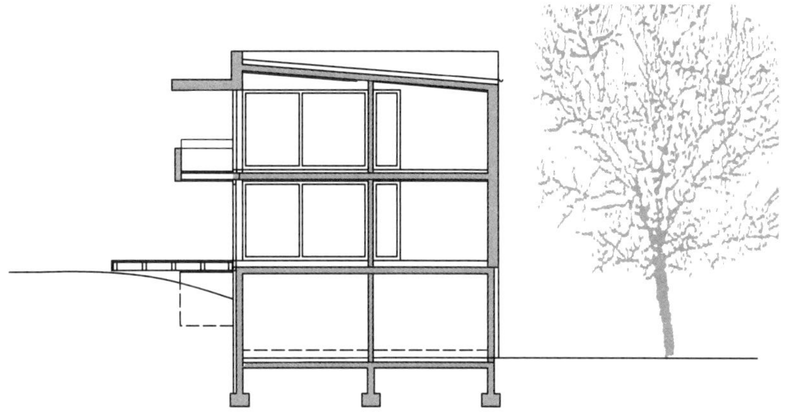

5

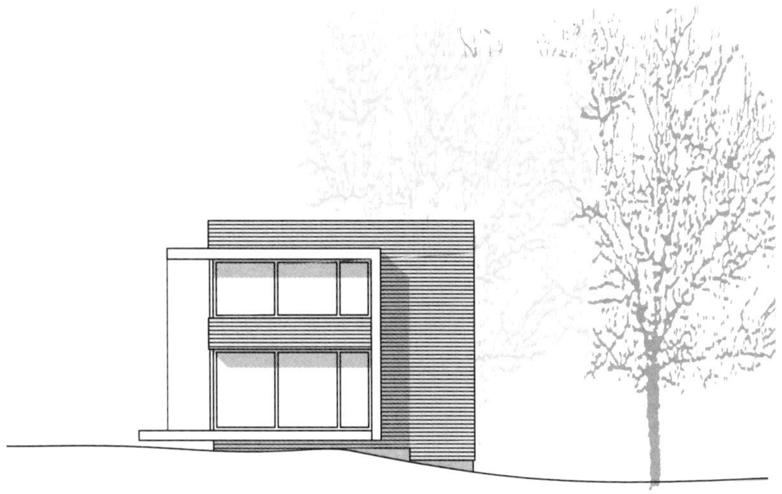

6

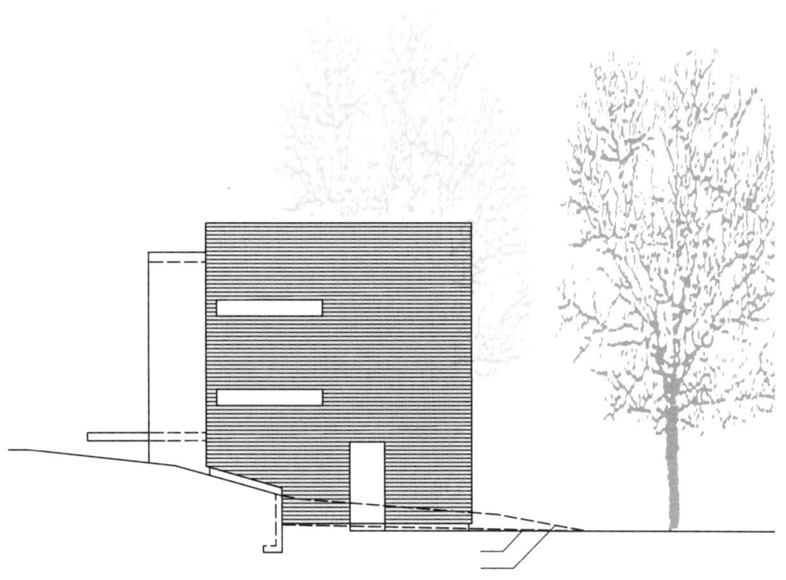

HOUSE S3

1

2, 3

1 Exterior view from west
2 Straight-lined stairwell
3 Floating stairwell

4 West elevation
5 Cross section
6 Façade detail
7 Exterior view from northwest

The detached house in Rhine-Hesse is characterized by its clear geometric design and staggered construction. A cantilevered cube also serves as a roof over the terrace and houses one of the five rooms. The linear staircase organizes the floor plan of the building with the characteristic wooden floating stairwell.

The oblong, rectangular window bands ensure a generous incidence of daylight. The light oak wood of the windows harmonizes with the white color of the interior. A variety of views and spatial experiences are made possible by an open path in the house. A roof terrace serves as a protected retreat.

The compact form of the building optimizes costs and energy. Energy is supplied by geothermics. With a primary energy requirement of 53 kilowatt hours per square meter per year, the building is designed according to the KfW 70 standard.

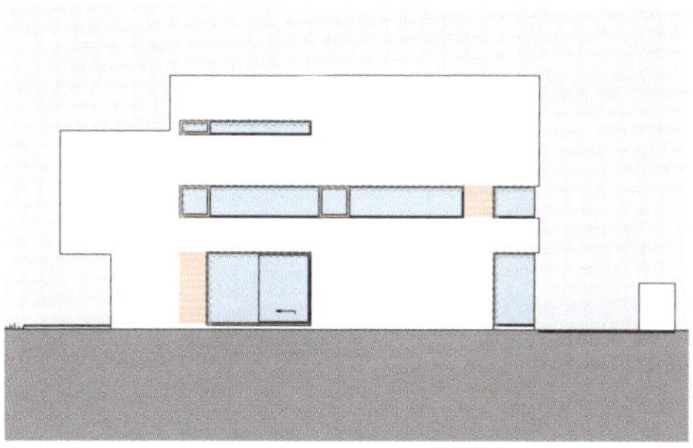
4

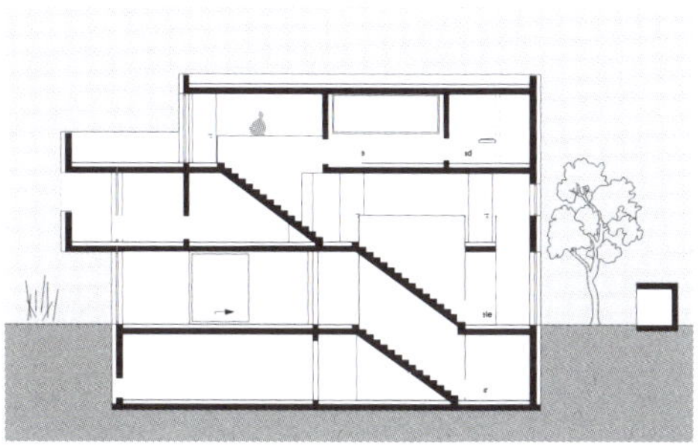
5

6

Architects: Hille Architekten + Stadtplaner
Year of completion: 2013
Location: Rhine-Hesse, Rhineland-Palatinate
Gross floor area: 380 m^2
Number of bedrooms: 3
Main materials / structure: plastered solid construction with full thermal insulation and green roof areas
Ecological features: energy supply via geothermal energy, triple glazing, energy requirement 20.4 kWh/m^2 a, KfW 70

7

HOUSE H IN FRANKENBERG

1

Architects: Studio Hajek with Kohlmayer Oberst Architekten
Year of completion: 2015
Location: Burghausen (Eder), Hesse
Gross floor area: 235 m^2
Number of bedrooms: 2
Main materials / structure: glass, natural stone, lime plaster, built-in furniture / solid construction
Ecological features: heat pump (brine-water)

2

The house on the edge of a quarry looks like a walk-in sculpture and has a magnificent view of the old town. At the ground level and without any barriers, the house offers exciting and at the same time functional rooms. Six cubes of different heights accommodate the private areas. In between there is a generous, floor-deep glazed living hall, which offers places to eat, work or simply views of the garden and the city.

Frameless glazing, the precisely manufactured built-in furniture and the lime plaster, used both inside and outside, make the transitions between the building and the extensive property almost disappear and extend the living space into nature. Without a single step, the building can also be used flexibly at an old age.

3

1 Exterior view from the garden
2 Exterior view at twilight

3 Staggering of the cubes
4 Cubes and living hall
5 Interior and exterior interaction
6 Exterior view from west

4, 5

6

1

2

3

1 Living hall
2 Guest room and study
3 View onto the city

4 Floor plan
5 South elevation
6 Longitudinal section

4

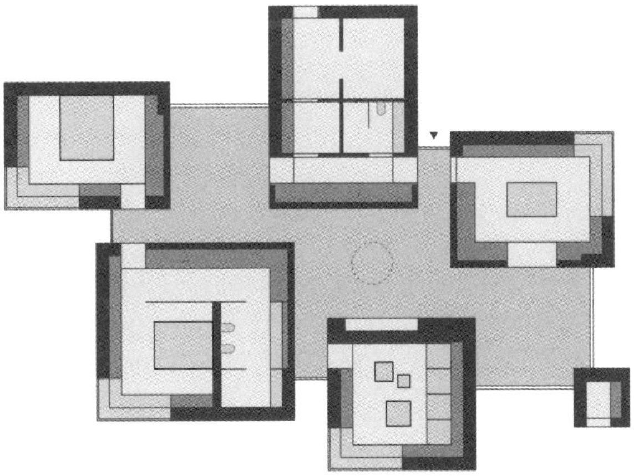

5

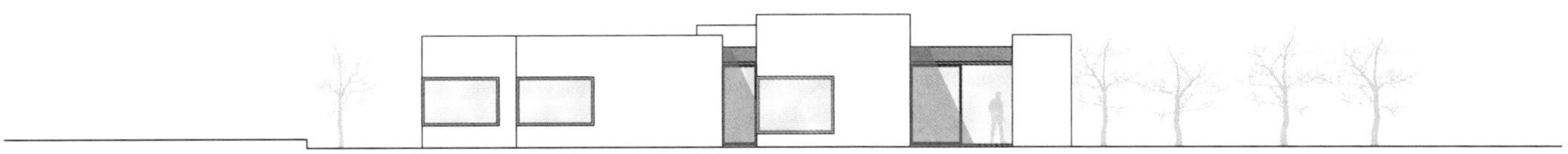

6

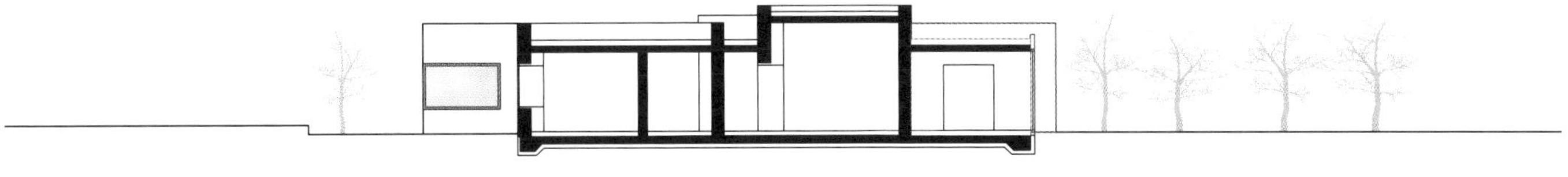

HOUSE S

1

2

192

Architects: VS Volker Schmidt Architekten
Year of completion: 2014
Location: Neuendettelsau, Bavaria
Gross floor area: 200 m^2 (including loggia)
Number of bedrooms: 3
Main materials / structure: wood / timber frame construction
Ecological features: use of renewable resources, local heat, wood chip heating

Located on the outskirts between a small weekend cottage and a large barn, the new building closes a gap in the small village. The residential house with carport and fence is arranged around the large oak, that divides the property into a semi-public area in the southwest and a private garden in the southeast.

The entranceway leads past the old oak tree. From the entrance there is a direct view into the landscape. The kitchen and the dining area open generously to the garden. The loggia attached to the living and dining area is oriented towards the landscape. A single flight of stairs leads to the spacious hallway with a workplace on the upper floor, with a view of the crown of the old oak tree. Here are the bedrooms and two bathrooms. The rooms are open to the roof and are lit from above by windows.

3

1 Exterior view entrance
2 First floor hallway

3 Hallway with shelf
4 Dining room
5 Staircase to the first floor

4

5

1

2

1 View from east
2 View from south

3 Site plan
4 Cross section
5 Ground floor plan
6 First floor plan

3

4

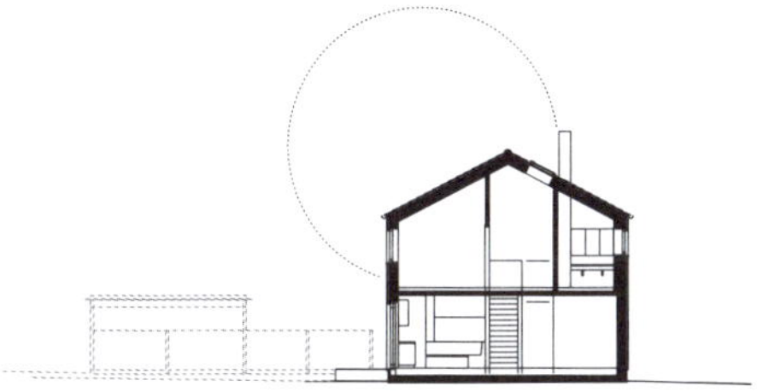

5

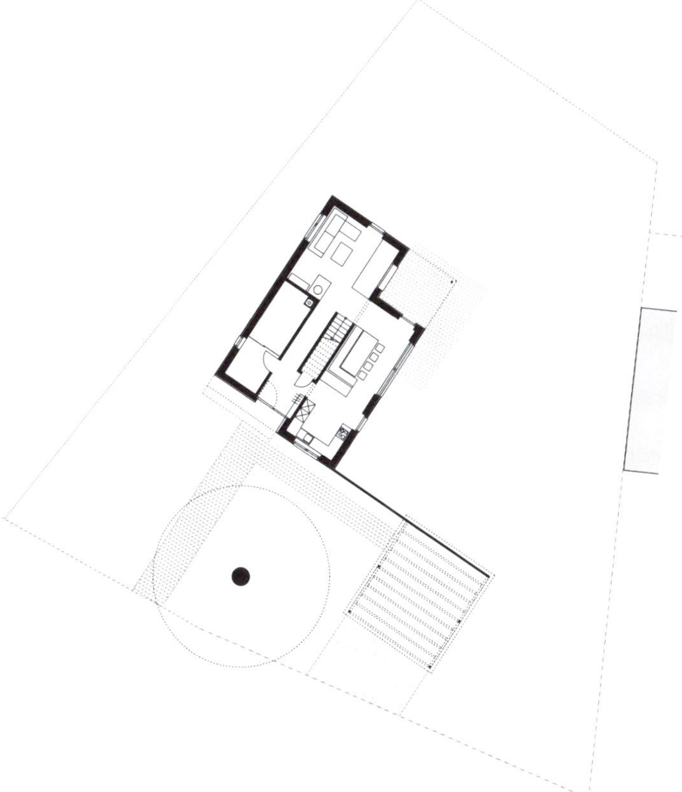

6

HOUSE AT THE TOWN WALL

1

Architects: Claus Arnold Architekt
Year of completion: 2017
Location: Würzburg, Bavaria
Gross floor area: 170 m²
Number of bedrooms: 2
Main materials / structure: solid wood / prefabrication
Ecological features: sustainable resources, space-saving and compact design

2

The project aimed for the integration of a new building block into a narrow, deep settlement structure typical of the region. This structure is taken up by the setting of the house and its traditional formal language and reinterpreted. The simple construction creates a fallow backyard situation. New defined spaces of different characters are created and engage into an exciting dialog with the historical city fortifications.

The use of simple materials, plaster, wood, glass and brick, conforms to the logic of the direct surroundings. The mineral appearance of the façade is structured by functionally set openings and reflects the clearly structured floor plan to the outside. This intelligently incorporates the peculiarities of the surroundings and reacts to the cycle of the times of day. The generous transparent wooden façade of the upper floor is oriented towards the most attractive part of the property, the garden to the west.

The authentic character of the used materials is continued in the interior and simply staged by a pleasant play of light. This small, manageable project plays soft tones and could be used as a role model for the post-densification of our cities It is an example for a harmonious coexistence of old and new.

3

4

1 Exterior view with the garden
2 Exterior view with the town wall

3 Living and dining room
4 Exterior view with town wall at dawn
5 Entrance area
6 Stairwell
7 Kitchen

5, 6

7

1

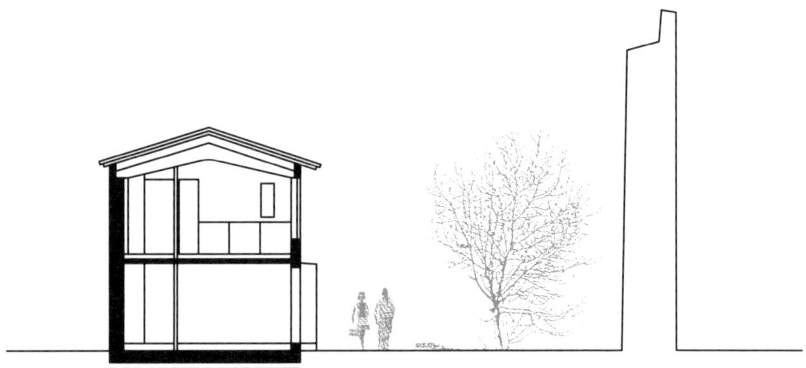

2

3

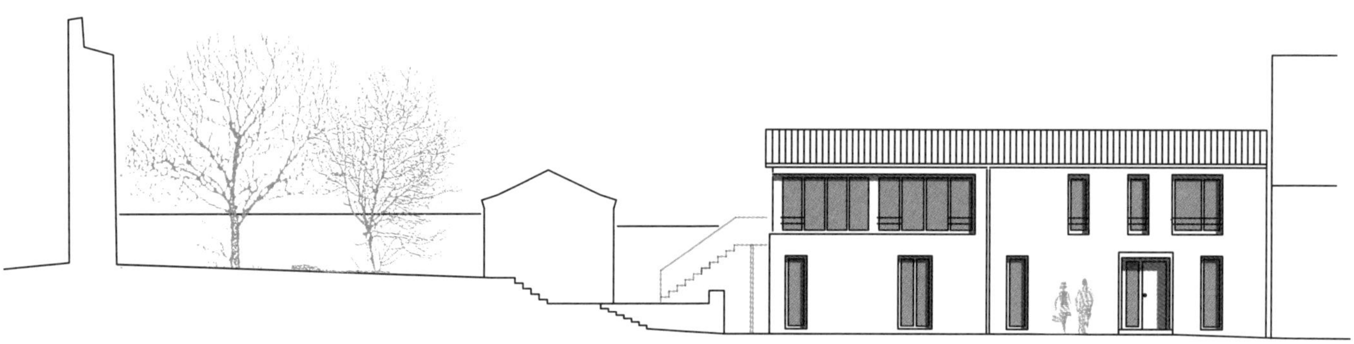

1 Section
2 Southwest elevation
3 Northwest elevation

4 First floor plan
5 Ground floor plan

4

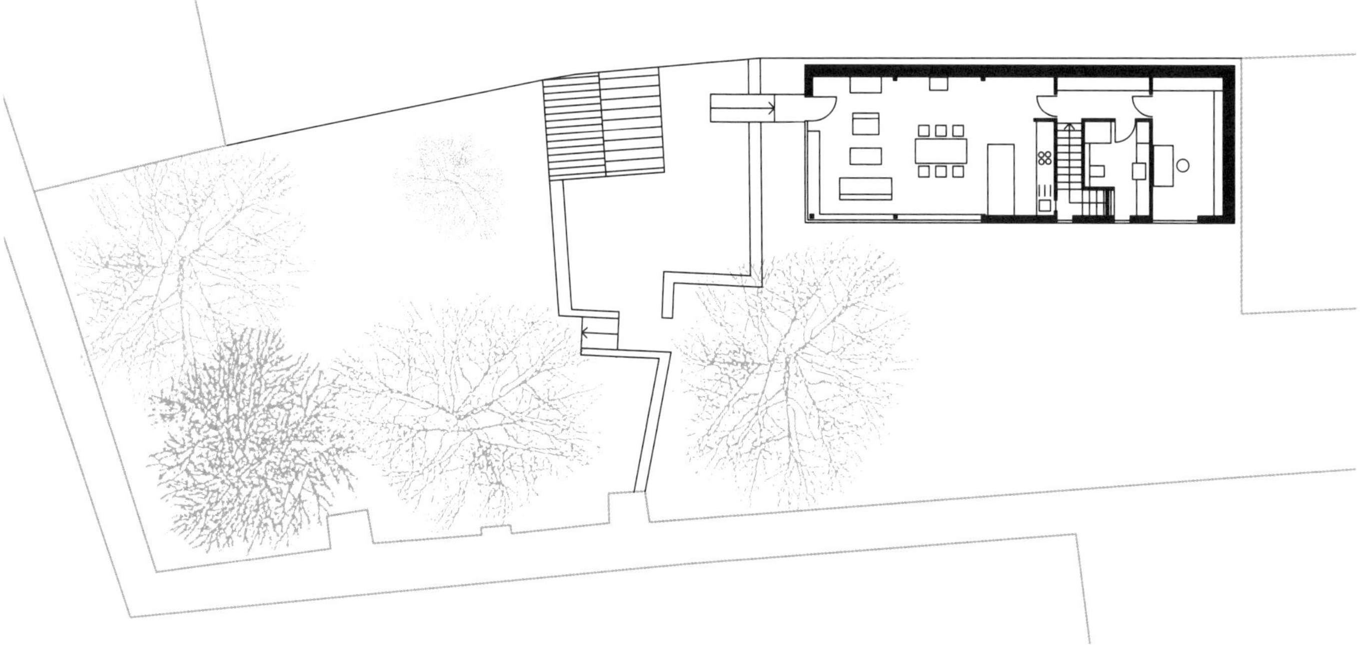

5

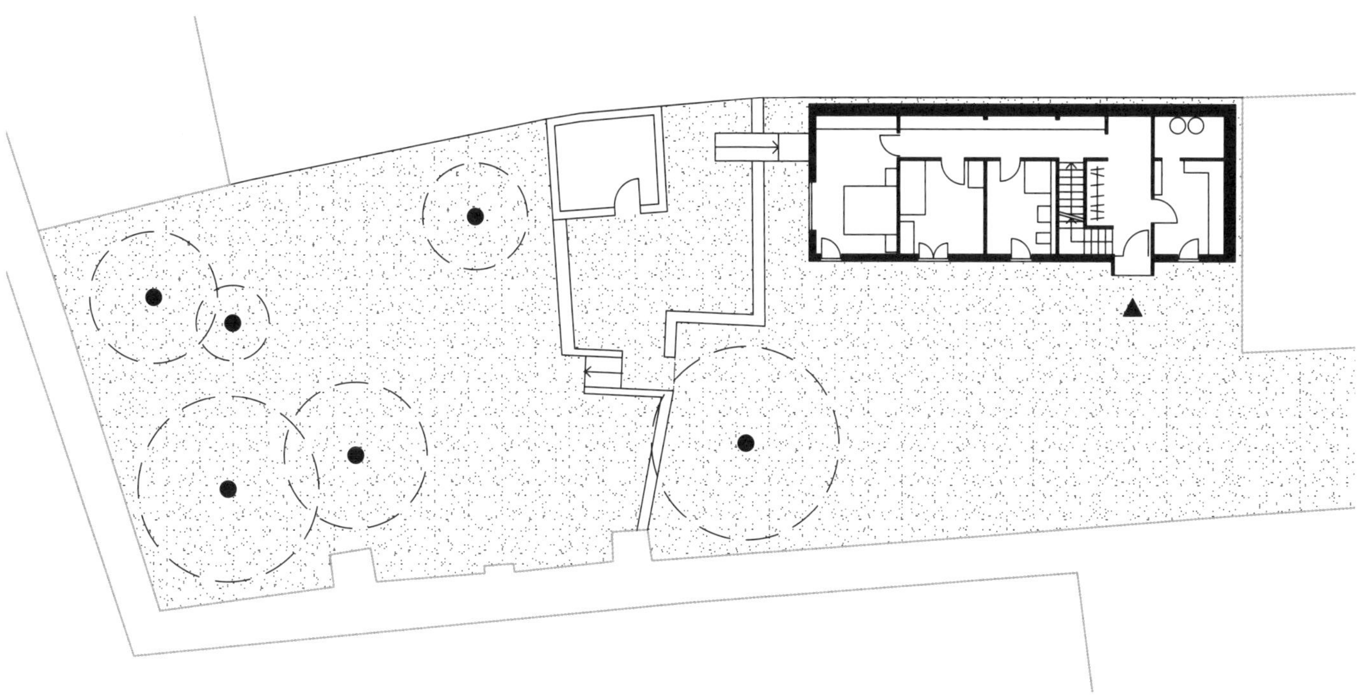

ET35

1

2

Architects: Gassner & Zarecky Architekten und Ingenieure Partnerschaft, Andreas Kellner
Year of completion: 2015
Location: Moosach, Bavaria
Gross floor area: 233 m^2
Number of bedrooms: 3
Main materials / structure: waterproof concrete / solid wood construction
Ecological features: wood construction with water-water heat pump as heating system

The architects were commissioned by a young couple with two children to build on a corner plot on the land with a sloping cut. It is integrated into the village on three sides and bordered to the south by a stream. Behind, the location on the outskirts of the village opens up a view of the landscape. The development plan correspondingly included strict specifications.

The concept of a solid, steady core that opens outwards and relates to its surroundings was implemented as a free-standing plinth building on the meadow. Its ground plan in the form of a parallelogram follows the property. This alignment creates a harmonious integration into the topography surrounding the building. An independent garage was integrated into the building volume in order to achieve a uniform overall character. A pergola connects the main building with a garden house.

Large openings on the ground floor create connections between entrance and exit as well as inside and outside. Kitchen and dining area optically extend to the west into the garden. Analogously, large flush seating windows on the upper floor invite to relax and enjoy the view. The wooden façade conceals the prescribed roof overhang and the irregular window openings behind the homogeneous, permeable shell.

The basement was constructed in exposed concrete as a solid construction in the area where there is groundwater. The house was built in solid wood, whereby the shell remains visible inside. The pre-grayed board construction in rough sawed larch sets a counterpoint to the machine plastered façades of the surrounding buildings and associates the appearance of simple rural development. The dark tiled roof forms a homogeneous unit with the grayish cladding. The generous glazing underneath is diagonal and aligned to the points of the compass and ensures balanced climate and light conditions.

3

1 Exterior view with pergola and terrace
2 Exterior view of the entrance area

3 Pergola details
4 General view of the pergola and terrace

4

1

2

3

4

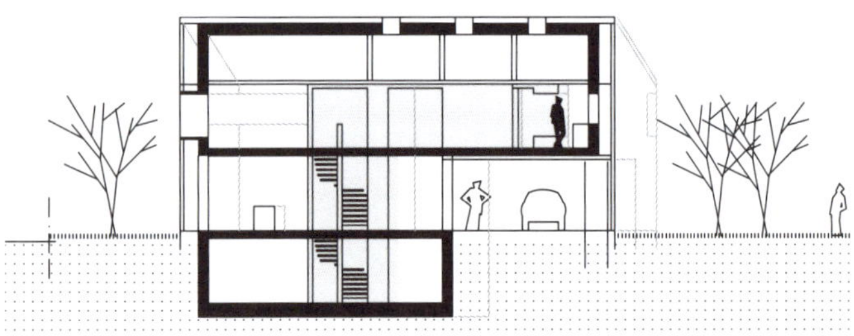

5

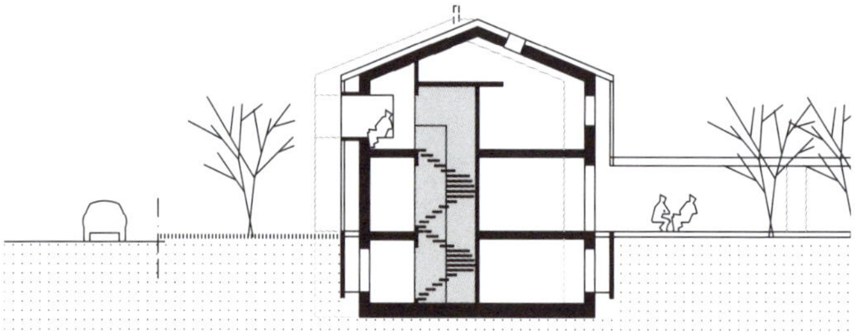

6

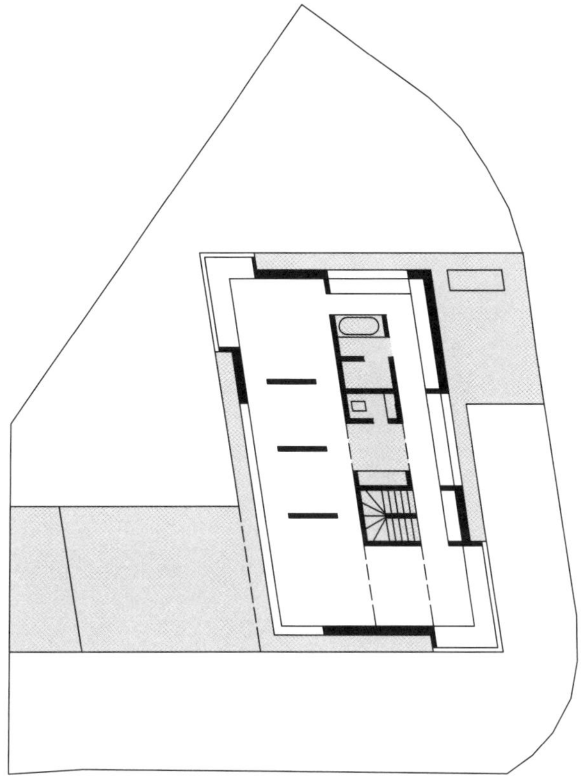

7

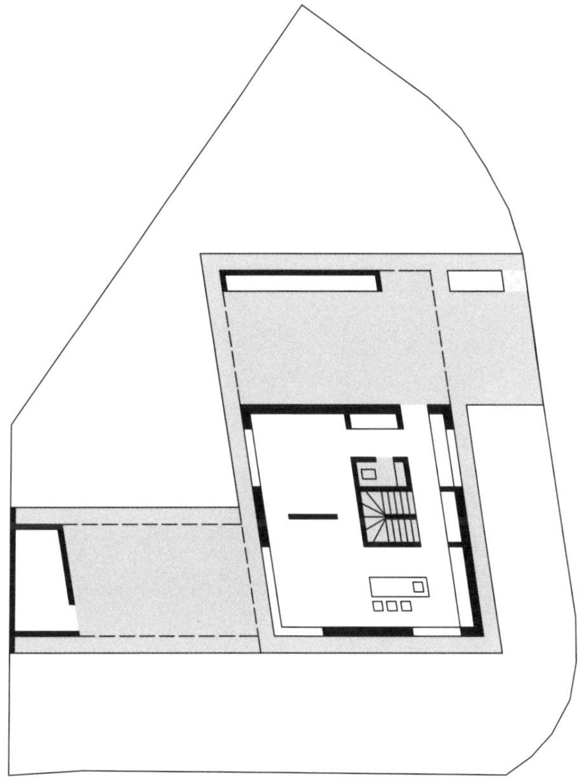

1 Bedroom
2 Interior view of the corner glazing
3 Bathroom
4 Longitudinal section
5 Cross section

6 First floor plan
7 Ground floor plan

HOUSE AT THE PETZINSEE

1

2

3

Architects: wolff:architekten gesellschaft von architekten
Year of completion: 2019
Location: Geltow, Brandenburg
Gross floor area: 216 m^2
Number of bedrooms: 2
Main materials / structure: plastered solid construction
Ecological features: secondary solar thermal for heating and hot water preparation

On a small plot of land near the Petzin lake it was necessary to accommodate an extensive space program for a young family. Despite the functional constraints, the building opens up attractively to the lake and offers surprising spatial possibilities.

The strict cubic formulation of the two-story, basement building resulting from the dependencies is broken on the north-eastern side by the indented entrance area. This sculptural work through gives the building its specific character. This is supported by the structuring of the façades with recessed, darkly accentuated plaster surfaces.

Inside, a skylight, in addition to the extensive glazing, allows plenty of daylight to enter. The open transitions in the living area and the choice of light colours also convey a feeling of spaciousness. A free-standing cooking island in the common living and dining area serves as the center of living together.

4

5

1 Exterior view from southeast
2 Exterior view from east
3 Entrance area

4 Living area and kitchen
5 First floor hallway and staircase area
6 Dining and living area

6

1

2

3

1 Kitchen with cooking island
2 First floor bathroom with open shower
3 First floor bathroom with bathtub

4 First floor plan
5 Ground floor plan
6 Cross section

4

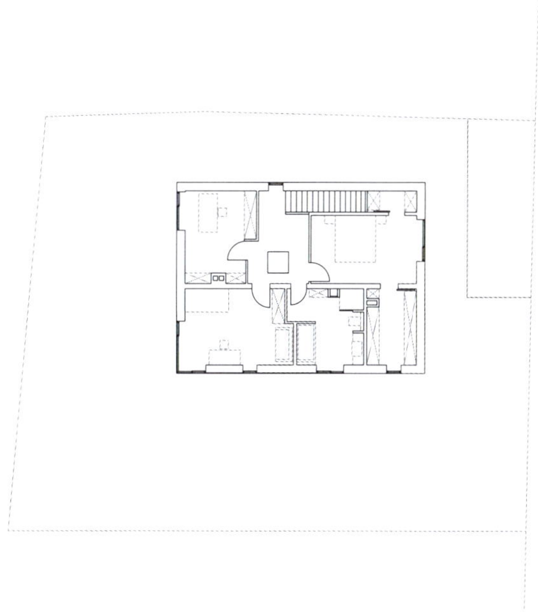

5

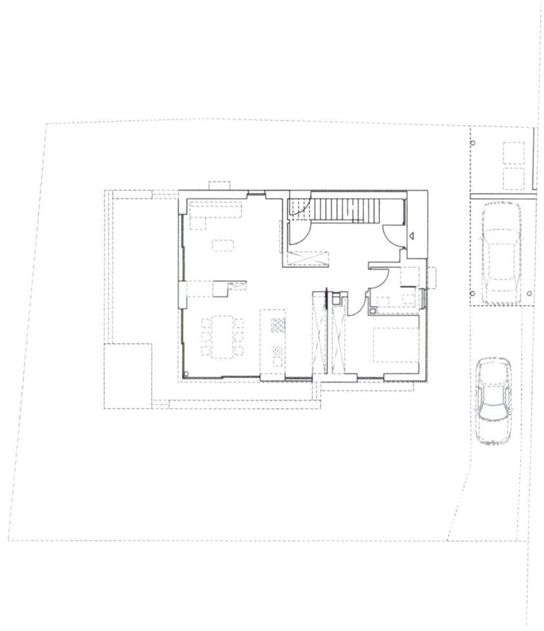

6

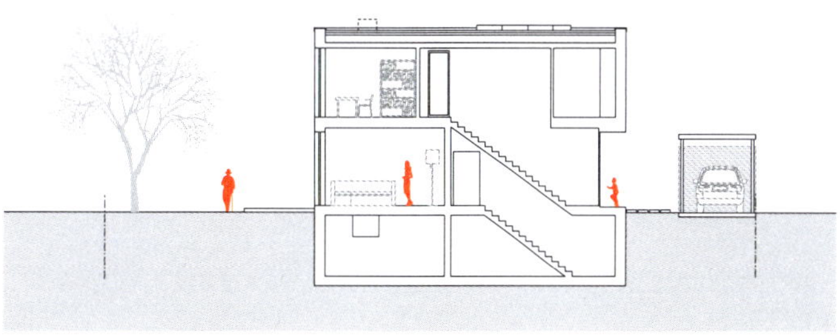

HOUSE M IN DÜSSELDORF

1

2, 3

Architecture: Geitner Architekten
Year of completion: 2015
Location: Düsseldorf, North Rhine-Westphalia
Gross floor area: 300 m²
Number of bedrooms: 4
Main materials / structure: wood formwork larch / timber frame construction
Ecological features: ecological construction method, use of local woods, air heat pump, ventilation system with heat recovery

The unusual cubature of the house is derived from the local dormers and gables. The basic form is the one-and-a-half-story single-family house with a saddle roof as specified in the development plan. On the street side, a lateral wall dormer was attached to the saddle roof and undercut in favor of an entrance canopy. On the garden side, a large dormer was formed on the side, which was connected with the dwarf gable to the roof surface in the ridge. This connection forms precise edges and develops a sculptural structure with a high degree of plasticity with the uniform materiality.

Only native woods were used for the exterior and interior. A ventilated outer skin of larch wood formwork surrounds the entire building, the color and reflection of which varies according to the incidence of light. Light, natural materials were chosen for the interior, analogous to the outer skin.

The house was built with prefabricated wood elements taking into account high energetic and ecological demands and fulfils low-energy standards.

4

5

6

1 Exterior view from the garden
2 Street side with wall dormer
3 Garden side with dormer

4 Living and dining area
5 Living area
6 Folded wooden staircase

1

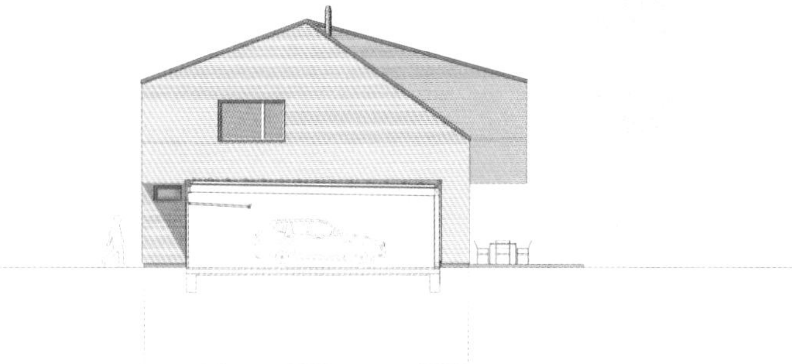

2

3

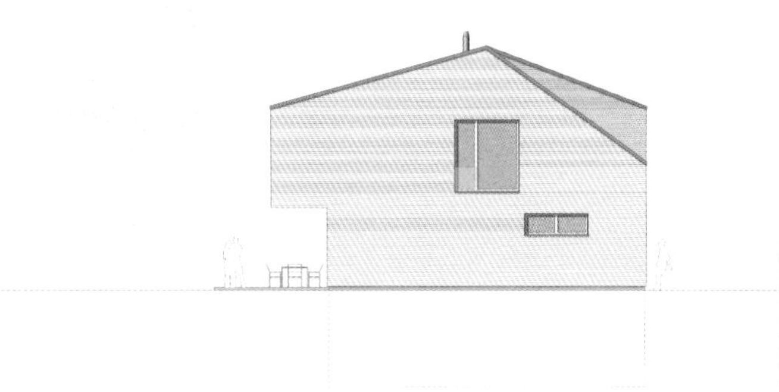

4

5

1 West elevation
2 South elevation
3 East elevation
4 North elevation
5 Cross section

6 First floor plan
7 Ground floor plan
8 Basement floor plan

6

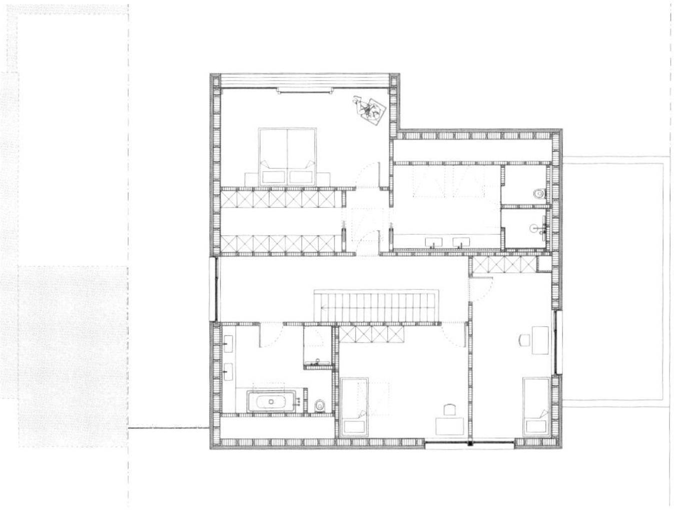

7

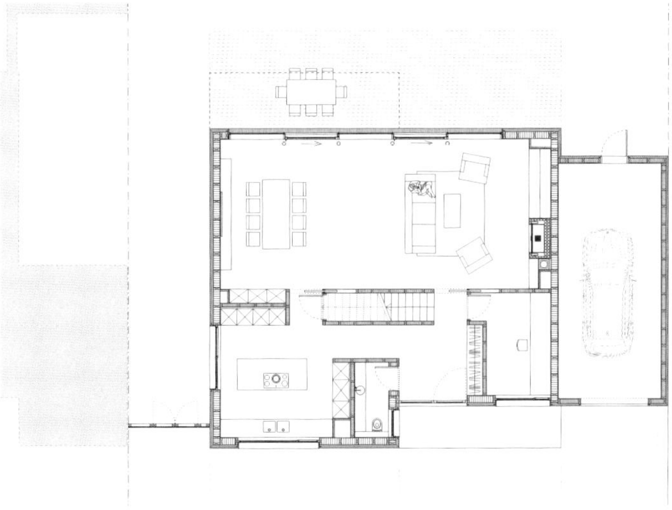

8

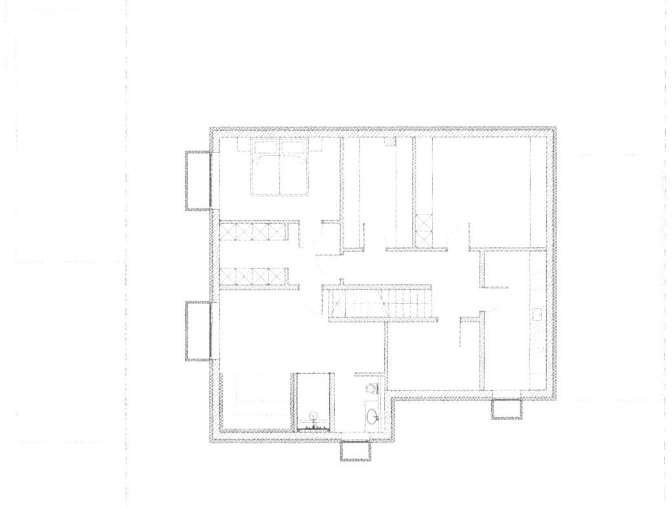

HOUSE F IN INGOLSTADT

1

2

Architects: Seidl-Architekten
Year of completion: 2017
Location: Ingolstadt, Bavaria
Gross floor area: 400 m^2
NUmber of bedrooms: 4
Main materials / structure: brick masonry, reinforced concrete, wood / solid construction
Ecological features: highly heat insulating outside walls, solar thermal system

Residence F is one of several detached houses that Christina and Roland Seidl built in the southwest of Ingolstadt. The challenge was to combine the special individual wishes of the clients with the local conditions in a sophisticated urban and architectural way.

House F offers spacious rooms for a family of five in the grown residential area of Haunwöhr. The replacement building blends discreetly into the surroundings, but sets individual accents with clear lines and careful detail planning. The design takes into account the origins of the building owners by picking up forms of the JuraHouse architectural style in the Altmühl valley from the flat inclined saddle roof covered with concrete roof tiles. The three residential floors are brightly designed and have an open structure. They are connected by a filigree, simple steel staircase.

The solid wood flooring has a warm appearance. On the upper floor there are bedrooms as well as an open corridor for playing with a striking corner window. The living and dining area on the ground floor, blending into one another, open up to a spacious terrace and garden with a room-high glass front. A characteristic design element is the corner pergola. To the street space the residential house presents itself rather closed with a wood entrance element, which combines house entrance door and garage door flush. The building services were implemented against the background of state-of-the-art technology, including solar thermal energy.

3

1 View from west with outdoor sitting area
2 View from south with the pergola

3 Internal access
4 View from east with entrance
5 View from southwest

4

5

1

2

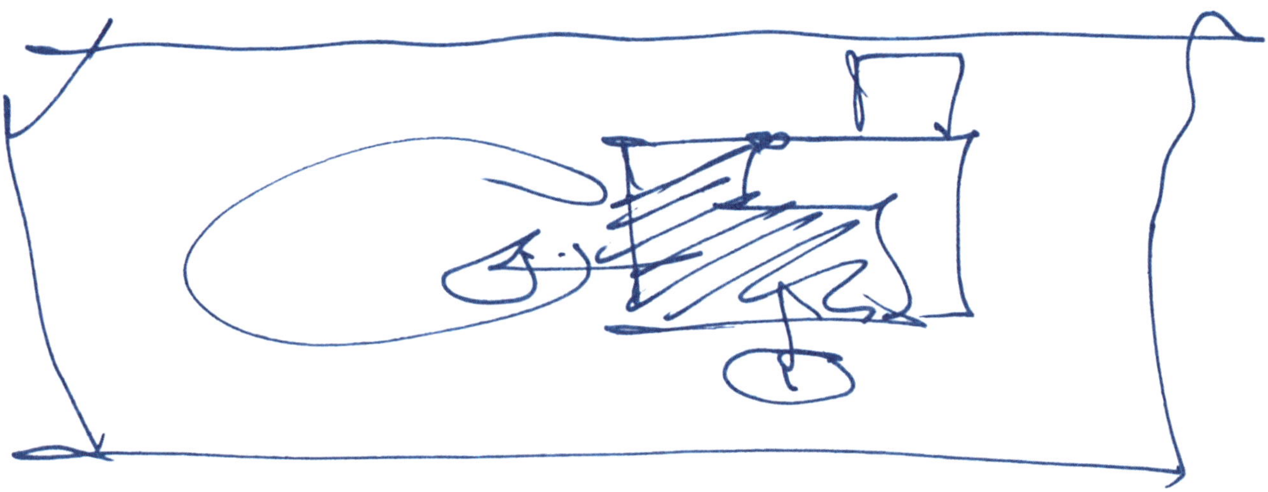

1 Sketch of the southwest view
2 Hand drawing of the design concept

3 South elevation
4 First floor plan
5 Sections
6 Ground floor plan

3

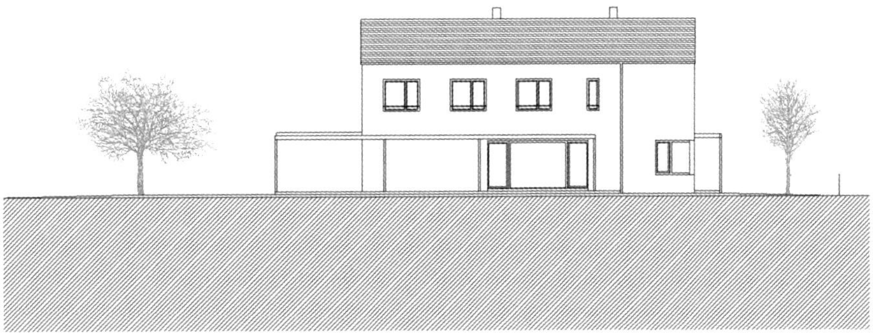

4

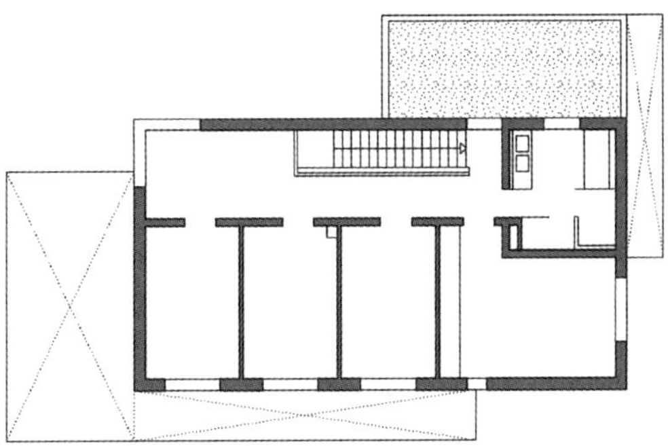

5

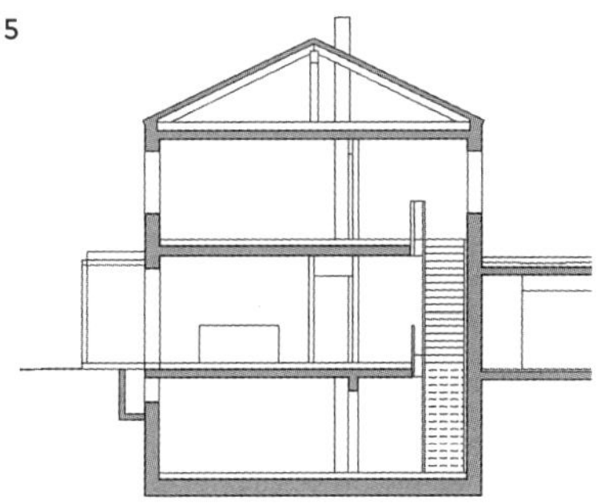

6

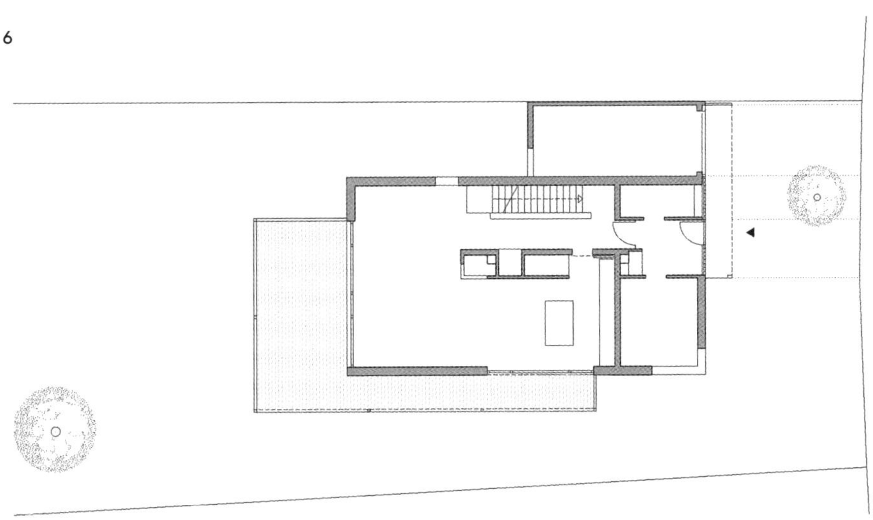

MANSION AS TWINS

1, 2

3

Architects: bauer architektur
Year of completion: 2016
Location: Weimar, Thuringia
Gross floor area: 298 m²
Main materials / structure: reinforced concrete, masonry
Ecological features: solar thermal, ventilation system with heat recovery, green roof

The family house on the eastern outskirts of Weimar is located next to the listed "Schießhaus". As the building is visible from four sides due to its location at the corner of a residential area, it also shows four main façades. No side is inferior to the other. This façade structure is created from the adeptly mirrored and rotated ground plan. The result are two apartments arranged side by side, each on two levels.

The interior of each apartment is generously illuminated from all directions. The ground floor has terraces directly connected to the garden. In the upper floor loggias offer view and farsightedness. This creates an extremely high quality living value – a villa with a panoramic view.

4

5

1 Exterior view from northwest
2 Exterior view from east
3 Exterior view from southwest

4 View onto the garden
5 View into the loggia
6 Exterior view from southeast

6

1

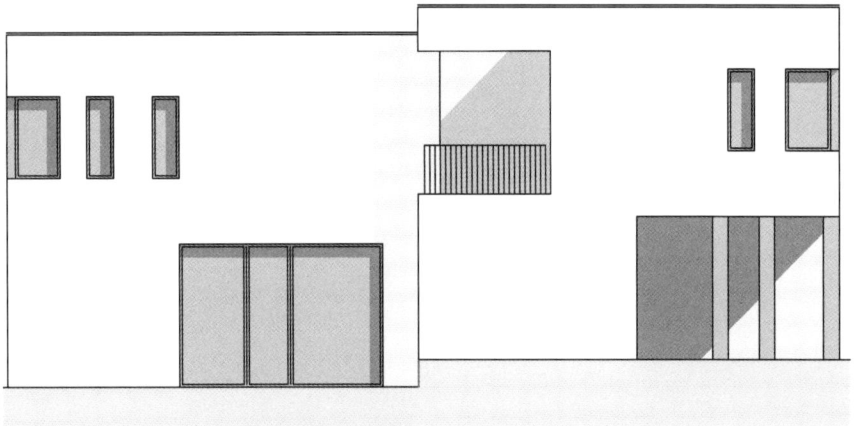

2

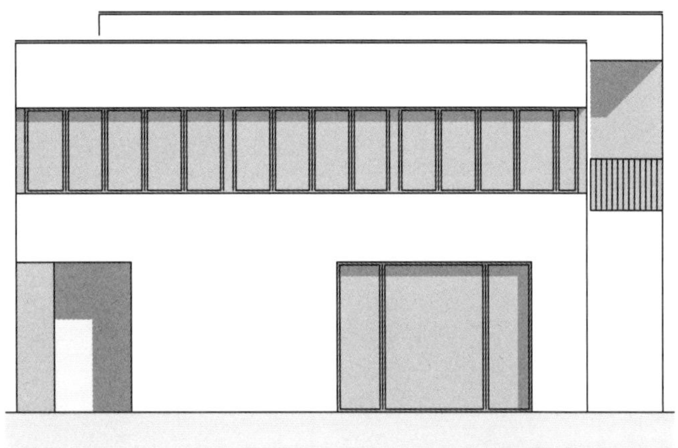

3

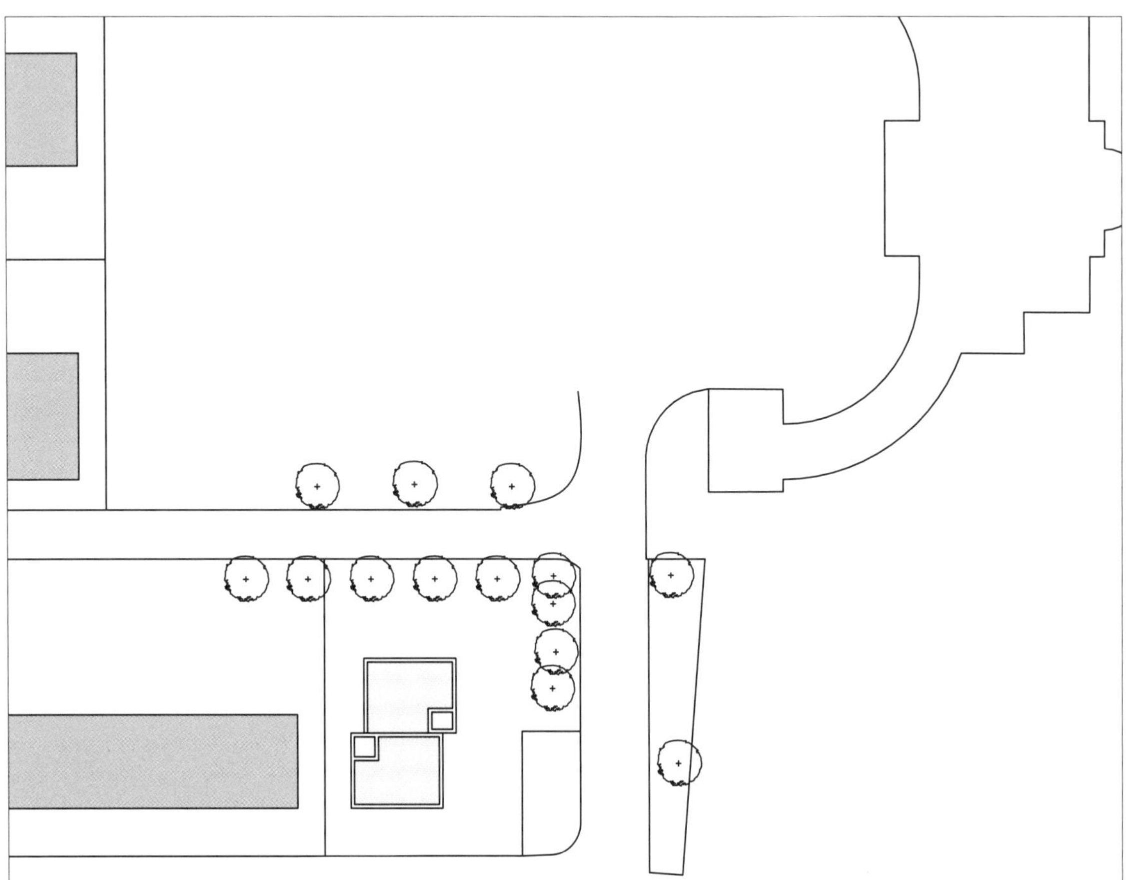

4

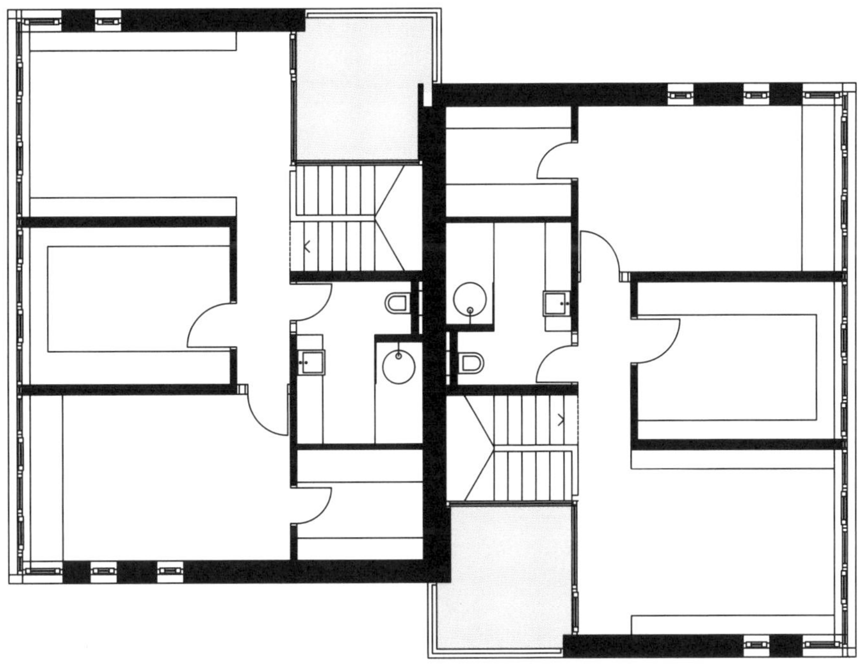

5

1 West/east elevation
2 North/south elevation
3 Site plan

4 First floor plan
5 Ground floor plan

HOUSE IN NETTERSHEIM

1

2, 3

Architects: Amonat Architektur
Year of completion: 2016
Location: Nettersheim, North Rhine-Westphalia
Gross floor area: 295 m^2
Number of bedrooms: 4
Main materials / structure: timber frame construction
Ecological features: solar system, ventilation system

In the Eifel in Nettersheim-Marmagen a house for a family of four was built in a timber frame construction. This enables a pleasant living climate. The visible ceiling rafters and the wood-aluminum windows in the same wood tone create a warm ambience in the interior. The exterior façade is also accentuated by a warm wood tone.

Visitors and residents are welcomed by a spacious entrance area that extends over two floors. From the entrance area one can look directly over the living area into the garden with far view. The living-kitchen-dining area is very spacious and open. As the main communication area in the family, the kitchen invites to linger. On the ground floor level there is a bedroom with a shower bath. On the upper floor there are the children's rooms with a gallery, the parents' bedroom with dressing room and the large family bathroom.

4

5

6

7

1 Street view
2 Garden view
3 Entrance area

4 Living area
5 Dining area
6 Cooking area
7 First floor gallery

1

2

3

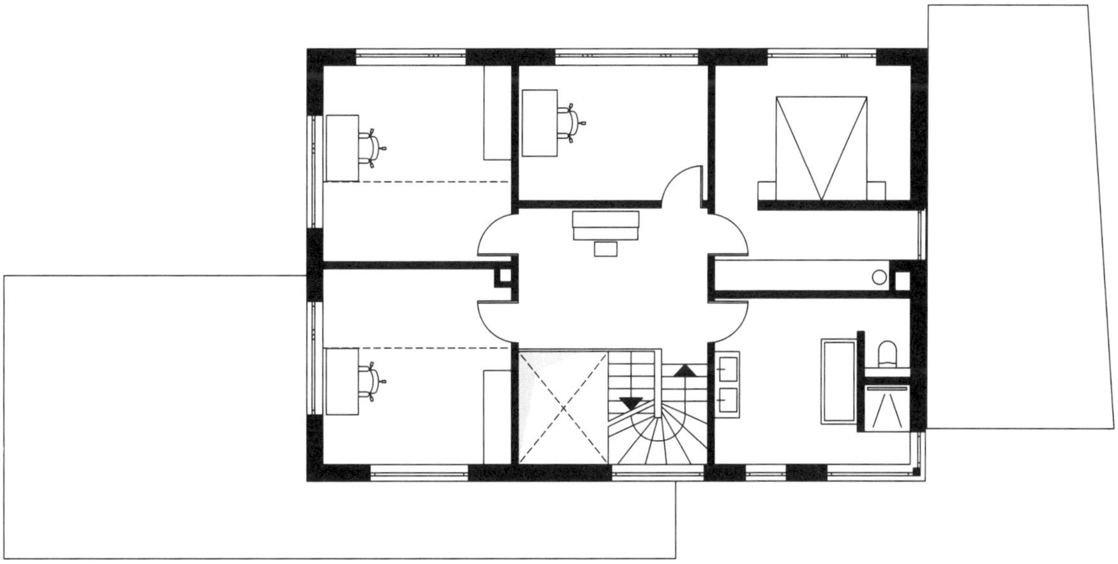

4

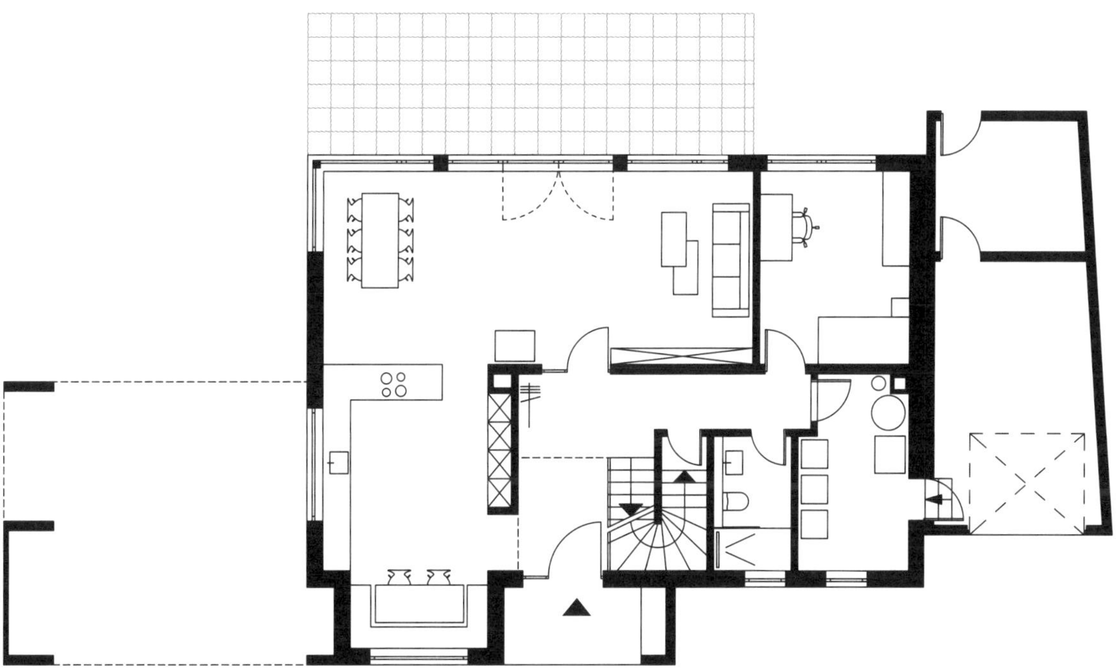

1 Ground floor bathroom
2 First floor bedroom

3 First floor plan
4 Ground floor plan

SOUTHERN STAR

1

2

Architects: fabi architekten
Year of completion: 2017
Location: Pentling, Bavaria
Gross floor area: 296m^2
Number of bedrooms: 3
Main materials / structure: tiles, reinforced concrete, wooden façade and titanium zinc elements for exterior use / solid construction
Ecological features: solar thermal system, controlled ventilation of living space with heat recovery

The residential building in the district of Regensburg is surrounded by meadows on three sides, the view to the west opens into the Danube valley. Due to its open location, the building is heavily exposed to the weather, which was taken into account in the building design. It is a modern, rural building with a red saddle roof and a natural coloring. The building protrudes above the basement and floats above the northern part of the property. The main features are the large, frameless all-glass pane in the north, which lies in a larch lamella form-work, and the two-story cut of the loggia in the south.

The basic mood of rural modernism continues in the interior. Rustic oak wood for built-in furniture and floors contrasts with black furniture fronts and concrete-colored tiles. A long bench connects the dining area with the living room and elegantly merges into the living rom furniture. On the ground floor, next to the barrier-free access with large wardrobe, there are the main living rooms. The attic floor with the individual rooms is accessed via a staircase.
In the centre of the building, the fully glazed, loggia-shaped building recess connects the floors vertically. Here, a room-high window directs daylight deep into the basement. On the upper floor, the cut is designed with a wooden terrace deck as an outdoor area for bath and sauna use.

3

4

1 Exterior view from northwest
2 Exterior view from northeast

3 Bathroom
4 Terrace
5 Kitchen
6 Dining area

5

6

1

2

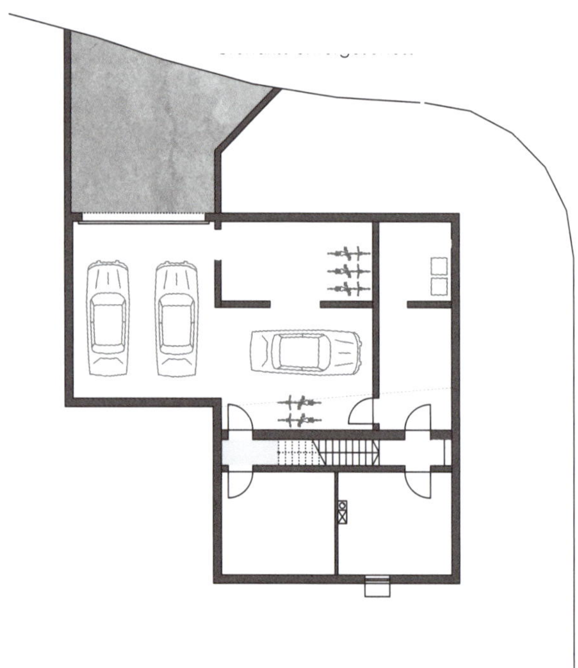

1 West elevation
2 Basement floor plan

3 First floor plan
4 Ground floor plan

3

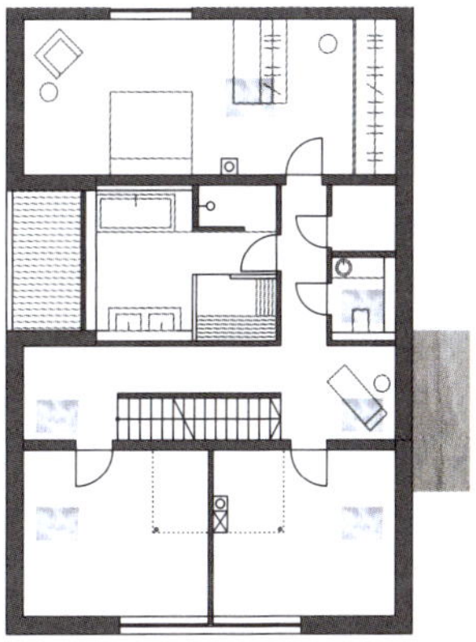

4

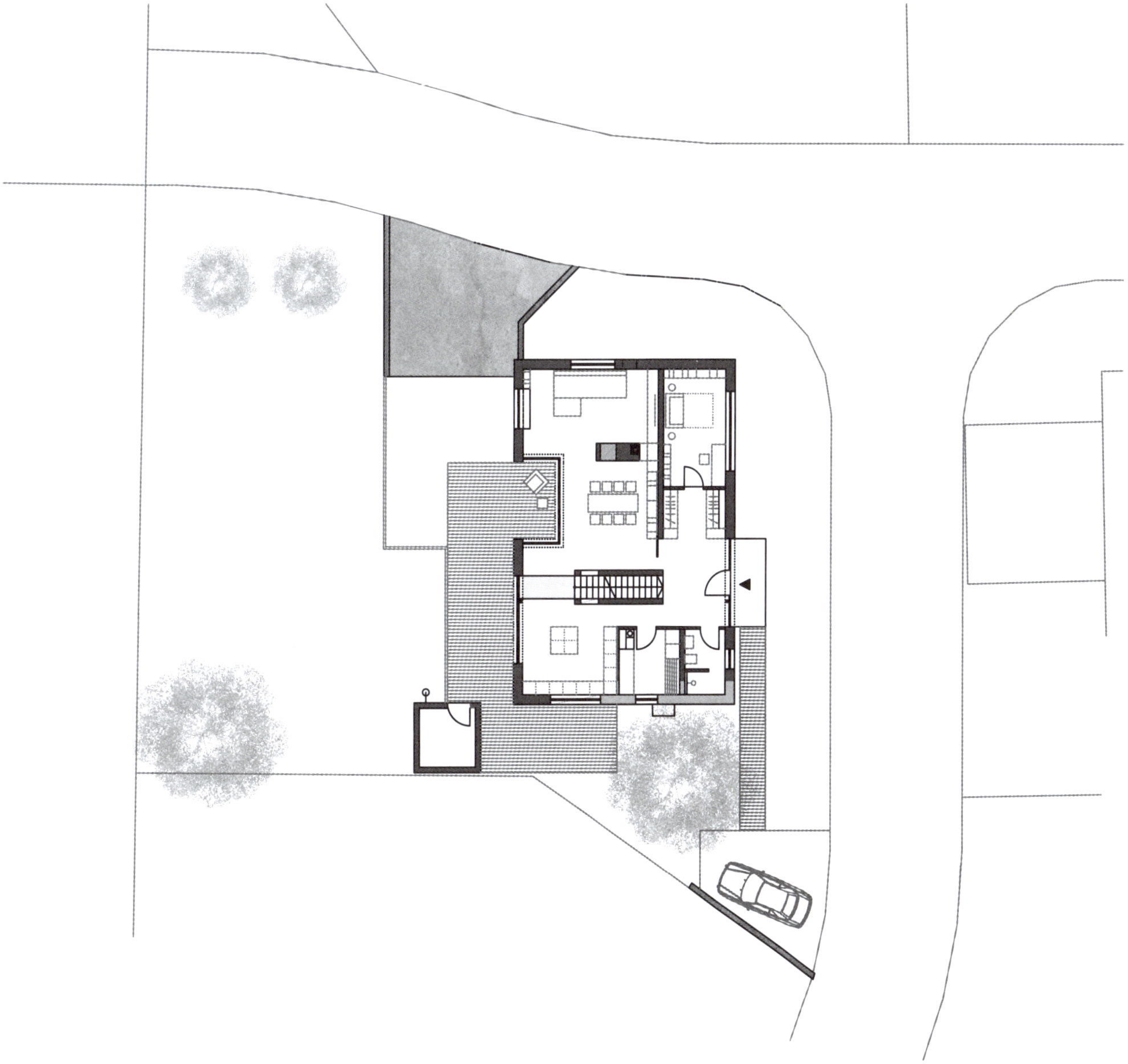

L18

1, 2

3

Architects: Grimm Architekten
Year of completion: 2016
Location: Ermreuth, Bavaria
Gross floor area: 237 m²
Number of bedrooms: 2
Main materials / structure: wood, natural stone / prefabricated timber frame construction
Ecological features: renewable resources, air-water heat pump, water-guided heating chimney, ventilation system

4

5

The building integrates modern and self-confidently into the existing structures of the location.
The entrance leads into the kitchen, which forms a unit with a cooking island and the dining room. The large fireplace between the dining room and the living room creates a retreat. The connection between the rooms is maintained. The fire is visible from both sides. The gallery above the dining room connects the two floors and allows the entire dimension of the house to be experienced in the interior. All the rooms are made of only a few materials. Oak wood floors with warm colors on the walls create a cozy atmosphere. A regional, gray jurassic stone was used in the bathrooms. The oak furniture and panelling provide a warm contrast.

The compact form, the good thermal insulation and the triple-glazed windows ensure a minimum of energy consumption. A water-supported heating chimney dissipates most of the heat into the central storage tank, which is needed for service water and underfloor heating. A ventilation system ensures heat recovery. The remaining heat required is generated by an air-water heat pump.

1 Entrance
2 Side view
3 Street view

4 Void and reading corner
5 Dining room with gallery
6 Dining room with fireplace and gallery
7 Staircase to the first floor

6, 7

1

2

3

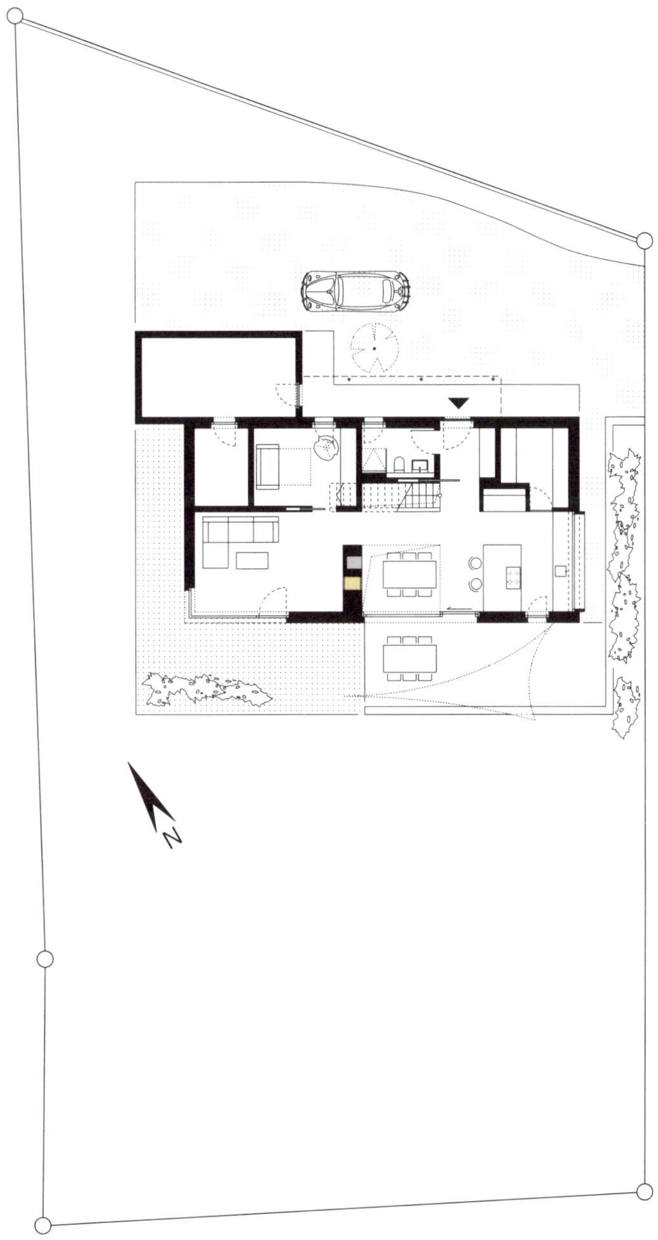

4

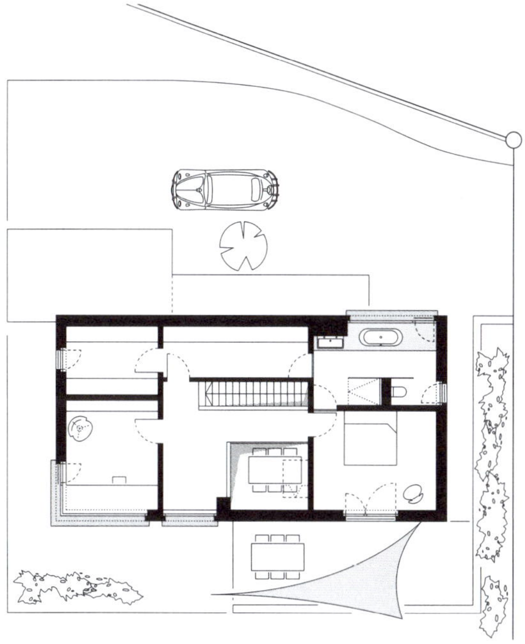

5

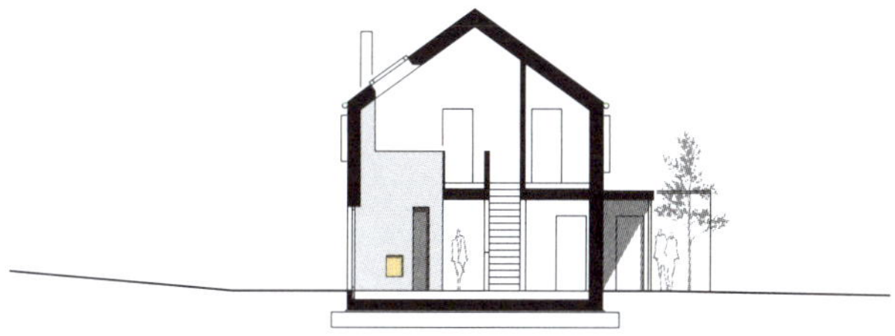

1 Bathroom in natural stone
2 Bathtub with distant view

3 Ground floor plan
4 First floor plan
5 Sections

AM BREITLE

1

Architects: andreas petermann architekt
Year of completion: 2007
Location: Augsburg, Bavaria
Gross floor area: 128 m²
Number of bedrooms: 1
Main materials / structure: timber frame construction
Ecological features: building components can be recycled, panel wall heating

2

On the outskirts of Augsburg, right on the city border with Neusäß, a housing estate was built in the 1950s. It was planned according to the respective zeitgeist: functional residential buildings, simple and clear, with gable roofs and generous properties of around 800 square meters. In 2007, the existing house was to be extended by a supplementary building. The former construction had to be kept; for the new building, another formal language had to be found. The simplicity and clarity of the former building is visible in the new construction as well, but was interpreted in a new and contemporary way, resulting in a simple, cubic building with two stories and a flat roof on a surface area of eight by eight meters.

The façades of the east, south, and west sides are composed of identical window and wall elements. The uniform design of the elements appears to be clear and generous. Moving the elements between the ground floor and the upper floor creates the necessary visual tension. With an oak façade, the new building contrasts pleasantly to the plaster façade of the old building. The material is allowed to change due to environmental influences and develops a silver-gray patina over time. Inside, there is no room division in a usual sense. The entire ground floor is an open space uniting cooking, dining, and living areas. It is structured by built-in furniture with a glossy white surface, thus reflecting the surrounding materials and lighting conditions. On the upper floor there is a studio or a study as well as the sleeping area with a bathroom.

3

4

1 Exterior view with wood panels from south
2 Garden view from southeast

3 Dining area and terrace
4 Bedroom with bathroom
5 Living and cooking area

5

1

2

3

4

5

6

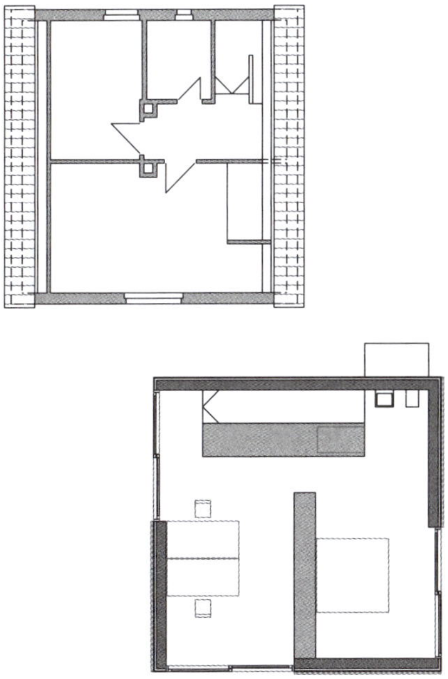

7

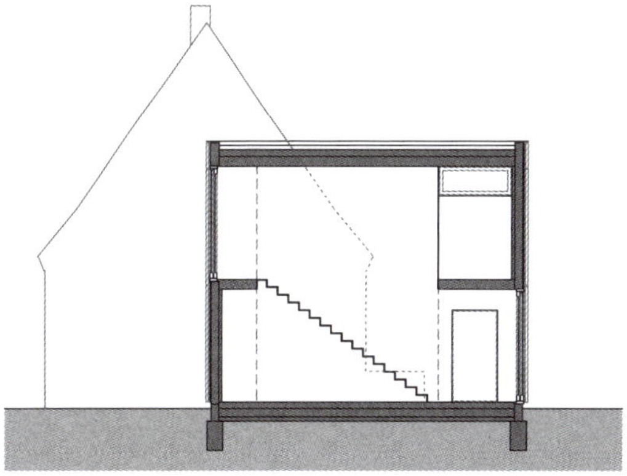

1 North elevation
2 East elevation
3 Ground floor plan

4 South elevation
5 West elevation
6 First floor plan
7 Cross section

HOUSE J

1

2, 3

Architect: Herbert O. Zielinski Architekt
Year of completion: 2002
Location: Frankfurt am Main, Hesse
Gross floor area: 230 m^2
Number of bedrooms: 3
Main materials / structure: brickwork, flat roof
Ecological features: low-energy house, condensing heating technology with underfloor heating, flat roof with extensive greening

The task was the reconstruction of a semi-detached house from the 1920s as well as the extension of the living space by a new building. Because of the condition of the existing building, a gutting of the existing building down to its basic structures was necessary. During the design phase, the decision was met to build an extension spanning over two stories, which is only connected to the old building by a narrow corridor, resulting in a spacious and open room layout. The former structure still remains visible and esthetically perceptible through the arrangement of the rooms. An open living area with high ceilings and an unusually large window front was created on the ground floor. The construction of steel and glass allows plenty of light to flow into the room, while a room-high sliding element extends the room into the garden. Vertical window slits on the front sides and squares on the longitudinal wall allow views all around. On the upper floor of the annex, there is the bedroom with adjoining bathroom.

4

5

1 Garden view at dawn
2 Street view
3 Garden side perspective

4 Living room with lodge-style floorboards
5 Connection between old and new building
6 Bathroom

6

1

2

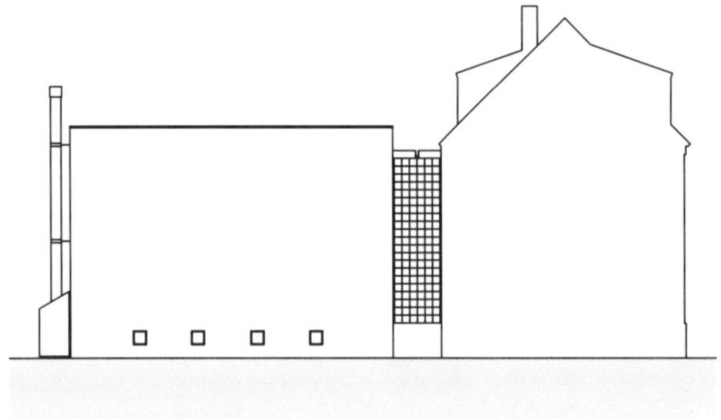

3

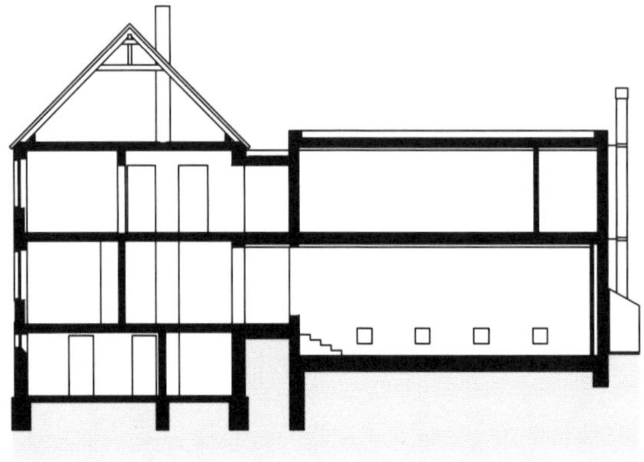

4

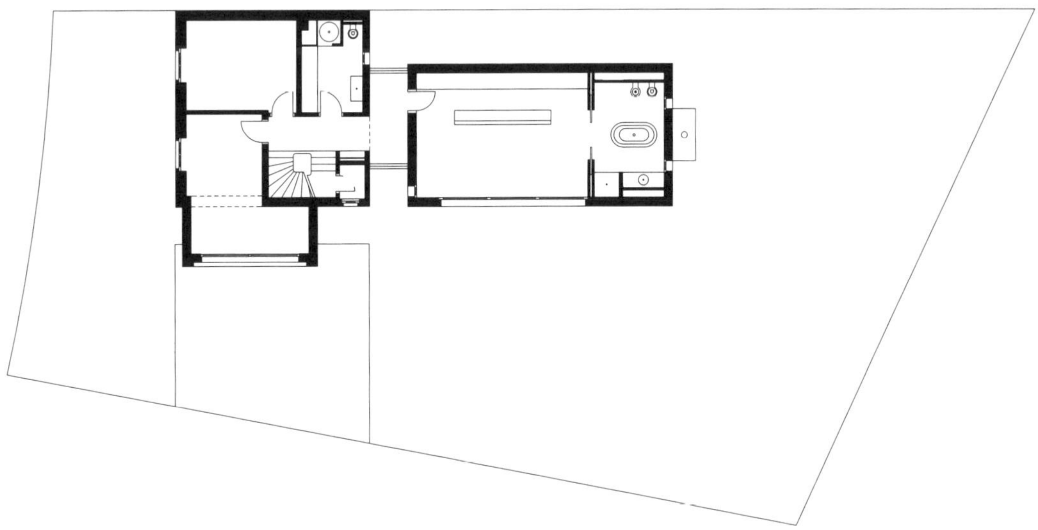

5

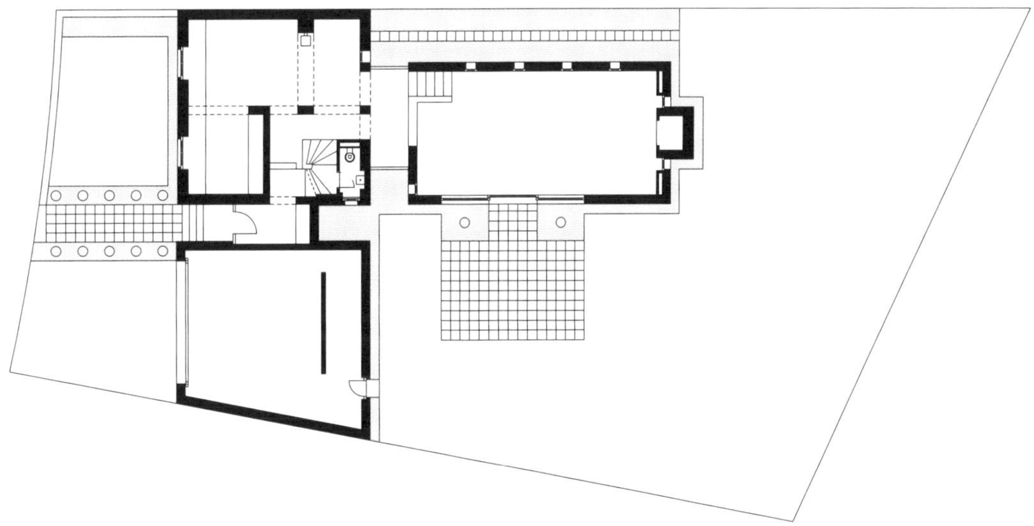

1 Southeast elevation
2 Northeast elevation
3 Section

4 First floor plan
5 Ground floor plan

BUNGALOW MÜHLENBERG

1

Architects: AHM Arnke Häntsch Mattmüller Architekten
Year of completion: 2014
Location: Arnsberg, North Rhine-Westphalia
Gross floor area: 363 m^2
Number of bedrooms: 2
Main materials / structure: water-struck bricks, exposed concrete precast elements, porcelain stoneware tiles, light oak / solid construction
Ecological features: collector surfaces for hot water preparation

2

The bungalow is characterized by its clear spatial organization and concise use of building materials. The L-shaped floor plan is divided into two areas by a central entrance. The open living space with the living, dining and kitchen area is extended to the southwest by means of a generous glass façade towards the garden. In contrast the bedroom, bathroom and study are much more introverted in the eastern part of the building. A continuous ceramic floor, covering of porcelain stoneware, connects the interiors and mediates between the interior and exterior.

On the façade, exposed brickwork alternates with room-high window elements, which are enclosed in the base and attic areas by a horizontal band of light exposed prefabricated concrete elements. For the exposed brickwork, a water-struck brick treated with a coal-fired process was chosen, which was laid in a wild combination. This way, a lively and varied surface was created which sets a high-contrast accent to the clarity of the geometry and organization of the building. The reduced choice of materials in the interior is complemented by smoothly plastered walls and floor-to-ceiling door elements made of light oak.

In addition, the system clearly distinguishes itself from its structural surroundings. A surrounding garden wall subtly separates the building from the given topographical situation and the heterogeneous environment. The slight elevation of the ground level on the property side towards the garden wall in combination with the dense planting creates an introverted and view-protected living situation.

3

4

1 Living area
2 Bathroom

3 Corridor to living area with garden
4 Entrance area
5 Panorama of bungalow with garden wall
6 Interior

5

6

1

2

1 Living area with terrace
2 View from the garden

3 Section I vertical plan
4 Ground floor plan

3

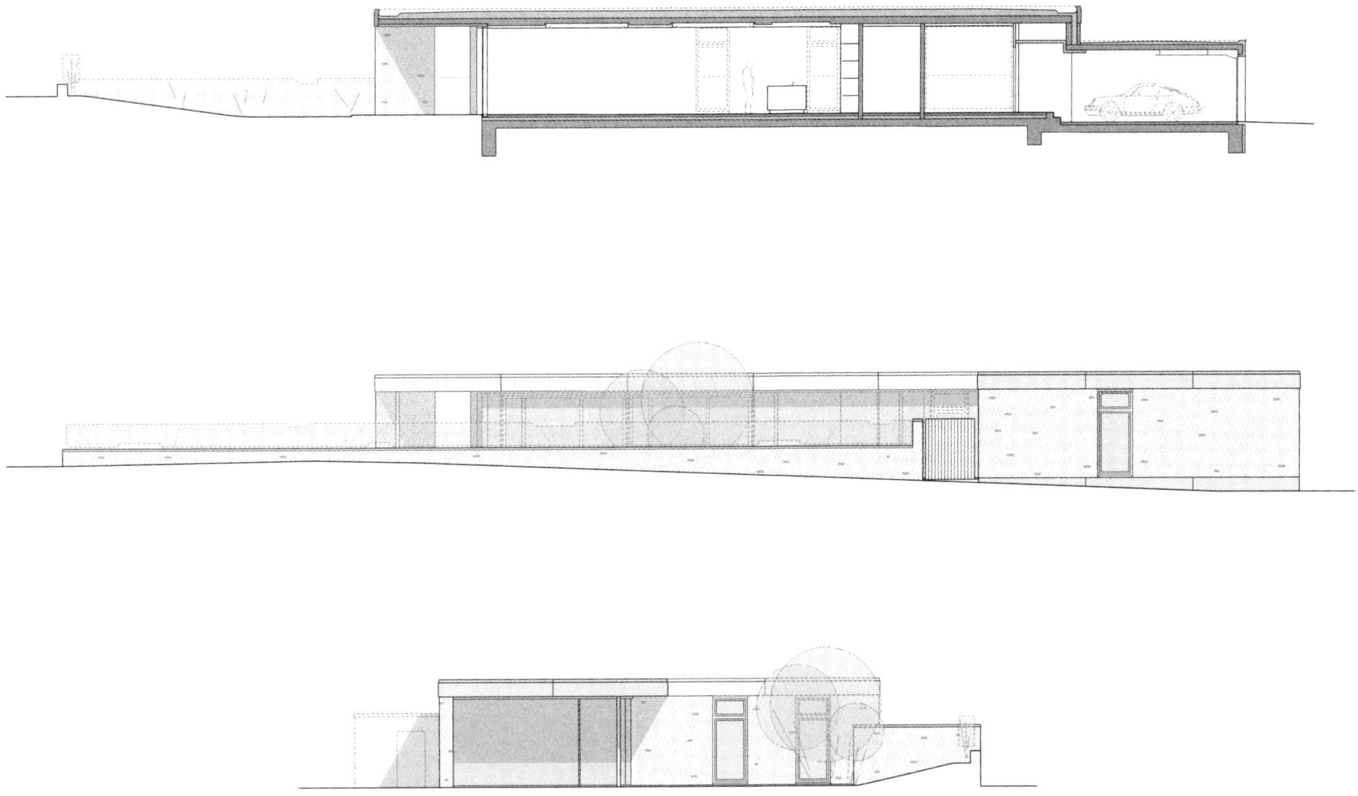

4

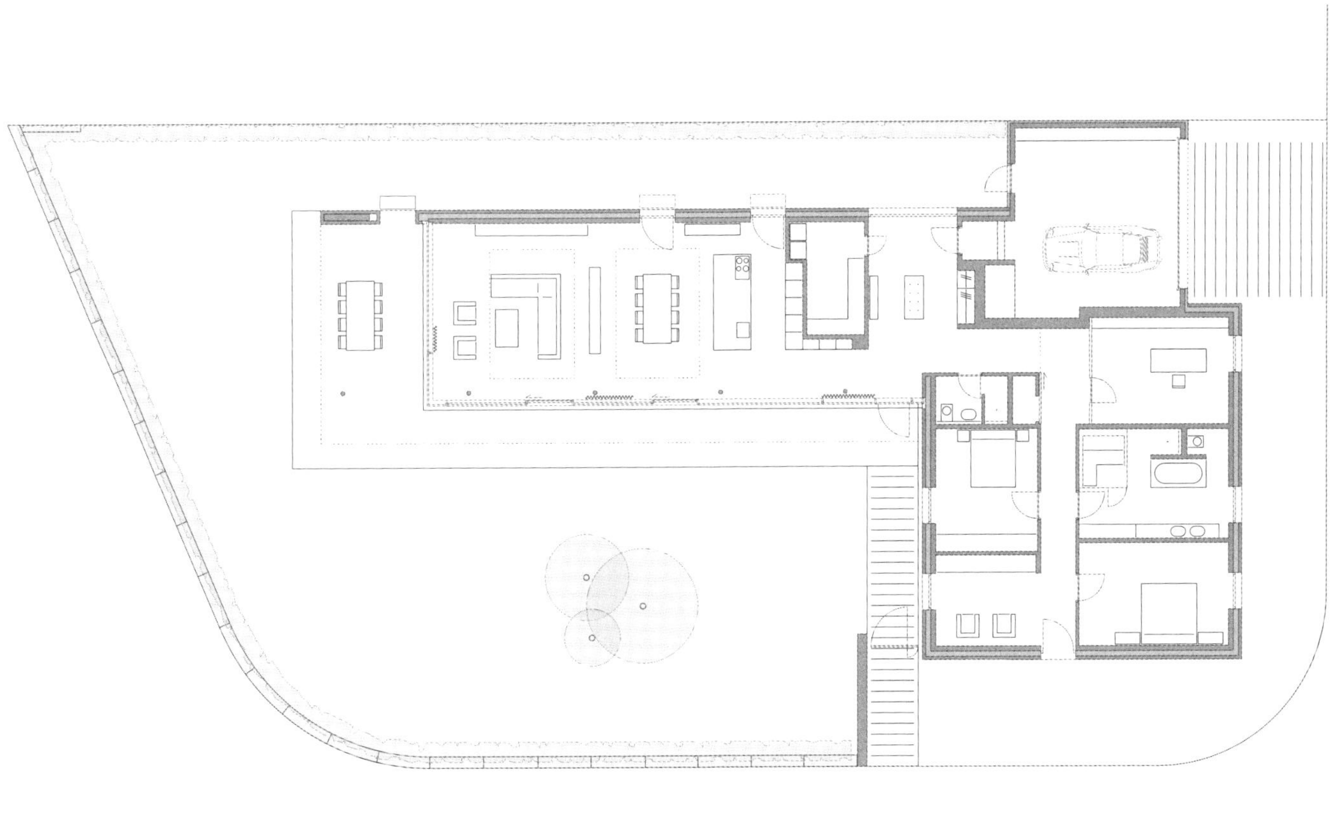

SMALL HOUSE IN A SMALL VILLAGE

1

2

3

244

Architects: Norbert Pakusch
Year of completion: 2013
Location: Prutting, Bavaria
Gross floor area: 151 m²
Number of bedrooms: 3
Main materials / structure: brick masonry, larch, fir planks, visible screed / solid construction
Ecological features: low-energy building

The building is located in the village Haidbichl-Prutting in Upper Bavaria. The construction task was to build a low-cost house for a family of four on a small plot. Only a smaller house could be built, corresponding to the small plot. This kept construction costs low, however, as every square meter of built area costs money. In addition, this leads to lower costs for heating and operating the house. The aim was to achieve a certain generosity despite the minimal living space. This was achieved through room-high windows and reduction to the essentials. This approach of simplicity is already part of traditional rural building. Thus the house is very modern in many design points, but at the same time takes up materials and surfaces of Upper Bavarian farms. For example, wood is the determining element for the roof truss, the larch wood windows and the pine floor boards. In contrast to the warm wood, the walls, plastered in traditional white technique, and the gray visible screed stand. The small house thus acquires a puristic, but also timeless character.

4

5

1 View from above
2 Driveway and entrance
3 Exterior view from south

4 Ground floor hallway and staircase
5 First floor hallway

1

2

1 Dining area
2 Dining area with kitchen

3 Sections
4 First floor plan
5 Ground floor plan

3

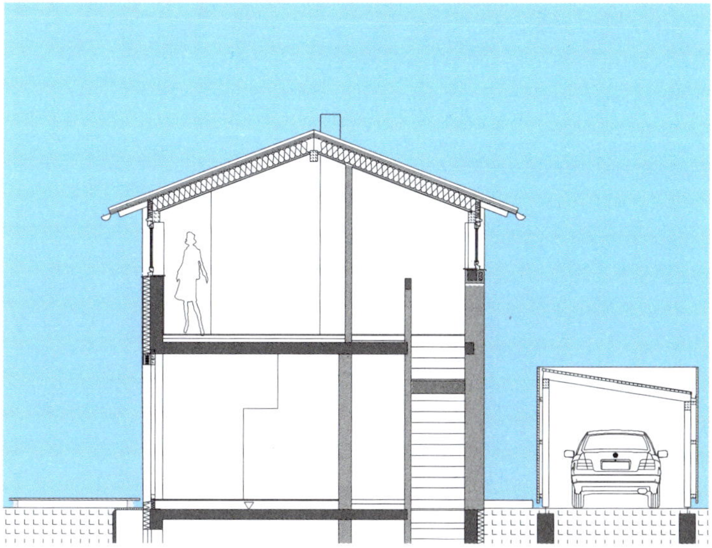

4

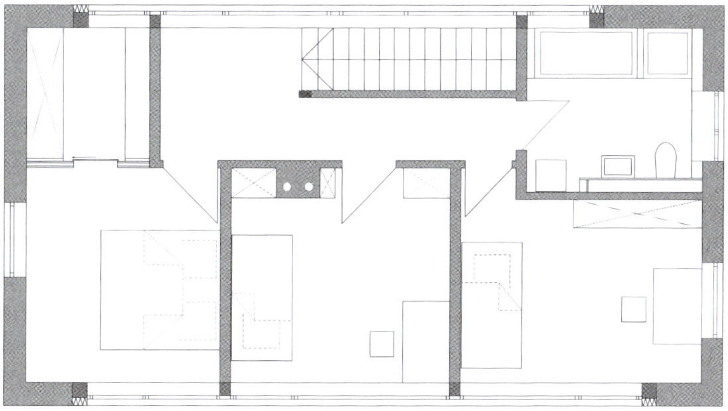

5

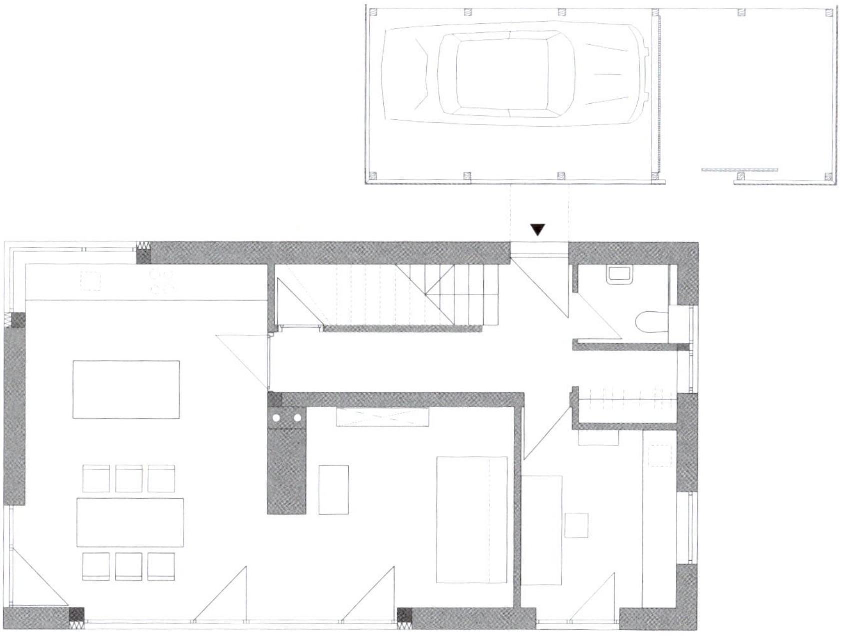

HOUSE KR

1

2, 3

1 View from east
2 Eastern window façade
3 Garden from southeast

4 Ground floor plan
5 Cross section
6 South side with view
7 Log building construction

In an unpretentious rural village structure that has so far been largely spared from mediocre DIY products, the owners decided to build a new building. The building site drops off from the village road to the east and offers an unobstructable view over meadow hills to the Allgäu mountains. A simple, elongated wooden building volume reflects the rural surroundings and stands in solid wood construction for contemporary living.

From the basement dug into the slope, the adjusted wooden construction develops upwards on the valley side. The log construction consists of a modular support and girder system up to under the open roof space and thus automatically attracts the floor plan and the generous glazing along both long sides. The log building technique in white fir creates a warm room atmosphere without superficial hometownism. The construction was carried out with a high quality timber loam insulation, heating by means of a geothermal heat pump and the use of local and renewable materials.

4

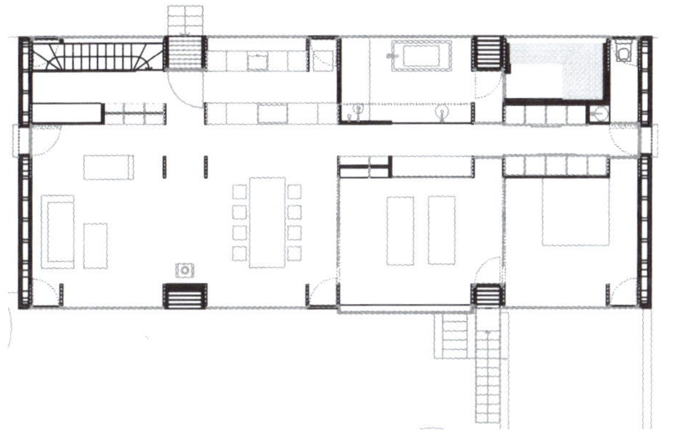

5

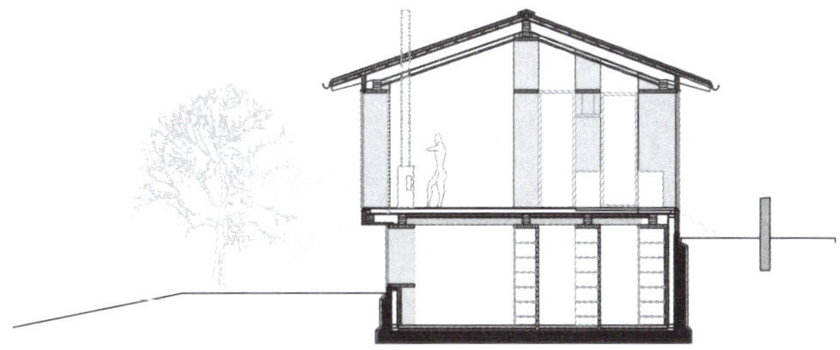

6

Architects: Becker Architekten
Year of completion: 2012
Location: Rettenberg, Bavaria
Gross floor area: 286 m^2
Number of bedrooms: 2
Main materials / structure: fir wood / log building
Ecological features: low-energy building, local building materials

7

SEMI-DETACHED HOUSES M

1

2, 3

4

Architects: Herbert O. Zielinski Architekt
Year of completion: 2017
Location: Reutlingen, Baden-Württemberg
Gross floor area: 150 m^2
Number of bedrooms: 2
Main materials / structure: oil-finished oak parquet, concrete, masonry / solid construction
Ecological features: flat roof with extensive greening, combined heat and power unit for heat generation

The two semi-detached houses with atrium were built in a quiet, sophisticated residential area with old buildings. With their minimalist architectural language, the buildings set a modern accent in this area. The houses are divided into a basement with a living space of around 36 square meters and an atrium of 11 square meters. There is a second fitted kitchen and a bathroom with bathtub. A floor-to-ceiling window front extends across the entire width of the atrium. On the ground floor, with an area of 47 square meters, is a guest restroom with a floor-level shower, the living and dining area with open fitted kitchen and access to the terrace and garden. Here a room-high window front repeats itself over the entire width of the house. The upper floor measures 41 square meters with a bedroom, a bathroom with toilet and bathtub. The balcony on the upper floor also has access from the bedroom and bathroom.

Both houses were built according to the KfW 70 standard. Heating and hot water are provided by a combined heat and power unit.

5

6

1 Southeast façade with entrance
2 Living space with view into the garden
3 View across the corner
4 Exterior view from northeast

5 Customized kitchen
6 Living space with view towards the kitchen
7 First floor bathroom
8 First floor balcony

7, 8

1

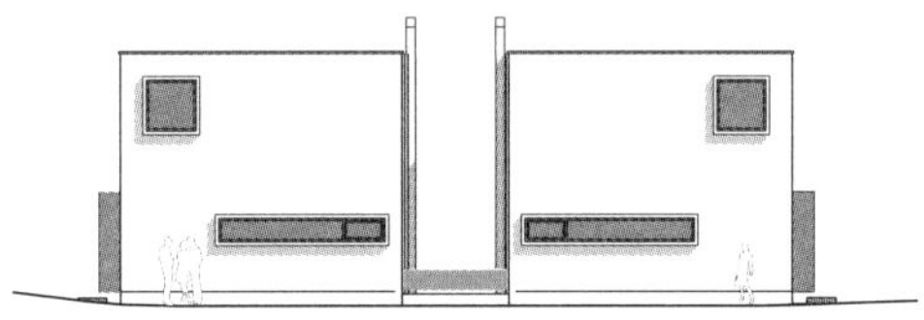

2

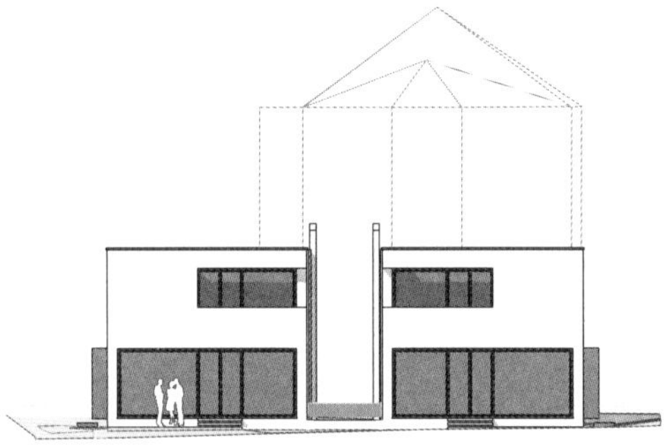

3

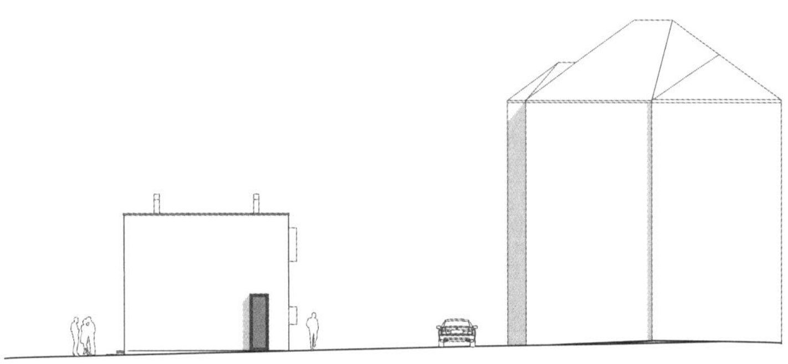

1 Northeast elevation
2 Southwest elevation
3 Southeast elevation

4 First floor plan
5 Ground floor plan
6 Basement floor plan

4

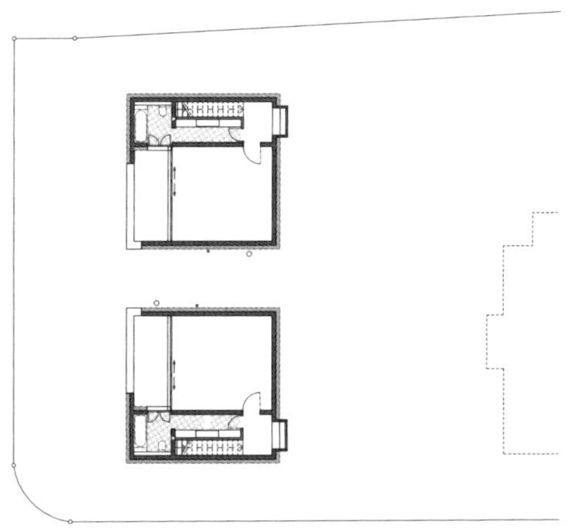

5

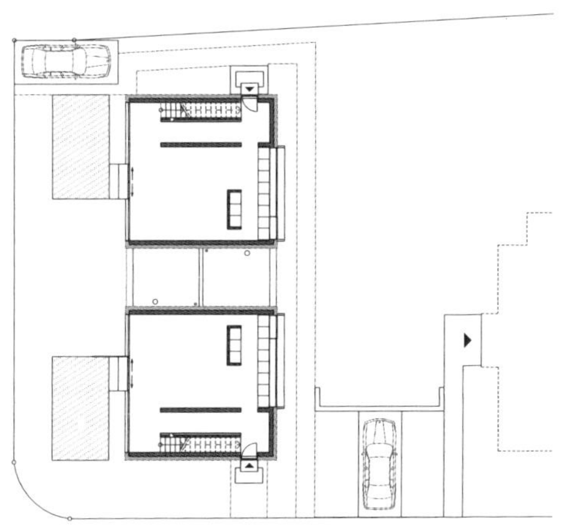

6

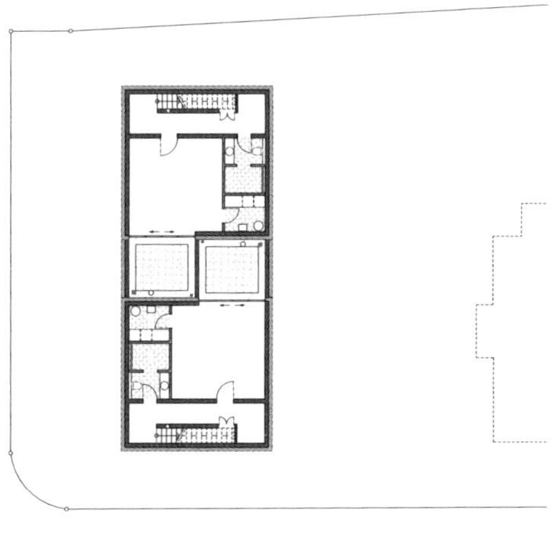

THE LITTLE BLACK ONE

1

Architects: f m b architekten
Norman Binder, Andreas-Th. Mayer
Year of completion: 2016
Location: Weil der Stadt, Baden-Württemberg
Gross floor area: 166 m^2
Number of bedrooms: 4
Main materials / structure: vertically perforated bricks, concrete, oak floors / monolithic solid construction

2

This detached house situated on the outskirts impresses with its clear form, simple typology and compact construction. The monochrome, umbra gray and smooth plastered structure reacts in its orientation like a black peep box with a panoramic view to the untouchable landscape conservation area. The new and unattractive environment of the mixed area is largely faded out. According to the development plan, only one full story was permitted on the building site, so a quarter of the ground floor area on the upper story had to be subtracted. The result was a roof terrace and the extension of the children's rooms to include a protected outdoor area.

The slender windows and doors, which open outwards and are flush with the masonry, enlarge the space inside and specify the cubic, monolithic form from the outside. The construction of the house is limited to exterior walls of 36.5-centimeter-thick vertically perforated bricks, strictly designed to the dimensions of the masonry. Only parts of the middle corridor wall on the ground floor support the interior. All other interior walls are drywall. Room-high oak doors with filigree floor frames and skylights separate the main rooms from the adjoining rooms and give the small rooms a large appearance.

From an energetic point of view, the orientation of the building makes it possible to dispense with external sun protection while at the same time orienting and opening up to the landscape conservation area. Expensive bricks filled with insulating material and triple glazing could therefore be dispensed with. Nevertheless, the building, heated with an air-water heat pump, falls short of the EnEV requirements by about 15 percent. Given the difficult building ground and for cost reasons, a basement was also dispensed.

3

4

1 Exterior view from south
2 Exterior view from west

3 Kitchen
4 Staircase
5 Entrance
6 Roof terrace
7 View from the roof terrace

5, 6

7

1

2

3

1 Kitchen with living area
2 Living area
3 First floor children's room

4 Ground floor plan
5 First floor plan
6 Section
7 Site plan

4

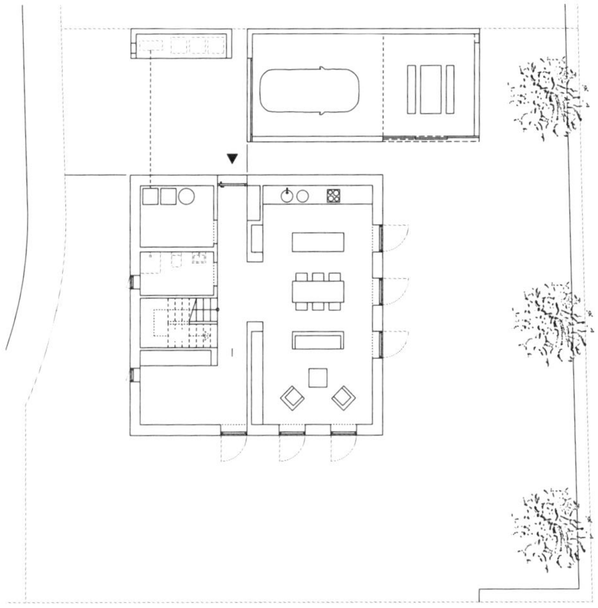

5

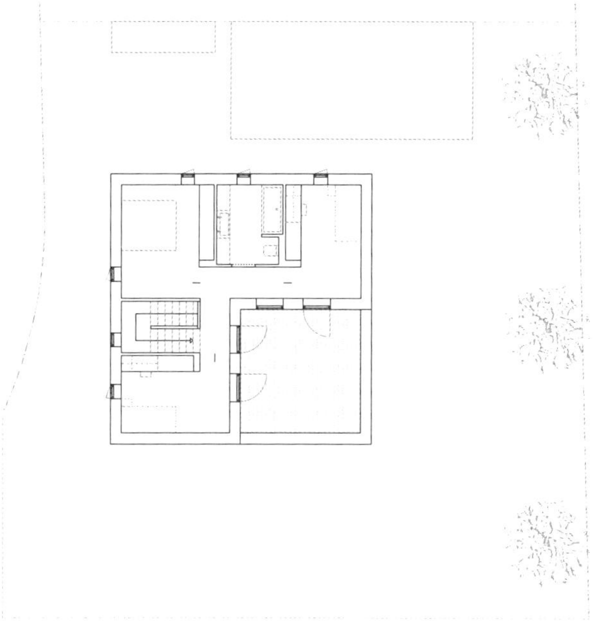

6

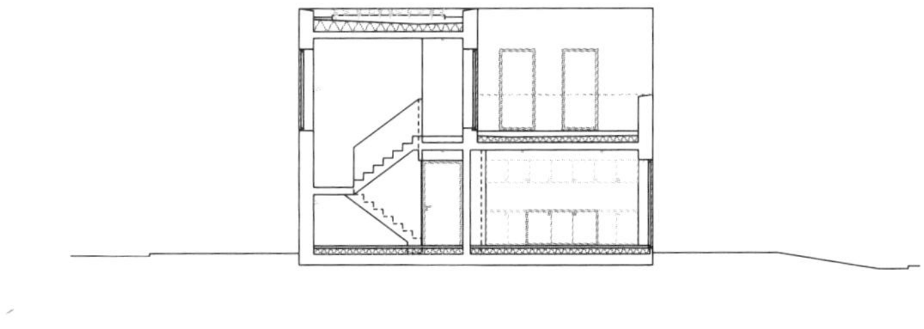

7

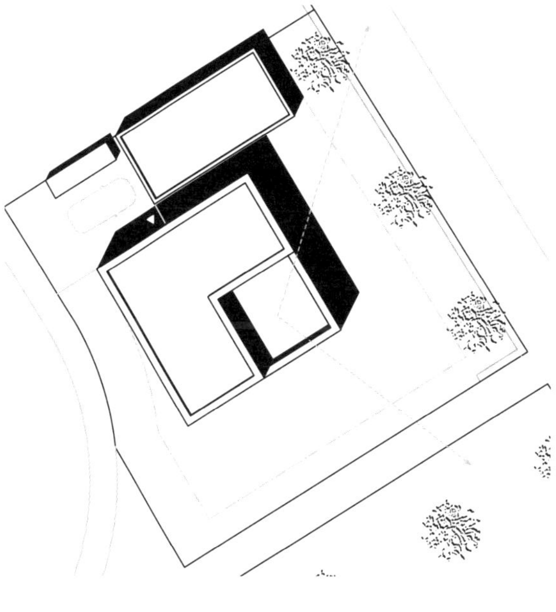

KBS 32

1

2, 3

Architects: Fischer Rüdenauer Architekten, FRA (former fischer architektur)
Year of completion: 2017
Location: Stuttgart, Baden-Württemberg
Gross floor area: 175 m^2
Number of bedrooms: 1
Main materials / structure: concrete, glass, silver fir / solid construction
Ecological aspects: compact design, low energy, heat pump with photovoltaics

This new building is a good example of moderate development in the conurbation of Stuttgart. An unused garden plot allows a small but fine single-family house, which contributes to an acceptable density while preserving the privacy of the neighbors. Two stacked and staggered cubes on the ground floor contain a kitchen, dining and living area as well as a restroom. The bedroom and bathroom are accessible via a gallery on the upper floor. The staggered arrangement of the cubes results in a roof terrace on the upper floor and a covered forecourt on the ground floor.

The building was constructed as a reinforced concrete structure. The interior staircase, ceilings and a wall panel remain visible in concrete. All permanently installed furniture is individually planned and made to measure. Walls become cupboards, furniture become space-forming elements, materials flow into each other. The upper floor was completely clad with pre-patinated silver fir on the outside and forms an opposite pole to the lime plaster on the ground floor.

4

5

6

7

1 Street view with roof terrace
2 Back view with outside area
3 Street side with forecourt

4 Materiality
5 First floor gallery
6 Terrace door
7 Staircase

1

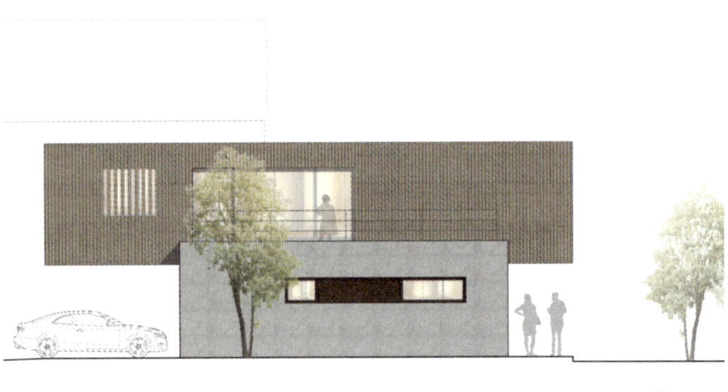

2

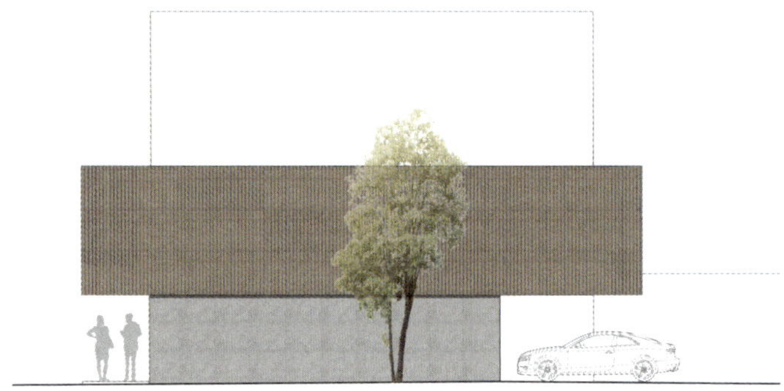

3

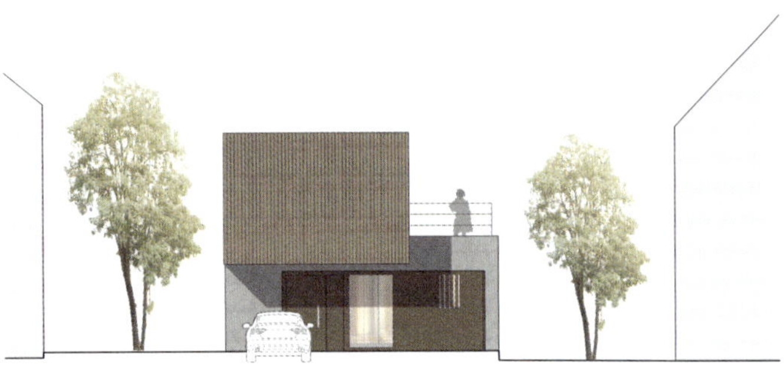

4

5

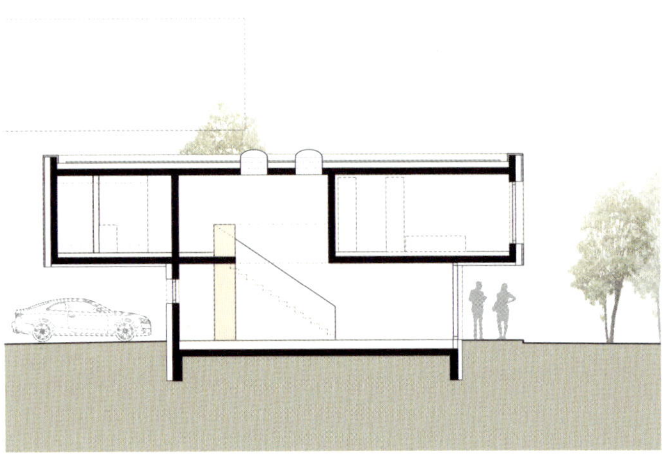

6

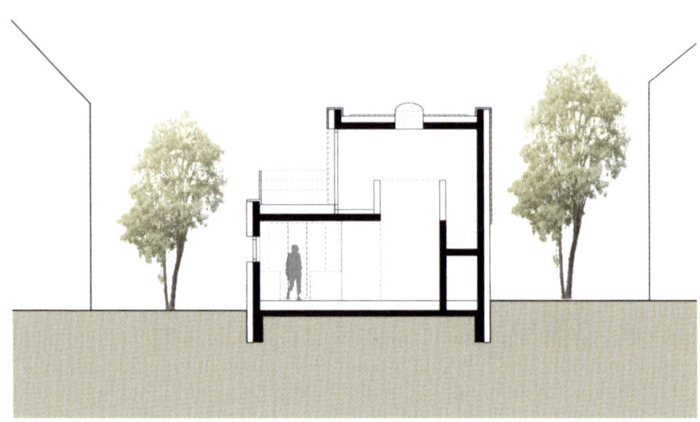

1 West elevation
2 East elevation
3 North elevation
4 South elevation
5 Longitudinal section
6 Cross section

7 First floor plan
8 Ground floor plan

7

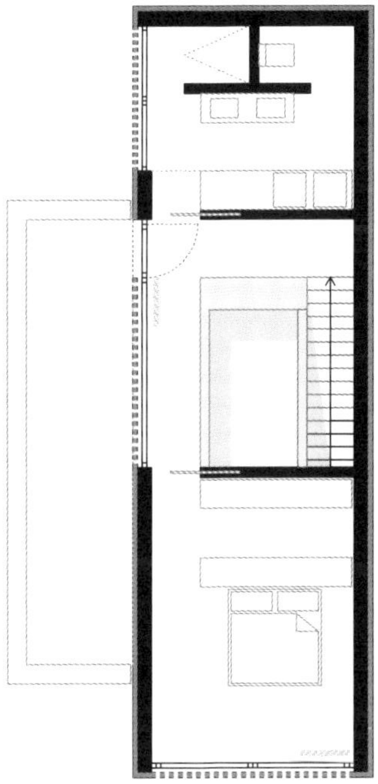

8

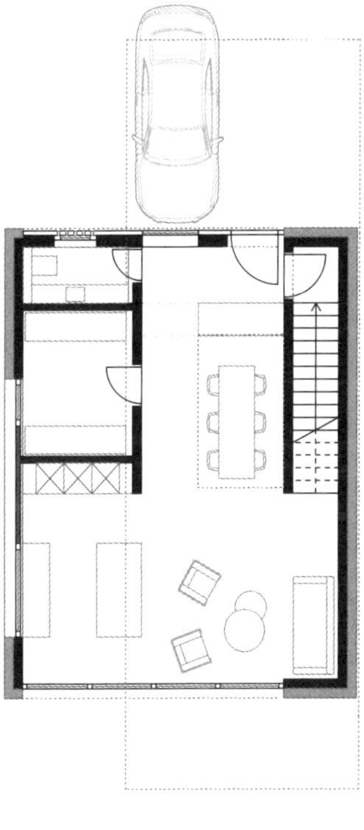

HOUSE T

1

2

1 Front view
2 Back view

3 Dining area
4 Gallery towards the living room
5 Dining area towards the living room

The starting point for the project was the wish of a family of three to stay in the historic city center and to develop new architecture tailored to their needs. The plot to be built on opens up from the existing garden of a secluded house, one of the last few gaps in the compactly built city of Husum. The street is lined with historic buildings with Gründerzeit villas and old trees. The new building was to fit into the existing row.

This requirement was met by a self-confident yet restrained architecture. Historical elements from the surrounding area are quoted and interpreted in a modern way. The steep classical saddle roof, the slate-like roofing, the Danish red tile, the zinc plate and the raised ground floor reflect some of the neighborhood's construction methods. Large window areas with a rich contrast are almost frameless inserted into the façade. The house is based on a flowing spatial concept. It does without any access corridors. Instead, two galleries connect the two floors and underline the airy, modern and family-friendly character. Only bedrooms, bathrooms and ancillary rooms are closed and form correspondingly intimate retreats.

The open kitchen and dining area forms the family's central living space. A three-meter-long dining table and a bench fitted into the window offer space for many family activities. The living room joins the open sequence of rooms. It is located two steps lower and, despite its openness, is zoned by it. This creates an artificial topography and leads the occupant over short and long concrete and Douglas fir stairs through the building. All rooms are opened up to the ridge and the two galleries are hardly limited by glass balustrades. This reinforces the open, communicative impression of the building.

3

Architects: TIMMTIMM Szenografie + Interior Design
Year of completion: 2016
Location: Husum, Schleswig-Holstein
Gross floor area: 258 m^2
Number of bedrooms: 3
Main materials / structure: brick, solid wood flooring / solid construction
Ecological features: geothermal heat pump

4

5

1

2

3

4

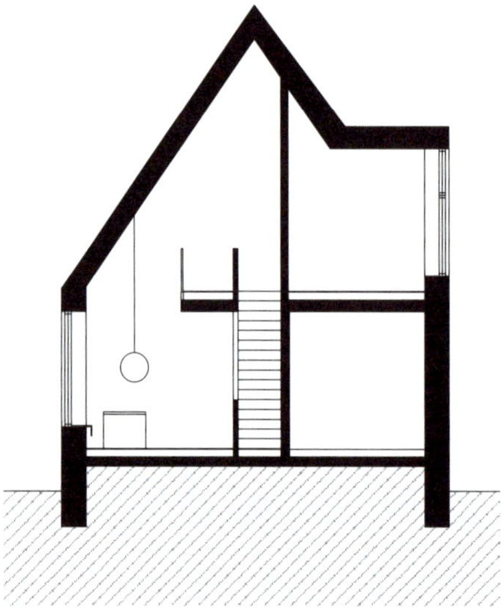

1 Staircase on ground floor
2 Gallery and staircase
3 Site plan
4 Cross section
5 First floor plan
6 Ground floor plan

5

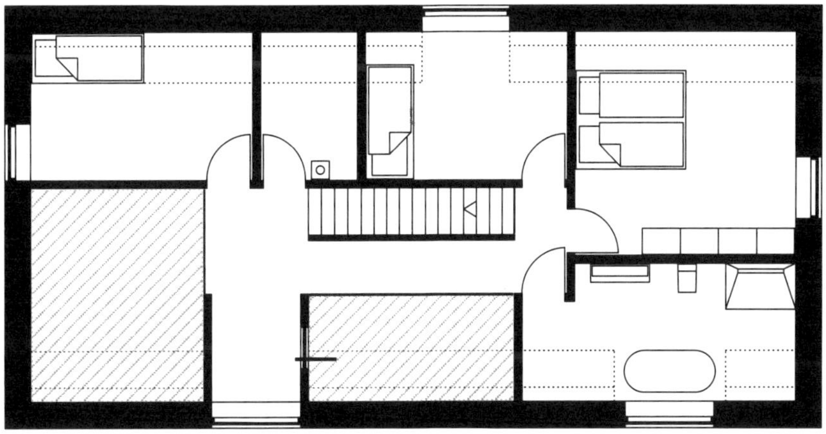

6

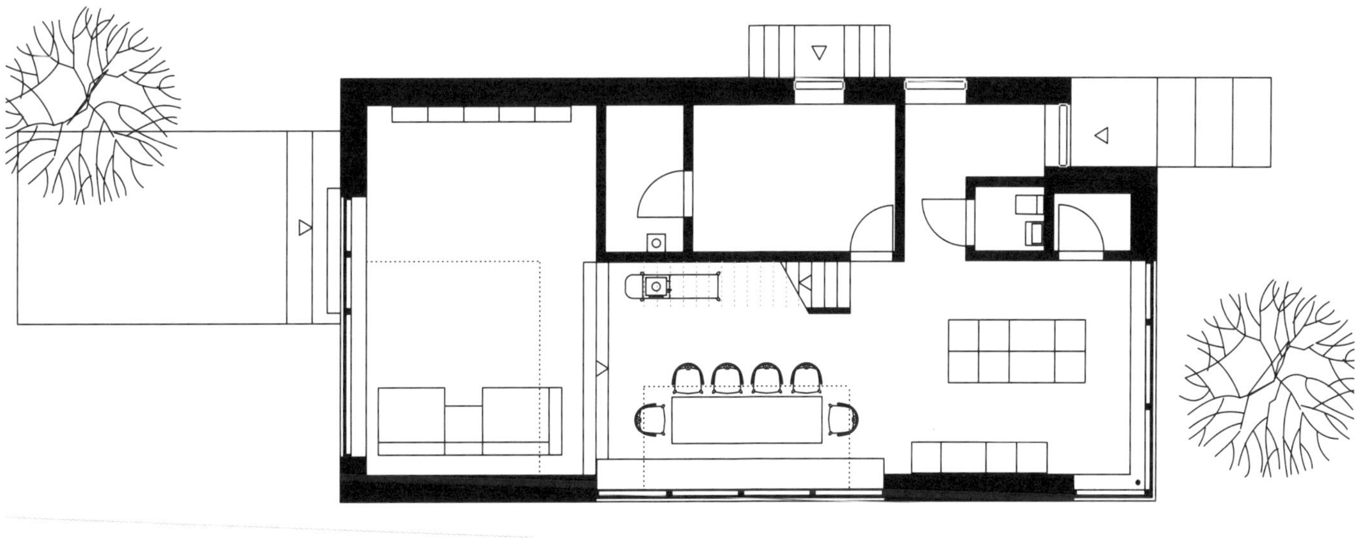

HOUSE H IN ALTLUSSHEIM

1

Architects: Thomas Fabrinsky Freier Architekt
Year of completion: 2016
Location: Altlußheim, Baden-Württemberg
Gross floor area: 383 m²
Number of bedrooms: 4
Main materials / structure: concrete, sand-lime brick / solid house with wooden roof framing
Ecological features: controlled ventilation

2

House H is located at the edge of a new development area in the Rhine plain in the Rhine-Neckar district, which is similar to many new development areas in the whole republic. The charm of the property lies in the peripheral location with adjoining, open field and wide view as well as the garden orientation to the southwest. Behind the concept was the claim to set striking accents in an environment characterized by everyday architecture without becoming pretentious and obtrusive. Balanced but exciting proportions, materials and colors were combined to form a harmonious whole.

House H captivates with clear lines, sharp edges and a flowing floor plan concept. The light-colored structure has precise incisions, the window frames are as dark as the glass surfaces in order to prevent them from being divided into small parts. The golden roof structures create a striking but unobtrusive color accent.

The asymmetrical roof cross section together with the generous glazing conveys a villa-like character. This impression is additionally supported by the expansive garden terrace with large-format slabs. From the dormer windows on the garden side of the bedrooms the continuous roof terrace, which is protected from view, is accessible.

Inside, the continuous larch plank floor is impressive, visually connecting all areas. Fine furniture and high-quality surfaces stand in pleasant contrast to the exposed concrete wall leading through the building. Bathrooms, kitchen and wardrobe were planned in detail, the nursery uses the height of the open attic with a sleeping gallery like a tree house.

3

4

1 Garden view by night
2 Main entrance in the evening

3 Kitchen area
4 Cooking, dining and living area
5 Main entrance
6 Garden view
7 View from northeast

5, 6

7

1

2

3

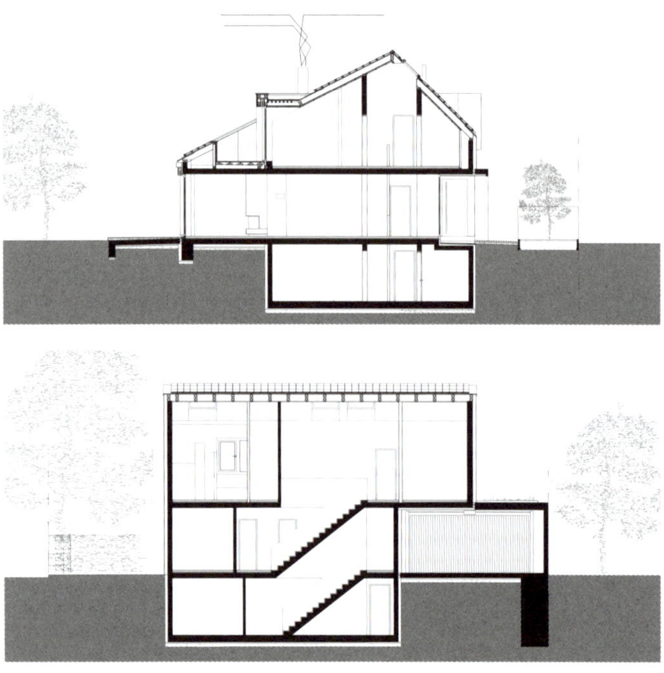

4

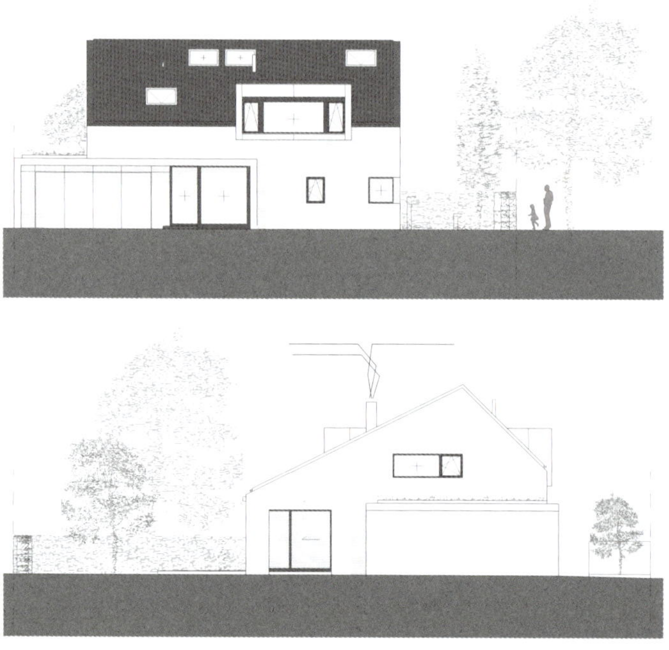

1 Nursery
2 Bathroom
3 Sections
4 Southeast and southwest elevations

5 First floor plan
6 Ground floor plan

5

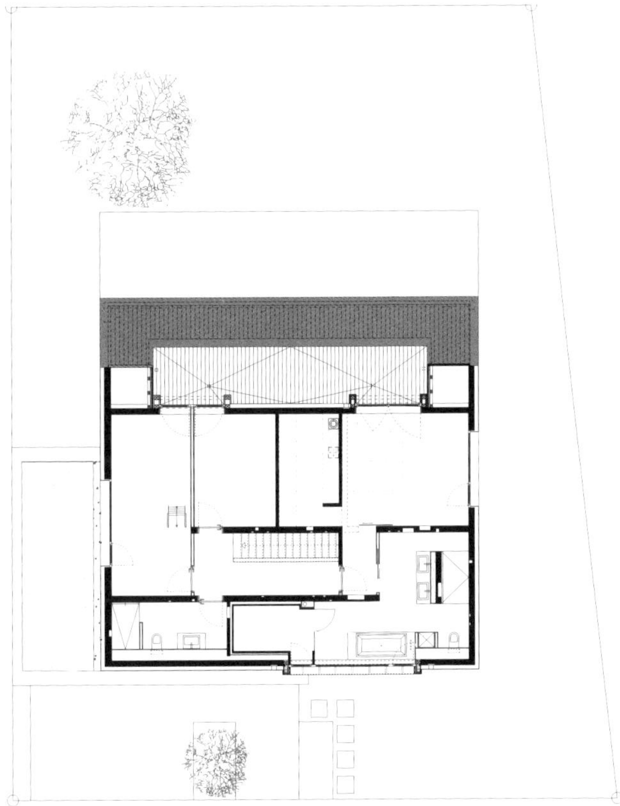

6

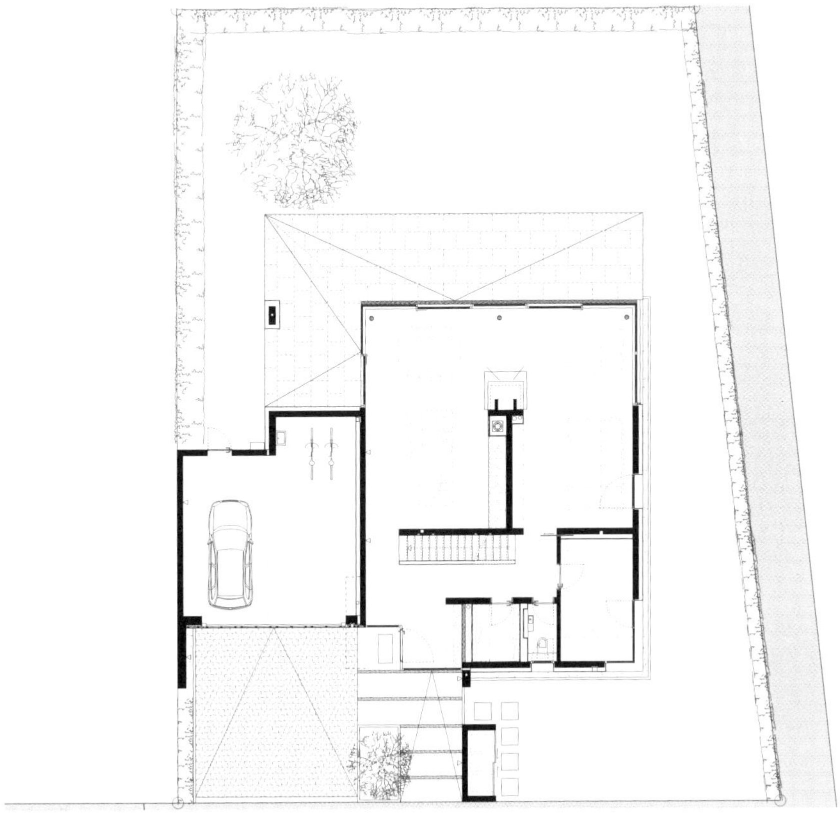

LAKESIDE HOUSE

1, 2

3

4

Architects: arcs architekten
Year of completion: 2012
Location: Berlin
Gross floor area: 120 m²
Number of bedrooms: 3
Main materials / structure: exposed concrete, oak wood
Ecological features: core insulation in combination with air-water heat pump

At an excursion lake near Berlin, the building law of the horticultural statutes only permitted one building structure on a surface area of 60 square meters. Architectural tricks, optimal use of space and maximization of building regulations resulted in a two-story structure with a total of 120 square meters of living space, sufficient for a family of four.

The building blends harmoniously into its surroundings thanks to its restrained design. On the lakeside, the building was fitted with maximum glazing to take advantage of the view and visually bring the surroundings into the house. The entrance side is single-story, the only opening is the access door. The basement is supplied with daylight on the lake side by a slope. Since a roofed terrace was not permitted, the roofing was changed to a bracket and defined as an architectural element not relevant to building law. The building was planned with all furniture fixtures in order to meet all requirements in the smallest possible space.

5

6

1 Back side made of exposed concrete from the northwest
2 Footbridge in front of the house
3 Reduced back of the building from the north
4 View from the lake onto the building

5 Maximum glazed living area
6 Bedroom with terrace
7 Ground floor hallway
8 Basement floor hallway

7, 8

1

2

3

4

5

1 Basement bathroom with view towards the lake
2 Basement bathroom with mosaic tiles
3 Bedroom with view onto the lake
4 Ground floor bathroom
5 Bedroom

6 Elevations
7 Cross section
8 Ground floor plan
9 Longitudinal section
10 Basement floor plan

6

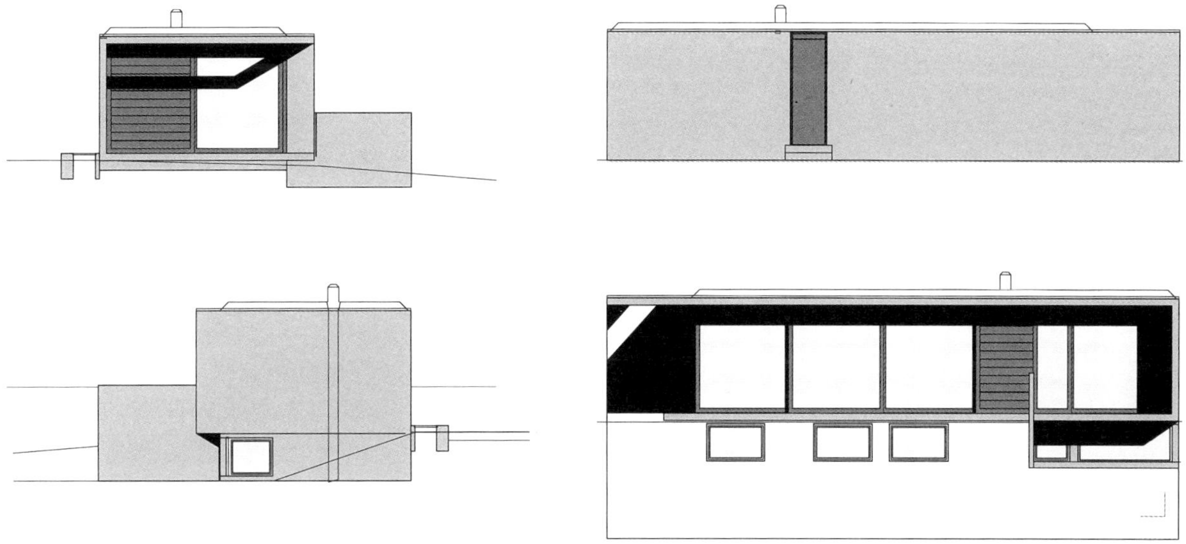

7

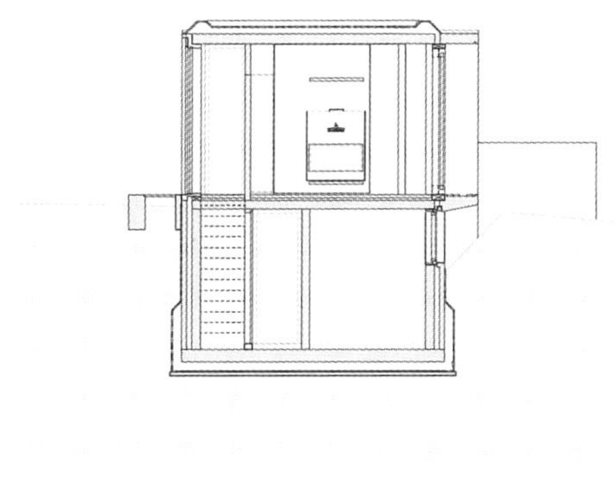

8

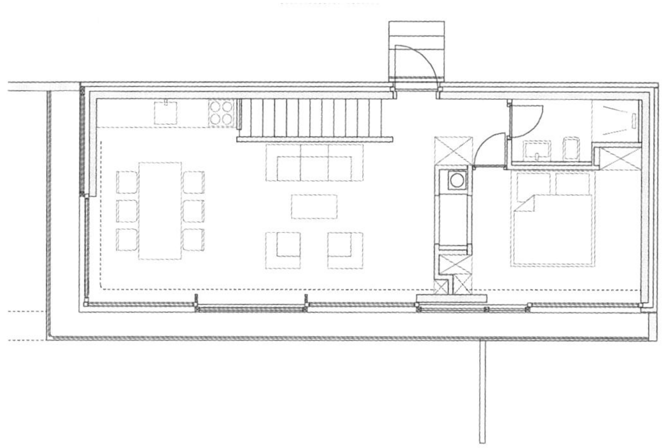

9

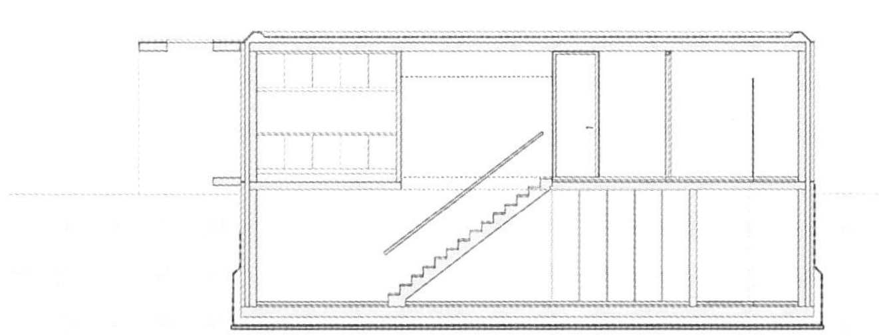

10

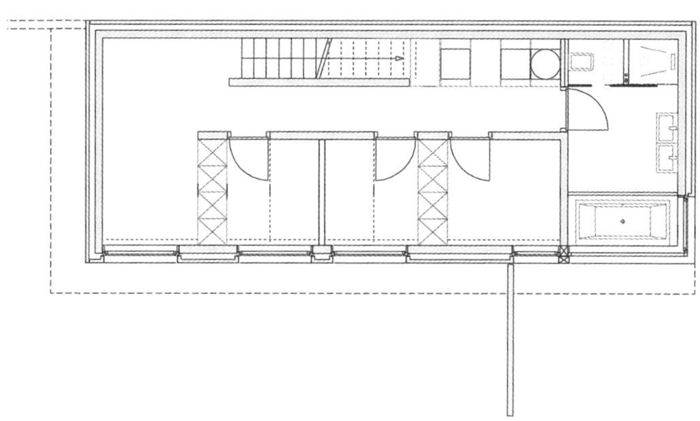

HOUSE L

1

Architects: Haack + Höpfner · Architekten und Stadtplaner
Year of completion: 2012
Location: Munich, Bavaria
Gross floor area: 241 m^2
Number of bedrooms: 2
Main materials / structure: glass, aluminum, wood, fiber cement boards / wood panel construction
Ecological features: construction in wood, passive sun protection, high thermal insulation

2

House L is an extension to a settlement house from the 1940s with renovation and reorganization of the interior. The existing building is preceded by a structure whose silhouette with an identical cross section is abstract and separated by a glass joint. On the ground floor, the extension serves to extend the previously cramped living spaces. A triple glazing system following the house profile between the new and old building allows for exposure into the depth of the building, the structural intervention becomes visible. On the upper floor of the new building there is a generous bedroom, which is separated from the living space at the joint by glazing. A glass bridge connects the two buildings in the attic and opens up the bedroom from the old building.

The façade of the side walls and the roof are clad with anthracite-colored fiber cement panels. The gable façade is completely glazed and covered with a homogeneous screen of horizontal aluminum profiles. This screen serves as privacy, glare and sun protection and from the inside as a visual space closure. This results in a changing play of light and shadow in the interior during the course of the day and depending on the season.

In the space between the glass façade and the aluminum construction, a small balcony is integrated on the upper floor, from which a motor-controlled folding and lifting mechanism makes it possible to open the façade as required. The puristic austere façade thus becomes a living image of everyday family life.

3

1 General day view
2 General night view

3 Glass joint
4 Façade appearance

4

1

2

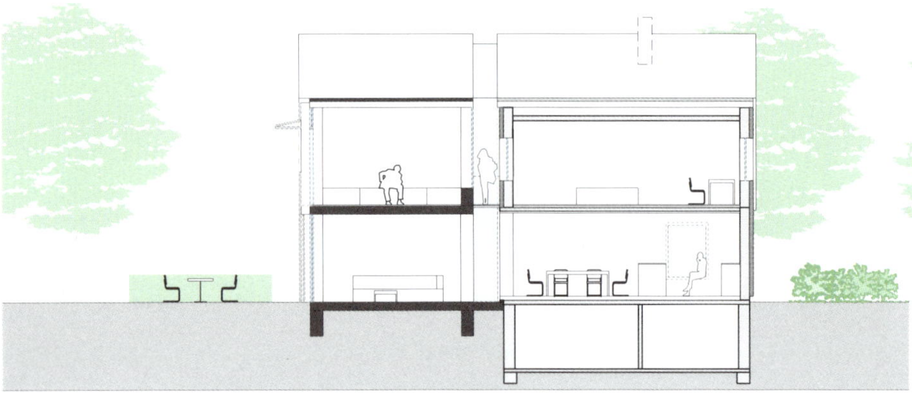

3

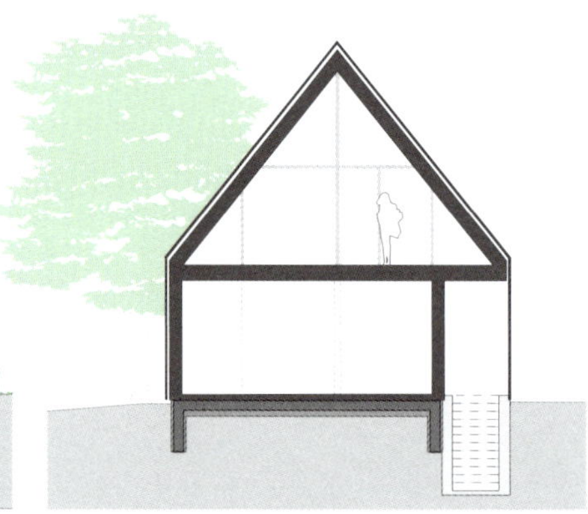

1 Interior space
2 Longitudinal section
3 Cross section
4 First floor plan
5 Ground floor plan

4

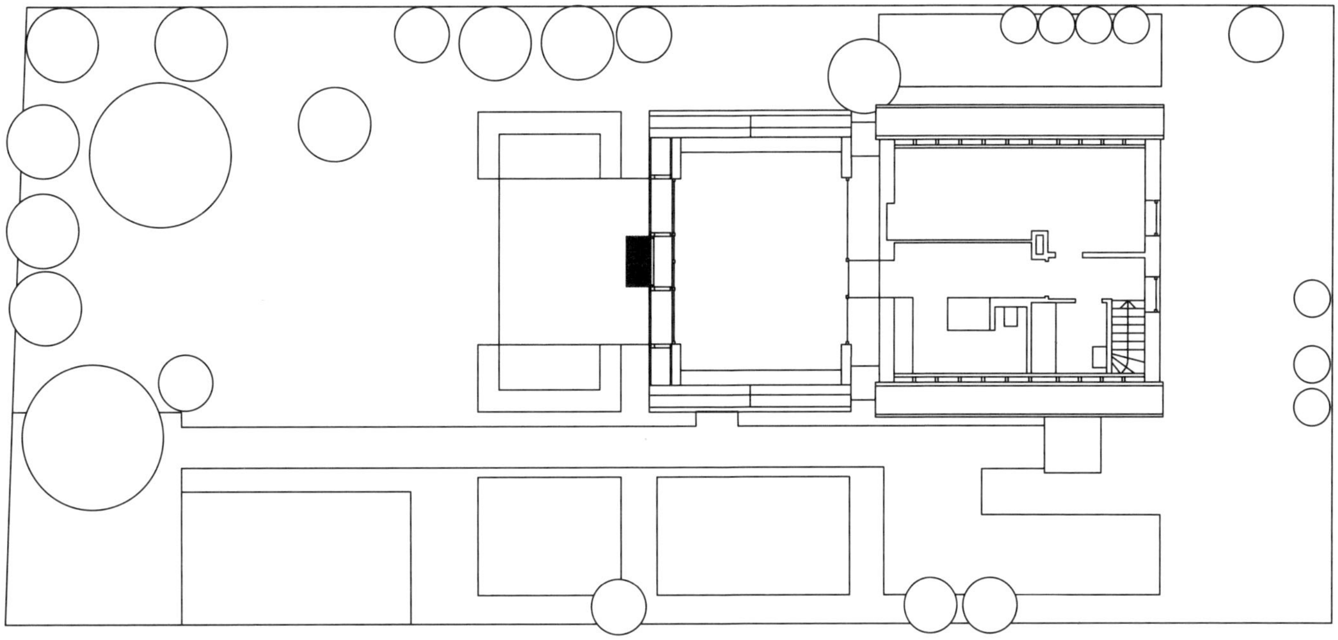

5

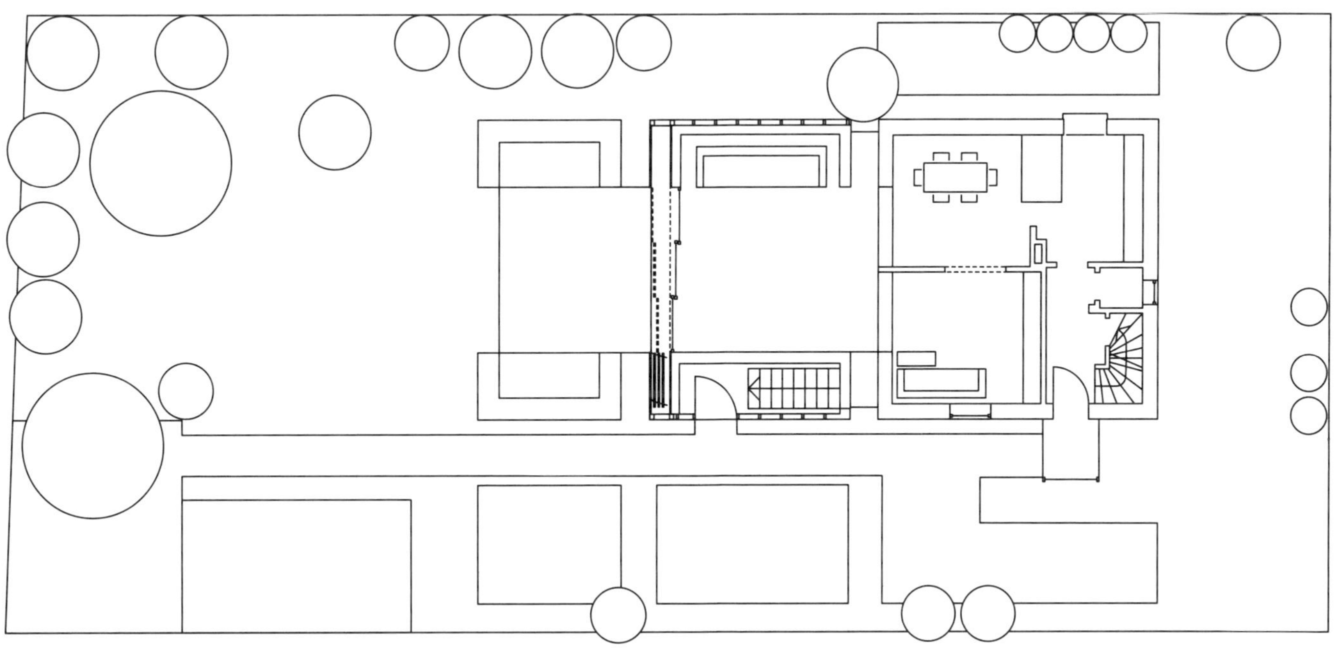

HOUSE M IN OSTFILDERN

1

2

Architects: Frey Architekten
Year of completion: 2015
Location: Ostfildern, Baden-Württemberg
Gross floor area: 430 m^2
Number of bedrooms: 3
Main materials / structure: reinforced concrete, masonry, wood / solid construction
Ecological features: gas condensing boiler, solar thermal heating and drinking water support

Situated at the interface between a context marked by detached houses and the foothills of a nature reserve with extensive orchards, the building has a breathtaking view of the Swabian Jura. The living spaces open up generously to the landscape, while the façades facing the street are only structured by a few precisely set window openings. This impression is reinforced by the exposed concrete garage, which forms a protective caesura towards the garden. The façade on the ground floor, which is set back, offers weather protection and welcomes both guests and inhabitants.

Inside the building, the differentiation between spacious and open areas as well as private and quieter spaces is the central design approach. Behind the entrance door, the ground floor opens to the south and again offers a view into the wide landscape. By merging the dining and living rooms with an open fireplace, the floor forms a spatial continuum that can be easily adapted to everyday situations by sliding doors. The kitchen is open and can only be separated from the dining room by adjusting the kitchen unit. The living rooms are characterized by light, warm oak planks – the exposed concrete surfaces form a deliberate contrast with their raw surface.

In order to transfer the openness and transparency to the upper floor, a generous and light-flooded void forms the focal point of the private rooms. The view from the framed panorama window allows one to relax and enjoy the landscape. This creates a quiet retreat despite the great openness. While the children's rooms and a study are connected to the airspace, the parents' floor is reached via the gallery. This forms the pivotal point between the spacious bathroom and the bedroom.

A smooth exterior plaster in a warm earth tone underlines the precise setting of the window openings and the sharp-edged modeling of the building's body. The black window profiles and external chimneys form a contrast to this. This appearance is rounded off by the deliberate omission of external rainwater downpipes and gutters. The roof was covered with smooth roof tiles.

3

1 Overall impression of the nature reserve
2 South façade and garden

3 Exterior view street side
4 Entrance area with garage

4

1

2

3

4

5
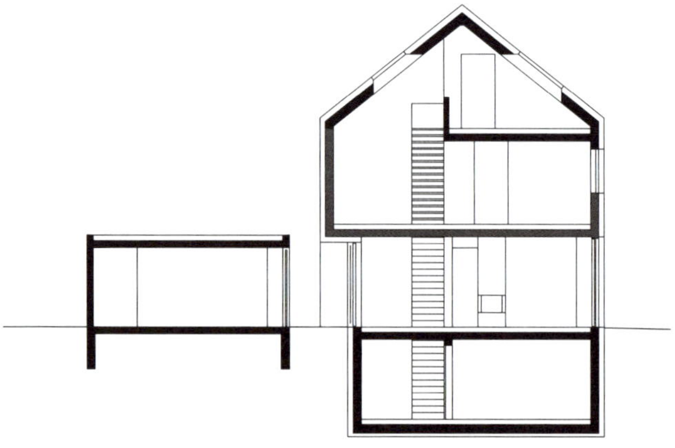

6

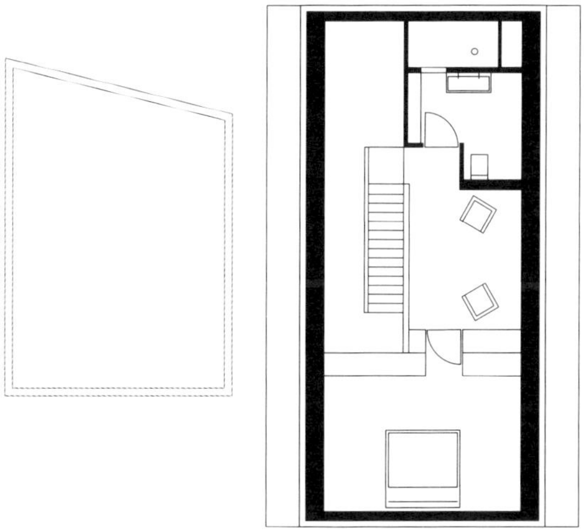

7

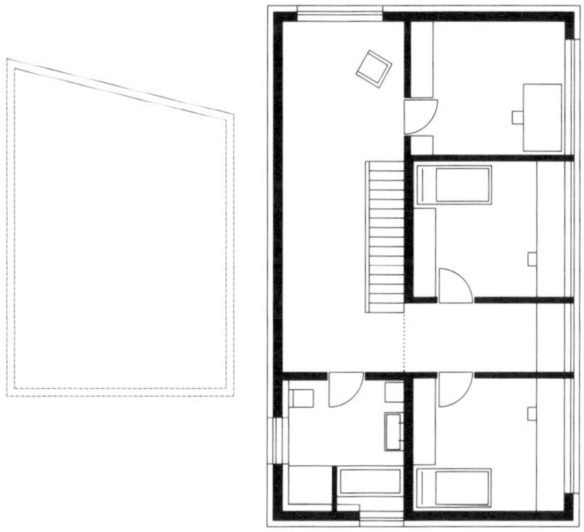

8

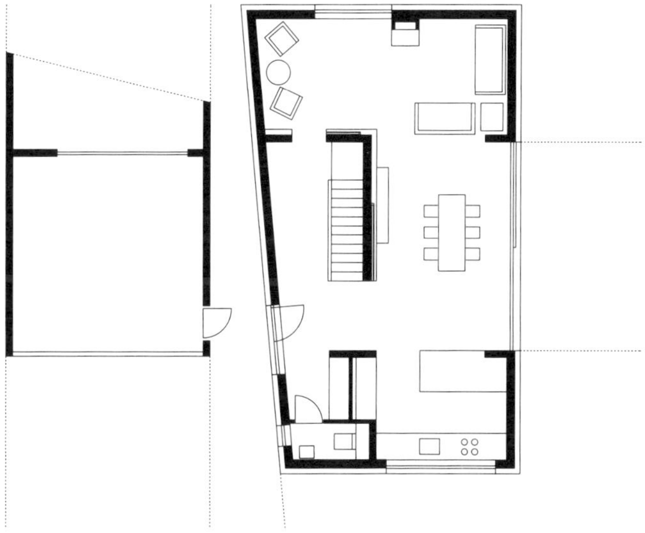

1 Seat window with a view of nature
2 Fixed furniture at the gallery used as partitions
3 Entrance situation
4 Site plan
5 Section

6 Attic floor plan
7 First floor plan
8 Ground floor plan

INDEX

A

B

C

D

E

F

G

H

I

J

K

L

M

INDEX

X

Y

Z

PICTURE CREDITS

Architekten Lenzstrasse Dreizehn
→ pp. 134–136

Johannes Armanazi
→ pp. 204–205, 206 nos. 1, 3

Karsten Bauer
Architekt
→ pp. 170–171, 216–217

Becker Architekten,
photographer: Franz Schröck
→ pp. 248–249

Thomas Beyer
→ pp. 72–73

Nikolaus Biederstedt, Haack + Höpfner .
Architekten BDA
→ pp. 274–276

bild_raum Stephan Baumann
→ pp. 266–268

Gunter Binsack
www.gunterbinsack.de
→ pp. 64–66

Bertram Bölkow
www.bertramboelkow.de
→ pp. 18–20

Claudia Bolle
→ pp. 110–112

Herbert Bucher
→ pp. 14–17

Clemens Bachmann Architekten
→ pp. 154–156

Dautfest Fotografie
→ pp. 132 nos. 1–2

Klaus Ditté
→ pp. 150–152

Maria Dorner
→ p. 92 no. 2

Annika Feuss
→ pp. 56–58

Nadja Filimonow
→ pp. 146–148, 130–131, 132 no. 3

Thomas Fischer
→ pp. 142–144

Flacke + Otto Architekten,
Isabel Podeschwa
→ pp. 26–28

Udo Geisler Photographie
www.udo-geisler.de
→ pp. 232–233

Daniel George Photography
→ pp. 188 no. 1, 189–190

Christoph Göckel
→ p. 123 no. 7

Michael Grimm
→ pp. 228–230

Janosch Gruschczyk
→ pp. 98 no. 1, 99 nos. 4–6; 100 no. 2

Antje Hanebeck
→ pp. 270, nos. 1, 3–4; 271–272

Dirk Hennings
→ pp. 186 nos. 1–2, 187

Jörg Jäger
→ pp. 278–279

Isabel Jasnau
→ p. 186, no. 3

Sebastian Kautz
→ pp. 220–222

keenco3
→ pp. 94–95

Andreas Kellner
→ pp. 200–202

Markus Kirschnick
→ pp. 98 no. 2, 99 no. 3, 100 no. 1

Christiane Koch
www.ck-fotografie.com
→ pp. 36–38

Henning Koepke
Munich
→ pp. 30–32, 102–104

Elena Krämer
→ pp. 52–53

Carolin Kreutzer
→ pp. 106–108

Dieter Leistner
→ pp. 196–197

Peter Litvai
→ pp. 22–23, 34–35

Rainer Mader
→ pp. 10 nos. 2–3; 11 no. 6, 12

Andreas-Th. Mayer
→ pp. 254–256

Waldemar Merger
→ pp. 118–119

Maik Mersmann
→ pp. 174–176

MS Planwerk
→ pp. 126–127

Stefan Josef Müller
Berlin
→ pp. 250–251

Nehse & Gerstein Architekten
→ pp. 84–85

Ivan Nemec
Prague
→ pp. 236–237

Peter Neusser
→ pp. 240–242

Norbert Pakusch
Prutting
→ pp. 244–246

Peters Fotodesign
Amerang
→ pp. 182–183

Detlef Podehl
→ pp. 158–160

Georg Poensgen
→ pp. 10 no. 1, 11 nos. 4–5

Wolfgang Pulfer
→ pp. 92 no. 1, 93 nos. 6–8

Michael Reisch
Düsseldorf
→ pp. 114–116, 208–209

Andreas Riedel
→ pp. 44–45

Thomas Rudolf
→ pp. 60–62

Christian Sandweger
→ p. 270 no. 2

Stefan Schilling
→ pp. 178–180

Patrick Schmidt
www.patrickschmidt.photography
→ pp. 48–49

Volker Schmidt
→ pp. 192–194

Michael Schnell
→ pp. 88–90

Mark Seelen Photography
→ pp. 262–264

Roland Seidl
→ pp. 212–213

Martin Stoll
www.buerostoll.com
→ pp. 40–41

Herbert Stolz | Fotografie
www.herbertstolz.de
→ pp. 224–225

Thomas Streitberg
→ pp. 258–259

Daniel Sumesgutner, banz + riecks
→ pp. 80–81

Tischlerei Hubert Schmitt GmbH
Welschbillig-Ittel
→ p. 77 no. 6

Daniel Vieser
www.dv-architekturfotografie.de
→ pp. 122, 123 nos. 5–6, 8

Frank Vinken
www.frankvinken.com
→ pp. 138–140

Johannes Vogt
Mannheim
→ pp. 166–167

stefan warter fotografie
→ pp. 206 no. 2

Joachim Weber
→ pp. 76, 77 nos. 1–5, 78

Günter Richard Wett
→ p. 188, no. 2

Christian Willner Photographie
→ pp. 68–69

wolff:architekten
→ pp. 162–164

Cover front: **Herbert Bucher**
Cover back (from left to right, from above to below): **Thomas Rudolf, Wolfgang Pulfer, Frank Vinken, Detlef Podehl, wolff:architekten**

IMPRINT

The Deutsche Nationalbibliothek lists this publication in the Deutsche Nationalbibliografie; detailed bibliographic data are available on the Internet at http://dnb.dnb.de

ISBN 978-3-03768-253-1

1st edition 2020

Project coordination: Editorial office van Uffelen
Editorial staff and layout: Julia Habenicht, Sylvia Gatzka, Jonas Haas
Graphic concept: Die Brueder Publishing
Reproduction: Bild1Druck GmbH, Berlin